COMMUNICATION
FOR
SUSTAINABLE DEVELOPMENT

About the Author

Dr. B. Balaswamy received M.A. and Ph.D. degrees in Communication from the Department of Communication, Sarojini Naidu School of Performing Arts, Fine Arts and Communication, University of Hyderabad. At present, he is Associate Professor in the Department of Communication and Journalism, Osmania University, Hyderabad. Earlier, he worked as Lecturer and Reader in the Department of Mass Communication, Assam University, Silchar. For the last nine years he has been teaching Mass Communication. He has several published research papers and articles to his credit.

COMMUNICATION
FOR
SUSTAINABLE DEVELOPMENT

B. Balaswamy
Associate Professor
Dept. of Communication & Journalism
Osmania University
Hyderabad

CONCEPT PUBLISHING COMPANY, NEW DELHI-110059

Cataloging in Publication Data—DK
Courtesy: D.K. Agencies (P) Ltd. <docinfo@dkagencies.com>

Balaswamy, B., 1970-
Communication for sustainable development / B. Balaswamy.
p. cm.
Study conducted at the Medak District of Andhra Pradesh, India.
Includes bibliographical references (p.)
Includes index.
ISBN 8180693473

1. Communication in economic development—India—Medak (District). 2. Sustainable development—India—Medak (District). I. Title.

DDC 338.954 840 7 22

ISBN : 81-8069-347-3

First Published 2006

Published and Printed by
Ashok Kumar Mittal
Concept Publishing Company
A/15-16, Commercial Block, Mohan Garden,
New Delhi-110059 (India)

Phones : 25351460, 25351794
Fax : 091-11-25357103
Email : publishing@conceptpub.com

Foreword

The present book 'Communication for Sustainable Development' has come in a particular context in the communication studies. In order to realize its importance and further strengthen this area of research, we need to understand the background to the context of this book. It has come when the concept of development passed through various phases and evolved as sustainable development, encompassing almost all spheres of human life. This new concept has widened the scope of development significantly. While the earlier concept of development was meant by and large for Third World countries, sustainable development is for the entire globe and into a distant future, calling for intragenerational and intergenerational equity, demanding the participation of people from individual to global levels. The communication potentialities of man also increased manyfold, particularly since 1990s and became an essential ingredient in enabling the man to fulfill various goals of sustainable development. It is pertinent to have insights into the diverse phases of development communication to appreciate the present work.

Ever since the end of the Second World War, development became a commonly shared concern of the world countries. It became a concern of scholars belonging to various disciplines, including Communication. Communication being considered as a missing link in the development chain, the uses of communication for development became an important concern of the communication scholars, which has been termed as development communication. The objective of this development communication was to augment the development process in newly emancipated countries from the colonial rule, which came to be known as Third World countries. In this direction, describing the role of media in developing countries, theories and models have emerged and media strategies were formulated and implemented in third world countries.

Development communication has witnessed different trends at different stages. In 1950s and 60s oblivious of the colonization aspect, it was believed that by following the foot prints of developed countries, the Third World countries could develop at faster rate than the developed countries themselves reached the stage of development. The industrialized western countries were taken as role models of development. But this approach did not yield the result. The gap between developed and developing countries could not be bridged, rather it widened. Even within developing countries, the gap between rich and poor increased. Hence a realization dawned among the third world scholars that there cannot be one single way/route for development to be followed by all countries, but every country can have its own development path, taking into consideration the socio, economic, political and economic conditions prevailing in that country. This approach continued for some time and came to be known as *Another Development.* While the first stage was dominated by the Western scholars, in the second stage, the scholars from Third World countries took an active role. In terms of communication it was realized that not only mass media but all media including the traditional folk media, group communication channels and interpersonal communication channels must be utilized effectively.

With people's participation in the planning and implementation of development programmes assuming significance, in the alternative approaches of development, participatory communication and development support communication assumed significance in the field of development communication.

The western model of development which emphasized industrialization, urbanization and modernization as essential routes to development left some dangerous consequences on environment. The industrialization and urbanization led to different types of pollution from local level to global level posing threat to various life sustaining systems. The United Nation Conference on Human Environment, held at Stockholm in1972 drew the attention of world countries to think about the development at the cost of environment and to take measures to protect the environment. While the IUCN advanced the idea of sustainable development, the World Commission on Environment and Development (WCED) firmly established it. Various summits such as Earth Summit (1992), Kyoto Summit (1997), Summit on Sustainable Development held at Johannesburg (2002) etc., have strengthened and sought to provide a direction to sustainable development. Interestingly, the globalization and the concern for sustainable development are taking place simultaneously with some complementary and contradictory features.

Though sustainable development is over a decade old concept and continues to be the only solution for healthy and productive life into a distant future, proper attention has not been paid to this aspect in development communication. This book fills this gap and it is crucial work in the field of *development communication*. This book deals systematically with various dimensions of sustainable development and the importance of communication in general and various communication channels in particular in meeting the different goals of sustainable development.

Medak District of Andhra Pradesh is a concrete example for underdevelopment, industrialization, pollution and environmental movements. The author has selected this district for empirical study and studied different dimensions of sustainable development from communication point of view.

The concept of sustainable development has widened the meaning of development and embodies a treasure of philosophy. It is concerned with all human beings, irrespective of the national boundaries. Every human being has a responsible role in today's world. It is common concern of the global people to broaden the humanism. Today the humanity is facing more challenges. The world resources are enjoyed quite inequitably. We can see the glaring contrasts between developed and developing countries. Though infant mortality rate has decreased significantly, still it continues to be high among the developing countries. On the other hand while four industrialized countries, viz., the United States of America, Japan, Germany and United Kingdom are responsible for 33 per cent of carbon dioxide emissions, the largest populated China and India are accountable for 16 per cent of carbon dioxide emissions. The rest of the world is responsible for about 50 per cent of the carbon dioxide emissions.

As the Secretary General of U.N., Koffi Annan rightly pointed at the Summit of Sustainable Development in Johannesburg (2002) the efforts of global people for sustainable is at the beginning stage only. We have to promote action and address some of the most pressing concerns of poverty and the environment. The commitments made to increase access to clean water and proper sanitation, to increase access to energy services, to improve health conditions and agriculture, particularly in dry lands, and to better protect the world's biodiversity and ecosystems, have to be materialized.

Dr. Balaswamy has made a significant contribution by examining in depth the role of communication in sustainable development. This book will be useful to the academia, policy makers, media practitioners, students and students of Communication.

Prof. P.L.Vishweshwer Rao
Professor of Communication and Journalism
and Director, Educational Multidedia Research
Centre (EMMRC), Osmania University
Hyderabad

Preface

Development Communication has evolved as an important area in Communication studies. As a concept, Development has undergone a remarkable shift in the meaning after being extensively debated at various fora. It has become a shared concern of countries across the globe during the last five decades. Initially, following the western model, industrialization, urbanization and modernization were considered routes to development. The limitations of this approach were realized in 1970s.

In the wake of various environmental problems, serious efforts were made to integrate the development and environment in 1980s, which resulted in the emergence of the concept of sustainable development. This new approach became an important trend in 1990s and was endorsed at various international summits — Earth Summit (1992) to Johannesburg Summit (2002). Sustainable development continues to be an inevitable solution for the healthy living of present and future generations. The scope of sustainable development is not confined only to Third World countries. It extends to the entire globe and to the distant future too. Today's slogan is think globally and act locally. The advent of new communication technologies, particularly, in 1990s have made the concept of global village a reality. The changing shift in the meaning and focus of development also necessitated the change in communication approaches for development. The present book is a doctoral thesis for which research was conducted during 1994-2001. Hence, the statistics, policies and programmes of government will reflect up this period only in this book. It examines the role of communication in sustainable development in the backdrop of changes in the fields of development and communication.

I hope this book will be useful to students and teachers of Communication and Journalism, and all those interested in environmental and developmental issues and for the betterment of society.

Dr. B. Balaswamy

Acknowledgements

The present volume, which is the result of painstaking efforts, would not have seen the light of the day without the guidance, help, co-operation and encouragement of several persons. Words are not adequate to express my gratitude to them all. Nevertheless, I will be failing in my duty, if I do not acknowledge their invaluable help.

I am grateful to my teacher and Ph.D. Supervisor, Prof. P.L. Vishweshwer Rao for introducing me to this new area of Development Communication and for his constant encouragement and guidance throughout the period of my research. I am deeply indebted to Prof. N. Sudhakar Rao, Dean, School of Social Sciences, Assam University, Silchar, for his valuable suggestions and extensive discussions. Prof. B.P. Sanjay, Director, IIMC, New Delhi; Dr. Vinod Pawarala, Sri P.K. Manvi, Mrs. Naga Mallika of the Department of Communication, University of Hyderabad and Dr. K. Stevenson, Dr. V. Shyam Sunder, Sri M. Srinath Reddy, Dr. K. Nageshwar and Dr. K. Narender of the Department of Communication and Journalism, Osmania University, have been a source of encouragement for the completion and publication of this work. I express my gratitude to them.

I owe a lot to the Project Director, DRDA, Medak District, Assistant Project Officers; MDOs and VDOs of Sangareddy and Medak mandals for their co-operation in data collection. My special thanks to Soma Narayana, VDO, Sangareddy Mandal for his help and encouragement. The staff of District Planning Office, DPAP, Sangareddy also extended their cooperation. I am thankful to the VAOs, Sarpanches, teachers, gram sevaks (Village Assistants) and people of the villages — Uttarpalli, Pathuru, Ponnala and Chitkul for participating in the survey. Mr. M. Sangita Rao of the Department of Telugu, University of Hyderabad, accompanied and helped me during the field-work for which I express my gratitude to him. I am thankful to Mr. Samuel Raju for helping me to process data. I express my gratitude to Prof. Ranga Rao of CIEFL for going through the proof.

I am thankful to Prof. S.C. Saha, Vice-Chancellor, Assam University for sanctioning study leave to complete this work. My thanks to my colleagues, friends and well-wishers Dr. Sisir Basu, Dr. H. Srikanth, Dr. Mala, Dr. Afeefa Bhanu, Dr. Hemanth Kumar and Dr. Musthafa for extending their support.

I am grateful to the library staff of the University of Hyderabad, Osmania University, Assam University, Silchar, ASRC, Hyderabad, Department of Forests, Hyderabad, National Institute of Rural Development (NIRD), Hyderabad, Centre for Economics and Social Sciences (CESS), Hyderabad, Indian Institute of Mass Communication (IIMC), New Delhi and CEE, Ahmedabad for their co-operation and help. My friends and seniors, Mr. P. Kennedy, Dr. Uday Kumar, Mr. Sudhakarudu, Dr. Sanjay Asthana and B. David have been a constant source of encouragement. My family members and in-laws were with me at the time of joy as well as difficulties. Especially, my mother Nagarathnam, my wife Hanna, and my brother B. Yesudas helped me by constantly inspiring and bearing with some difficulties. I am thankful to them. I express my gratitude to Concept Publishing Company and to all those who have helped me directly or indirectly in bringing out this book.

Contents

List of Tables

List of Figures and Maps

List of Maps

1 Introduction

Last five decades have witnessed a remarkable shift in the meaning and focus of development. Besides, these decades also witnessed a tremendous advancement in communication technologies. Though the concept of sustainable development is over a decade old, it being the latest and present trend of development, this book deals with the issue of sustainable development and the role of communication in sustainable development. Whether its role in sustainable development is the same as that of it in relation to the previous trends of development or different? If it is different, to what extent? Why and how? It becomes very pertinent to ask these questions for two reasons: one, the scope of sustainable development is broader than the earlier notions of development. While earlier development was the concern of a few economists, policy makers and administrators, sustainable development has become everybody's concern. Two, it is pertinent to find out the implications of tremendous changes that have taken place in communication in relation to sustainable development. Before a detailed discussion on this is made background presentation of the emergence of the concept of sustainable development would be useful.

The Background

Any kind of development like life itself, ultimately depends upon Nature. Nature has provided mankind with a protective cover as well as a supportive resource base. The protective cover is designed to protect mankind and other living beings from the harmful effects of certain elements of nature such as ultraviolet rays. The supportive resource base is provided for the sustenance of mankind and other living beings. This life supporting system is fragile and for the healthy condition of its various parts, they are interdependent on each other. Until the dawn of industrial revolution in Europe and America, man's activities did not disturb this fragile system. The progress in science and technology from the middle of 18th century onwards, resulted in industrialization, urbanization and modernization. The impact of industrialization on environment was not considered at that time. It was felt that the sky was so vast and clear that nothing could ever change its colour, that our rivers so big and their waters so plentiful that no amount of human activity could ever change their quality, and trees and natural forests so plentiful that we will never finish them. After all they grow again (Chitepo, 1986). Economic growth through industrialization became the obsession of some countries. Due to their prosperity and material wellbeing the industrialized countries became subsequently the models of development for underdeveloped countries. With the emergence of the concept of 'development' as an important concern, it also became the concern of scholars, belonging to various disciplines, including communication (Narula, 1994). As the focus and meaning of development has been changing over the last five decades and with the advent of new technologies, particularly satellites and telematics, the communication strategies are also planned according to the focus of development.

The Concept of Development

Development has been a highly debated and probably the most commonly shared concern of the world nations. It emerged as a distinct concept during Second World War. Between the years 1940 and 1944, the Allied countries were keen in adopting higher productivity, greater welfare and democratic governments as goals for the colonial territories (Brook-field, 1975). With the formation of the United Nations Organization (UNO) in 1945, the disparity between the rich and poor countries became a matter of international concern.

At the end of the Second World War, the countries of Asia, Africa and Latin America were liberated from colonial rule. These countries are also known as Third World countries, backward countries, underdeveloped countries, developing countries and less developed countries (LDCs). In the early post-war years, the attention of the UN and its most influential member, the United States of America (USA) was concerned with relief and rehabilitation work in war ravaged Europe. But starting in the fifties and going on into the sixties, this attention turned increasingly to the Third World where two-thirds of the world's population resided. Concern for the plight of these people moved US President Harry S. Truman to propose Point Four Programme. He observed: "More than half of the people of the Third World are living in conditions approaching misery. Their food is inadequate. They are victims of disease. Their economic life is primitive and stagnant. Their poverty is a threat both to them and to more prosperous areas." The key to prosperity and peace he said, was, 'greater production' through a wider and more vigorous application of modern scientific and technical knowledge (Daniels, 1951). The outcome of this proposal was called 'development'. Relieving Third World suffering consisted of making available the western cornucopia of advances in agriculture, commerce, industry and health (Melkote, 1991).

How to develop the underdeveloped societies just emancipated from colonial rule became an important concern among 'developed' nations. Therefore, the scholars in developed countries started formulating the theories and strategies for the development of under-developed world. In this process, they recapitulated the unique West European and North American transition from traditional to modern societies. One basic character of these countries is their economic growth due to the process of industrialization based on vast investments of capital, high level application of science and technology to productive process and organizational functioning. It resulted in a degree of economic development and improvement in material well-being of people. Therefore, the solution for solving the problems of underdevelopment in Asia, Africa and Latin America was considered to be simple and straightforward : by retracing the development path of the European countries (barring the colonization aspect), the Third World could be speeded through the different stages at a rate faster than the advanced countries themselves. This orientation came to be known as Dominant Paradigm (Melkote, 1991).

There were four main elements in the Dominant Paradigm (Rogers, 1976):

1. Economic growth through industrialization and accompanying urbanization, approximately equivalent to passing through the Industrial Revolution. Development performance was quantified in such economic terms as GNP (Gross National Product) and per capita income.
2. Capital intensive, labour saving technology, mainly transferred from industrialized nations.

3. Centralized planning, mainly by government, economists and bankers, in order to guide and speed up the process of development.
4. The cause of underdevelopment lay mainly within the developing nations, rather than in their trade or other external relationships with industrialized countries.

It was generally assumed that a nation became truly modern and developed when it arrived at that point where it closely resembled western industrial nations in terms of political and economic behaviour and institutions, attitudes towards technology, innovation and social and psychic mobility (Fjes,1976). From 1940s to late 1960s economists, sociologists, psychologists and communication experts believed that industrialization, urbanization and modernization were the routes to development. Thus the meaning of 'development' in 1950 and 1960s was transition of traditional societies as complex modern societies or in other words, transformation of Third World countries into the form of industrialized, ' developed' countries, such as, USA, UK etc.

Development and Communication

In 1950s development as well as 'Development Communication' scholars recognized the importance and role of communication as vital in the process of development. Information was considered as the missing link in the development chain (Melkote, 1991). Some scholars stated that the major problem in developing countries was not a shortage of natural resources but underdevelopment of human resources. For example, Wilbur Schramm felt that the modernization of industry or agricultural sectors in developing nations required the mobilization of human resources (Schramm, 1964). Therefore, the utmost responsibility of modernizing human resources was entrusted to education and mass media. In the process of studying communication in relation to development, Development Communication emerged as a distinct discipline in the communication studies.

Indeed, the origin of development communication dates back to the application of agricultural extension education during 1945-50, launched in most of the developing countries. Initially it was popularized as agricultural communication. Later, when the scope of extension effort was enlarged to include other areas like health, education etc., it became popular as rural communication. With the emergence of development as a distinct concept in the international arena, communication applied for initiating and accelerating the process of development branched off as a serious study under the discipline of Development Communication or Development Support Communication (Rao. 1992).

The 1948 U.N. Conference on Freedom of Information and the subsequent U.N. General Assembly Resolutions of 1953 which emphasized the role of information media in education, economic and social progress, provided a fillip for a faster growth of development communication. The idea that development is dependent on effectiveness of communication and is conditioned to a large extent by the character of communication, gained momentum. It was widely appreciated that : (a) wherever communication existed on a planned level, development has been accelerated, and (b) that major developmental programmes will not reach their targets without adequate and planned communication inputs (Rao,1992).

The pioneering and landmark research in this area was done by Daniel Lerner (1958), Willbur Schramm (1964), Everett Rogers (1976) etc. According to Lerner (1958) mass media were both the indices and agents of modernization. The social change occurred in three phases, viz., urbanization, literacy, and a great spurt in the growth of modern mass media. He believed that literacy would lead to greater mass media exposure. Greater mass media exposure in turn would result in higher rates of literacy. Mass media exposure and literacy were seen as related to economic and political participation. The role of mass media was, therefore, to mobilize human resources by motivating change in attitudes, beliefs, and behaviours. So the mass media were seen as mobility multipliers, capable of producing empathy, the capacity to put oneself in the other's shoes and be able to relate to a rapidly changing environment, and to be future oriented, ambitious, competitive, rational, with a desire to progress and consume (Kumar, 1994).

Lakshmana Rao's study of two villages in India, Kothooru and Pathooru (1963) suggested that communication was the prime mover in the development process. It was the quality and quantity of information that triggered change in Kothooru. The mass media brought in modern ideas and values from outside. Traditional ideas and modes of behaviour as they existed in Pathooru were gradually dislodged. Education was given a great spur. The new developments led to new jobs and higher productivity (Melkote, 1991, p. 85). While Lerner suggested the role of communication as the harbinger of new ideas from outside, Rao felt that new communication helped to smooth out the transition from a traditional to a modern community. In his influential book Mass Media and National Development (1964) Wilbur Schramm strengthened the views of Lerner and Lakshmana Rao in favour of modernization through mass media which he termed 'the magic multipliers' (Kumar, 1994). He felt that the mass media were agents of social change almost miraculous in their power to bring about the change.

In the process of diffusing innovations also mass media channels were often considered to be most rapid and efficient means to inform an audience of potential adopters about the existence of an innovation, that is, to create awareness, while interpersonal channels were considered to be more effective in persuading one individual to adopt a new idea (Rogers, 1983).

Thus in Dominant Paradigm's communication strategies in 1950s and 1960s there were three approaches : powerful effects approach, diffusion of innovations approach, and mass media and modernization approach. In these three approaches also mass media were thought to have a powerful, uniform and direct influence on individuals, in blowing the winds of modernity to replace the traditional way of life in underdeveloped countries. Thus the bullet theory model of mass media effects seemed to hold in the Third World countries in the 1950s and 1960s, even though this model was discarded in North America in the 1940s (Melkote, 1991). According to Ascroft and Masilela (1989) Dominant Paradigm's approach to communication for development was, vertical in nature, authority based, top down, expert driven, non-negotiable, well intentioned and thus hortatory in orientation.

Though many Third World countries followed the model of Dominant Paradigm, the rift between the developed and under-developed countries, as well as, between the rich and poor within the underdeveloped countries, did not decrease. Rather, it widened. Therefore, in 1970s, realization dawned that the above model (Dominant Paradigm) cannot decrease the poverty of all but can certainly increase the affluence of a few. Majority of the nations and people continued to live in poverty. For scholars like Schumacher people did matter. For him "The farmer is not merely a factor of production" but, before any thing else, he or she is an end-in-itself, meta-economic, and in a certain sense ' sacred' (Lutz, 1992).

It was viewed that development could no longer just be economic development, or in a narrow sense, as economic growth. When one talks of development, the real indicators are a decrease in the rate of poverty, income inequality and unemployment. Besides, realizing the fact of the development of underdevelopment in Third World countries during colonial rule and socio-cultural circumstances specific to different countries, it was felt that there was no question of one best way, but each country will have its own perspective and pattern of development achieved through strategies forged in the country itself.

Therefore, in the light of above realization, the roles assigned to communication also changed. The focus in the newer approaches was not just top-down flow of information and ideas but equal knowledge-sharing between users and sources. Communication was now employed to conscientise the common people to their needs and problems; facilitate problem articulation; help in self-development efforts, foster cultural growth and autonomy; serve as a tool for diagnosis of community's problems; and serve as an important vehicle in bringing about community participation. Thus, there was a shift from development communication (DC) to development support communication (DSC), while the former was characterized by top-down communication which focuses upon the sender, the nation as a whole, and the media effects (James, 1994), the latter is participatory and goal oriented, and concerns itself with communication at grass-roots, message structure, message effects, and the ability of the target group to process development information effectively.

The Paradigm Shift : Sustainable Development

As mentioned earlier, industrialization, urbanization and modernization were considered to be the main routes for development, but they could not eradicate the poverty, inequality and other ills of the society. Besides, owing to the process of industrialization based on vast investments of capital, high level application of science and technology, excessive convenient and opulent lifestyle of affluent people and population explosion, some deleterious effects took place on environment and society, such as, social and economic inequalities, health hazards, soil erosion, desertification, acid rains and pollution of atmosphere. Today the human race faces enormous challenges to its very existence owing to the over exploitation of natural resources, carbon emissions of fossil fuels and the consequent warming up of the earth climate and damage to the ozone layer.

Since 1900 the world's population has tripled and global industrial production has increased 50 times. Some 80 per cent of the increase in industrial production has occurred since 1950 (MacNeill, 1989). In 1991 the annual product of the global economy was valued at $ 29,000 million which meant it produced in a mere 17 days the equivalent of the entire annual global product in 1900 (Brown *et al.*, 1991). Throughout a great period of the century there has been accelerating increase in the consumption of both renewable and non-renewable resources. Agricultural production has risen dramatically, so also desertification, soil erosion and the salinization of productive lands (Reid, 1995).

Energy generation, industrial processes, transport, high-input agriculture and domestic consumption continue to make bigger and bigger demands of the capacities of the earth and the atmosphere to absorb CO_2, Sulphur, Oxides of Nitrogen (NO_x) and methane emissions, Chlorofluorocarbons (CFCs), and a range of toxic chemicals. For example, Polychlorinated Biphenyl (PCBs), dioxins and other carcinogens, including radioactive wastes—which threaten widespread endemic pollution (Reid, 1995), certain environmental disasters alerted the people of various countries. For example, in the 1950s in Minimata Bay of Kyushu in Japan, dumping of a mercury based compound by a chemical company eventually killed 700 people and left 9000 crippled. In Sweden also lakes and rivers have become polluted by mercury from pulp, paper and pesticide industries (Sharma, 1994). In Love Canal, New York, in the 1970s communities were shocked when toxic wastes began to ooze out of the earth in their lawns and basements (Eddie,1992). In addition to that, pollution of major rivers in various countries made the people feel concerned for the environment all over the world.

Though United Nations (UN) has been showing concern for the environment since 1946, the first international conference on human environment held at Stockholm in 1972 was a landmark event (Chakraborty, 1994). It alerted the world countries on the need of protecting the environment and to re-think about the 'development' that is oblivious of the environmental deterioration.

It was felt that development and conservation are equally necessary for our survival and for the discharge of our responsibilities as trustees of natural resources for the generations to come (IUCN, 1980). The world conservation strategy of 1980 had advanced the idea of sustainable development and had recognized the challenge of integrating development and environment. Thus as Vandana Shiva (1991) observed the development has given way to sustainable development and growth has given way to green growth.

Though the concept of sustainable development was advanced, the world conservation strategy did not succeed in integrating economics with environment (Pearce, *et al.,* 1989). Therefore, in 1984 the U.N. General Assembly appointed the World Commission on Environment and Development, headed by Gro Harlem Brundtland. The Commission first met in October 1984, and published its report 900 days later in April 1987. Over those days, the following environmental disasters took place.

The drought-triggered, environment-development-crisis in Africa peaked, putting 35 million people at risk, killing perhaps a million:

- A leak from a pesticides factory in Bhopal, India (on December 2, 1984) killed more than 2000 people and blinded and injured 2,00,000 more.
- Liquid gas tanks exploded in Maxico city, killing 1000 and leaving thousands more homeless.
- The Chernobyl nuclear reactor explosion sent nuclear fall out across Europe, increasing the risks of future human cancer.
- Agricultural chemicals, solvents and mercury flowed into the Rhine River during a warehouse fire in Switzerland, killing millions of fish and threatening drinking water in the Federal Republic of Germany and the Netherlands.
- An estimated 60 million people died of diarrhoea related to unsafe drinking water and malnutrition; most of the victims were children (WCED,1987, p. 3).
- In 1986 a hole in the ozone layer above the Antarctica was discovered (WECD,1987, p. 33).

The report of World Commission on Environment and Development, titled *Our Common Future*, was published in 1987. The report firmly established the concept of sustainable development as the basis for an integrated approach to economic policy in the coming decades. The concept of sustainable development gained further strength and greater attention since the United Nations

Conference on Environment and Development, the largest international conference ever held (Popularly known as Earth Summit) in Rio de Janeiro in June 1992 (Reid, 1995).

Meaning and Definitions of Sustainable Development

The most widely accepted definition of sustainable development is provided by the UNO's World Commission on Environment and Development (1987), which described it as *the development that meets the needs and aspirations of the present generation without compromising the ability of future generations to meet their own needs.* This articulation of sustainable development has led to attempts to spell out in greater detail the specific features of this concept. Some alternative definitions that outline the content of sustainable development are as noted below :

> An economic definition places greater emphasis on the use of "renewable natural resources" in a manner that does not eliminate or otherwise diminish their usefulness for future generations (Goodland and Ledec, 1987).
> A technology based interpretation is that sustainable development includes a rapid transformation of the technological base of industrial civilization with the use of new technologies that should be cleaner, more efficient and less natural resource intensive (James Gustave Speth, 1989).
> An ecological definition of the concept is that it involves improving the quality of human life while living within the carrying capacity of supporting eco systems (IUCN, UNEP and WWF, 1991). From consumption point of view, sustainable development means a change in consumption patterns towards environmentally more benign products and a change in investment patterns towards augmenting environmental capital (Pearce, Anil Markandy, Edward B. Barbier, 1989).

As Akshay Jaitly (1993) observed, the Rio declaration contains numerous references to sustainable development. In the absence of an explicit definition, aproximate interpretation can be derived through an examination of the text of various principles:

(a) a healthy and productive life in harmony with nature (Principle-1),
(b) environmental protection is an inherent part of the development process (implying perhaps that development that does not protect the environment is not sustainable) (Principle-4),
(c) eradicating poverty (which is seen as an indispensable requirement for sustainable development (Principle-5),
(d) as related to production and consumption and appropriate demographic policies (Principle-8),
(e) involving exchange of scientific and technological knowledge and by enhancing the development, adoption and diffusion of new technologies, including the transfer of technologies (Jaitly, 1993, p. 30).

Sustainable Development—Intra Generational and Inter Generational Equity

Intra generational equity and inter generational equity are two important aspects in sustainable development. These two kinds of equities are embodied in the WCED's definition of sustainable development. Intra generational equity is for people living now who do not have access to natural resources or social and economic goods. If we look at the present situation, out of 5.6 billion world population, more than one billion people are living in extreme poverty—70 per cent of them are women. 1.3 billion people do not have access to clean drinking water and proper sanitation (Reddy, 1995). Every year 1.8 crore people are dying due to the diseases caused by hunger. Owing to the malnutrition every year 1.8 crore children are dying. Due to the deficiency of A vitamin, every year 25 lakhs children are going blind. On the other hand 86 per cent of the world industries, 78 per cent of trade, 85 per cent of chemical products, 90 per cent of motor vehicles belong to developed countries. On an average 1000 calories more of extra food is consumed by a person in a developed country than a person in an underdeveloped country (Manasa, 1995). But in poor societies people are struggling for their daily survival, often lacking the resources. In these societies, what is at risk is not the quality of life but life it self.

The poor are not preoccupied with the loud emergencies of global warming or the depletion of the ozone layer. They are preoccupied with the silent emergencies—polluted water or degraded land that put their lives and their livelihoods at risk. Unless the problems of poverty are addressed, environmental sustainability cannot be guaranteed (Human Development Report, 1994).

Intergenerational equity is the obligation of current generations to future generations. To define the notion of inter generational equity, it is helpful to view the human community as a continuous partnership across all generations, whose purpose is to realize and protect the well being of every generation and to conserve the resources of the planet for this purpose (Jaitly, 1993). Inter generational equity can also be defined in terms of inter generational inter-temporal externalities (Rowe, 1991). An inter-temporal externality would be one which involves benefits accruing to the present generation, reaped at the cost of future generations. It is the imposition of a cost at a time later than the time at which the benefit is received. If we observe today's consumption patterns, the north has roughly one-fifths of the world's population and four-fifths of its income and it consumes 70 per cent of the world's energy, 75 per cent of its metal and 85 per cent of its wood. Replicating the patterns of the North in the South would require ten times the present amount of fossil fuels and roughly 200 times of mineral wealth. And in another 40 years, these requirements would double again as the world population doubles (Human Development Report, 1994). This situation reveals the need to change the consumption pattern of the North and controlling the population of the South. Therefore, to fulfil the intergenerational equity, there is a need of conserving, reducing and recycling and thus transferring the environment or natural resources to next generations in good condition.

Importance of the Role of Communication in Sustainable Development

In the wake of the above discussion it is observed that sustainable development is a coin which consists of two obligations on its two sides. One side is the alleviation of poverty and the other, the protection of environment. Sustainable development is very much linked with the involvement and active participation of people. It is a holistic concept that can be on the global, national, local and individual scale. Communication is an intervening variable without which the materialization of different goals of sustainable development is not possible. Therefore, communication has the key role in facilitating the participation of people relating to sustainable development.

Conceptual Framework

The present study has been taken up with the following theoretical framework. There are a myraid of theories and models of communication, but there are only a few theories and models which deal with the question of development. Therefore, it is useful to discuss the relevant models and theories in the context of the present study as follows:

Development media theory deals with the task of media in developing countries. It emphasizes the positive uses of the media in national development and for the autonomy and cultural identity of the particular national society. To a certain extent elements of this theory favour democratic and grassroots involvement, thus promoting participative communication model (Mcquil, 1987). The one thing which gives unity to a development theory of the media is the acceptance of economic development itself and often the correlated nation building, as an overriding objective. To this end, certain freedom of the media and of journalists is subordinated to their responsibility of helping in this purpose. Collective ends rather than individual freedoms are emphasized.

With the failure of the Dominant Paradigm of development, and its communication approach in bringing about the expected change, there took place a rethinking about the alternative paradigm of development which led to the emergence of the concept of 'another development' and subsequently a more specific one, sustainable development. With regard to communication also, a major shift has taken place from top-down authoritative model of communication to a two way, horizontal and participatory model of communication.

Shirly, A. White (1994) distinguished the genuine participation from pseudo participation. When the development bureaucracy, the local elite, and the people working co-operatively throughout the decision-making process and when the people are empowered to control the action to be taken, then only there will be a genuine participation. He further emphasized that Freire's concept of conscientization is central to the theme of participation. To activate consciousness and critical awareness of one's situation and environment, one's identity, one's talents, and one's alternatives for freedom of action is an imperative to participatory action.

In Sri Lanka, Kanthowski (1980) observed that the *Shramadana* camps foster spiritual development of both the individual and the group. The development of the individual personality is brought about by the emphasis on four Buddhist principles, kindness, compassion, sympathetic joy and equanimity. Similarly four Buddhist principles guide group behaviour—sharing, pleasant language, joint work, and equality.

All these principles are put into actual practice through *Shramadana* or labour donating camps. Dissanayake (1984) notes that in these camps important village activities such as laying of roads, construction of schools, community centres and rural housing schemes, repair and construction of irrigation channels, and clearing land for agriculture, are performed through the active voluntary participation of local people.

Dissanayake compares the Buddhist model of communication as used in the *sorvodaya* movement with the typical Western or Aristotelian model. The Buddhist model emerges as an interactive, two-way process, bringing out the dynamic nature of communication,

Table 1.1 : Western and Buddhist Models of Communication

Aristotelian (Western) Model	*Buddhist Model*
1. Emphasis on communicator	1. Emphasis on receiver
2. Influence a key notion	2. Understanding a key notion
3. Focus on control	3. Focus on choice
4. Emphasis on out ward process	4. Emphasis on both out ward and inward processes.
5. Relationship between communicator, receiver asymmetrical	5. Relationship between communicator and receiver symmetrical
6. Stress on intellect	6. Stress on empathy

Source : Melkote (1991: p. 205).

whereas the western model uses the static, top down, one way model of Berlo as follows :

Thus, there has been a shift in the development communication theory from one way, non-participatory communication models to two-way participatory communication models. In the participatory communication model, emphasis is not on big media but appropriate media. Taking into consideration the broad goals of sustainable development and the importance people's participation in materializing these goals, participatory communication model is more relevant in the context of sustainable development.

Ramireg (1995) contended that in sustainable development there are multiple stake holders, all generating and exchanging information. There is, therefore, a need for building bridges, linking different view points and creating a common "language" among different stake holders. Communication for development is about aiding different types of actors interested in understanding needs and assessing opportunities jointly, it is about providing them with the methods and media to reach common meaning, and about enabling them to negotiate with other actors with contrasting perceptions and interests.

The Agenda 21 is evident that the need for sustainable development is a common goal of mankind. According to this, "in sustainable development, everyone is a user and provider of information considered in the broad sense. That includes data, information, appropriately packed experience and knowledge. The need for information arises at all levels, from that of senior decision makers at the national and international levels to the grassroots and individual levels." In the backdrop of the above theoretical framework, the present study deals with the sustainable development from the communication perspective.

Sustainable Development in India

India is a vast country with wide spread poverty, over population, and a number of environmental problems. In the post-independent India development became an overriding objective of the government. Consequently in the area of social environment, India has been able to eliminate famines common during colonial times. Though the concept of sustainable development is relatively a new one, some of its tenets were present in the Government of India programmes, even before the emergence of this concept. Government has been trying to achieve the goals of development through five year plans. For poverty alleviation a number of programmes were introduced. These programmes include, community development programme, Small Farmers Development Agency (SFDA), Jawahar Rozgar Yojana (JRY), Integrated Rural Development Programme (IRDP), Development of Women and Children in Rural Areas (DWCRA), Training of Youth for Self Employment (TRYSEM), Indira Awas Yojana (IAY), Swarna Jayanti Gram Swaroajgar Yojana (SGSY) etc.

For conserving environment also government introduced a number of programmes and Acts. As long back as in 1972, at the Stockholm

Conference Mrs. Indira Gandhi, the then Prime Minister, asserted that the objectives of achieving development and that of protecting the environment were not contradictory but complementary. (Ganguly, 1996)

Later she formulated the government's policy of achieving 'rapid economic development without ecological damage'. In keeping with this goal, the National Committee of Environmental Planning and co-ordination was constituted in 1972. The committee brought out the alarming proportions of environmental degradation and destruction of land and water resources in its draft report published in 1981. It revealed that, of the total land area of 304 million hectares, over 175 million hectare were environmentally endangered, due to deforestation, erosion and water logging. The area affected by the floods had doubled from 20 million hectares in 1971 to 40 million hectares entailing an average loss of Rs.700 crores. Only 12 per cent of the land surface was under adequate forest cover as against the target of 33 per cent by the 1952 national forest policy.

The concern for environmental conservation even as the process of social and economic growth and development should be maintained was reflected in the Sixth Five Year Plan (1980-85) document. It was stated therein that in preparing plans and programmes, a crucial guiding dimension must be an assessment of their impact on the environment. The two kinds of environmental problems faced by India, according to the Planning Commission, were people's poverty and underdevelopment on the one hand and the negative effects of the very process of the development on the other (The Sixth Five Year Plan, 1980-85). The Commission presumed that without checking the rate of the growth of population and enabling the people to meet their basic needs and improving the quality of their life, the environmental health of the country can not be truly protected.

To meet these objectives, the Department of Environment was entrusted with the task of undertaking environmental appraisal of different development projects proposed for inclusion in the plan. The department also monitored the level of environmental pollution and working of regulatory measures for pollution control, conservation of diverse bio-resources, marine eco system, etc. In India's Planning system it is now a compulsory requirement that environmental impact assessment studies are made in respect of all projects which are required to be cleared by the government or Planning Commission. Sanctions of projects, like river valley development, power generation, hydel, thermal or atomic, etc. are given only after the project is cleared after making such studies.

By introducing various policies and programmes for the development and conservation of environment, post-independent India has been able to eliminate famines common during colonial times. Many people now have access to safe drinking water and the number of under-weight children is declining. Child and infant mortality has dropped substantially and primary school enrolment has risen. The poverty rate has gone down.

Yet India is far from where it could be. The absolute number of poor has risen over recent decades. Roughly 300 million of our people, or 1 in 3 live below the poverty line (Parikh, 1999-2000). Most of India's poor live in rural areas and are engaged in agriculture. Over the period 1991-97, urban poverty declined, but rural poverty has remained broadly unchanged. In spite of the efforts of the government to control the population, the unabated growth of population has crossed 1 billion mark, aggravating the problems of unemployment, poverty and environmental degradation. The illiteracy rates of men and women are higher than the average of low income countries. The gap in literacy between men and women is among the highest in the world, one stark indication being that a girl is one-third less likely to attend secondary school than a boy.

According to the Water Commission, we have 3,600 dams that qualify as big dams. Yet, one-fifth of our population—200 million people — does not have safe drinking water and two-thirds—600 million lack basic sanitation. (Roy, 1999)

The country is passing through a number of environmental problems : air, water and sound pollution, deforestation, soil degradation, loss of bio diversity being some of these problems. In the recent years the country has witnessed severe floods and droughts in the states of Orissa and Gujarat respectively. The environmental deterioration is evident from the fact that safe drinking water, which was freely available some years ago, has become an economic goods. Commenting on the problem of droughts, Anil Agarwal (2000) wrote that India gets more rains than most, if rain water could be conserved, there need not ever be a drought. Clearly, India's problem is not water. It is the government that penalizes private initiative to harvest rain water simply because it owns everything, even our streams and lakes.

The short sighted policies of the government are also leading to various environmental problems and affecting the lives of people. Various environmental groups and movements are advocating the cause of protecting environment. For example, *Narmada Bachavo Andolan*

(NBA) is advocating and fighting for the cause of environment and the lives of people in the Narmada valley. But, unfortunately it is seen as a war between modern, rational, progressive forces of 'Development' verses a sort of neo-luddite impulse—an irrational, emotional 'Anti-development', resistance, fuelled by an agrarian, pre-industrial dream. On the other as a Nehru *vs.* Gandhi contest. In order to meet the goals of sustainable development, India needs to address all the above discussed problems.

Andhra Pradesh

Andhra Pradesh is the fifth largest and fourth poplous state in India. It lies between the 12° 14 N to 19° 54′ N latitudes and 76° 50′ to 84° 45′ E longitudes and is situated in the south eastern part of the Indian peninsula. Its total area is 2,75,909 sq.kms., with a population of 72 millions. The language spoken in the state is Telugu. It is bounded in the east by the Bay of Bengal, on the North by Orissa and Madhya Pradesh, on the south by Tamil Nadu and on the west by Karnataka and Maharashtra.

The state has 23 districts distributed in three regions, viz., Telangana, Rayalaseema and Coastal Andhra. The last two regions were the part of Madras presidency until a separate Andhra State was formed on October 1, 1953. Following the reorganization of states on the language basis on 1st November 1956, the Telangana region was merged with Andhra State to form the present state of Andhra Pradesh.

The literacy rate of the state is 43.2 per cent according to 1991 census much lower than the country's average (52.3 per cent). In 1987-88, the number of rural persons living below the poverty line in the state were 33.8 per cent, while in India this number was 33.4 per cent. For the alleviation of poverty, a number of programmes have been implemented in the state. These programmes are—integrated Rural Development Programme, Training of Rural Youth for Self Employment, Development of Women and Children in Rural Areas. Improved tool kits to Rural artisans, Maternity Assistance for women Agricultural labourers, failed well compensation scheme, Drought Prone Areas Programme, Integrated Wastelands Development Programme, financing self-help groups, involvement of voluntary organizations, rural water supply and minimum needs programme. (Govt. of A.P., N.D.)

Prior to 1980s, its economy was considered to be predominantly agriculture based. In the past three decades the state has continuously and deliberately tried to move from agricultural to industrial economy. From a modest beginning during independence with only 45 large and medium industries with an investment of Rs. 63 crores, the state has emerged as one of the major industrialized states in the country (Reddy, 1992). However, this industrialization tended to be clustered or concentrated in the capital city and one or two other centres with concommitant socio-economic and environmental problems.

In Andhra Pradesh most of the important lakes and streams are grossly polluted. Reportedly, only 25 per cent of state's inland water sources contain clean water with 3 to 5 parts for million of BOD (Bio-chemical Oxygen Demand an indicator of pollution). The state is also facing the problem of rampant air pollution and industrial pollution, caused by industries and automobiles. Though the state's forest area is considered to be 23.11 per cent. In reality, it has been reduced to 11 per cent. (Rao, *et al.*, 1990 : p. 17). Guntur and East Godavari districts of the state, occupy 1st and 4th positions respectively in the use of fertilizers. Deforestation and excessive use of fertilizers is leading to soil erosion and soil degradation. Thus the state is facing a number of environmental problems.

After coming to power, the present Chief Minister of Andhra Pradesh, Mr. N. Chandra Babu Naidu introduced several developmental programmes, including the *Janmabhoomi*, Joint Forest Management and Watershed Development Programmes to bring about sustainable development in the state.

He observed "my vision of Andhra Pradesh is one where poverty is totally eradicated; where every man, woman and child has access to not just the basic minimum needs but to all the opportunities for leading a happy and fulfilling life; a knowledgeable and learning society built on the values of hard work" (*Down to Earth,* Feb.,1999). He emphasized the involvement of people in development process and declared the rural development as his biggest priority. Environment is one of the focal points for the government programmes. The state government has given priority to environmental protection and promotion in the Vision 2020 (1998) a document prepared by the government to make the state by the 2020 as *Swarn Andhra Pradesh* (Golden Andhra Pradesh).

Earlier Studies

From the above points of view on sustainable development it is necessary to take stock of the research studies that focused on the role of communication in development.

Right from the time the role of communication in development assumed significance, a number of studies have been carried out relating to communication and development. There are also some studies on communication and environment as follows:

Based on his studies during 1950-51 in the Middle East (covering Iran, Egypt, Turkey, Syria, Lebanon and Jordan) Daniel Lerner (1958) found out that mass communication served as the great multiplier in development, the device that could spread the requisite knowledge and attitudes immeasurably, more quickly and widely than ever before. His analysis revealed that there is high correlation between media growth and national growth. He argued that the person who changes in a developing society is usually "a mobile personality" who has high capacity to identify with new aspects of his environment, and who can take in his stride the new demands upon himself that are out of his habitual experience. According to Lerner, the first element in social dynamics of development is the infusion of modern or mobile personality, the second element is the mobile multiplier; the mass media.

Lakshmana Rao (1963) in his study of two villages in India, viz., Kothooru and Pathooru found that among other things, the road brought new people, ideas, and the mass media into the village while at the same time facilitating the villagers to visit the urban centres. All this new information opened up people's minds in Kothooru. They were not only ready for change but demanding and expecting it. The new ideas and innovations were first available to the elite and then trickled down to other sections in the village.

Wilbur Schramm (1964) asserted that the mass media were essential for creating a climate for development intended to prepare populaces for the radical changes that modernization would bring upon them. The media were to become technological tools in the hands of Third World governments for educating their people about the imperatives of modernization as well for diminishing the potential for resistance to change.

Nora Quebral (1975), traces the genesis of the term development communication and its parameters. According to her, development communication grew out of the field of agricultural communication. The term was coined to include under it, apart from agricultural development, other areas as of national development such as population, nutrition, health, education, housing, development etc.

Everet M. Rogers has done extensive research on Diffusion of Innovations. According to him, diffusion is a special type of communication, in which the messages are concerned with the new idea (Rogers, 1983). It is this newness of the idea in the message content of communication that gives diffusion its special character. Newness hints that some degree of uncertainty is involved. It was found that most of the inter-personal network links connect individuals who are alike or similar in adopter category and socio-economic status. So innovations generally "trickle across" rather than "trickle down" in the interpersonal structure of a social system (Rogers, 1983: 392). By adopting innovations relatively sooner than others in their system, innovators and early adopters achieve windfall profits, thereby tending to widen the socio-economic gap between these earlier adopting categories *versus* laggards. He felt that this tendency towards gap widening need not occur, if special strategies are followed to narrow gaps.

Akhileshwari (1989) presented an account of the media coverage of environment in general and Patancheru and adjacent areas in particular. She observed that articles, documentaries, films and their like hardly sway the public opinion. Their influence on die-hard bureaucrats and politicians is even less unless they carry the by line of an Arun Shouri.

Meenakshi Subramaniam (1989) expounded the crusading role of media with regard to the threat to the Taj Mahal, the Silent Valley hydro-electric project, Pooyamkutty project etc. She pointed out that the media have stepped in wherever there were active disincentives and legal restraints on private individuals willing to raise and maintain natural resources, political pressures for regularising encroachment and land given for projects such as dams, reservoirs, mines and industries.

Amitava Mukharjee and V.K. Agnihotri (1993) noted that there is a necessity for incorporating ecological and environmental studies at all levels of education. They also observed that mass media play a very important educative role in protecting the environment. Identifying the dearth of trained people in the area of environment and ecology, to produce programmes for various target groups, they felt that there is need for giving proper orientation to journalists to work efficiently in these areas.

V.S. Gupta (1989) discussed the catalytic and stimulating role of media in creating awareness, in chronicling the activities of action groups, grassroots movements and voluntary agencies : in informing the readers of the trends and perspectives at the global level and in performing the watch dog function.

Pradeep Krishnatray (1989) contended that ownership determines the development priorities and strategies of media. According to him, the Bhopal gas tragedy exposed the divergence between media establishment and the working journalists. The Bhopal media greatly reduced and played down the writings of a few conscientious journalists. Government hand-outs, Carbide Version, and the visits of ruling party politicians were front-paged and the plight of the victims, after two or three days of the tragedy, relegated to inner pages. Delhi newspapers editorially condemned the arrest of Anderson, the Carbide Chief, when he was in India. Only a few of them made fly-by night visits to Bhopal and wrote learned commentaries.

Alwi Dahlan (1989) dealt with the environmental approach to mass media coverage. He pointed out that a reporter should look at the subject with critical environmental eye. "He does not stop at the regular 5WsIH formula, but also ask those questions in relation to environmental conditions. Asking the what, for instance, also includes what would this occasion, event, or factor, do to the environment? The question of where could be extended to : is the location of this activity being covered close to a vulnerable environmental area, for example, a river to be used as waste disposal of the factory ?"

Mani Shankar Prasad (1996) observed that the first attempt to generate common awareness in environment was the clarion call of Sanjay Gandhi in 1975-76 who vociferously publicized the urgency and importance of plantation of trees all over the country. Again when Rajiv Gandhi became Prime Minister, he revised Twenty-Point Programme and laid emphasis on the preservation of environment. Besides, Prasad emphasized the importance of education in creating environmental awareness.

Pandey, K.N. *et al.* (1990) studied the number, duration and subjects of environmental programmes aired by Doordarshan Kendra, Lucknow, television and All India Radio, Varanasi stations. They found that considering the importance of environmental issues, the time allotment for creating awareness and educating the masses is meagre.

Ascroft and Masilela (1994) pointed out that living organisms survive not just by ingesting energy in the form of food, water, and air but also by ingesting information necessary for enabling them to adjust to their changing environments and make their adjustments felt upon them. Where food energy is converted to work energy, information is converted to purposeful behaviour for channelling that energy, enabling organisms to roam their environments safely as they search for food, avoid danger, and cope with the vagaries of weather. Humankind and all living systems must constantly engage in energy exchange and information exchange processes to survive.

Graham Chapman *et al.* (1997) in their study 'Environmentalism and the Mass Media: The North-South Divide' found that the Indian public show little understanding on 'global environmental issues and such knowledge is more influenced by access to the press than to TV. Precise technical knowledge seems to be most influenced by the access to the English press. They observed that the biggest discriminators in India are clearly poverty and wealth, and this also mimics the distinction between the illiterate and literate, the less educated and the more educated, those who have access to media sources and those who don't, and perhaps the distinction between the many local public and the post-nationalist audience. On the other hand, in more homogenous and more developed Britain, the prime interest of people is with their local economy, particularly, employment. It is not that people are not concerned with environmental issues at all; it is just that they do not have a high priority unless they have a detectable local impact.

Srinivas, R. Melkote *et al.* (1992) studied the comprehension of agricultural messages among farmers. They emphasized on isomorphism between source and the target and found that comprehension levels are higher for farmers with greater degree of formal education and lower for the farmers with less education or no education.

B.S.S Rao (1992) in his study ' Television for Rural Development' which was conducted in five villages of Poona region, Maharashtra, found that for majority of the respondents interpersonal communication channels, such as fellow villagers and relatives were main channels of interaction. He further observed that by and large the villagers have a favourable image of television as a medium for the delivery of useful information. This could be properly exploited to create faith in its capacity to respond to the information needs of all occupational groups. Potential audience with no idea of what television could offer to them; apparently, have no interaction either direct or indirect with the medium. One of the immediate goals of television should be to reach them with some relevant messages.

S.L. Sharma (1996) observed that the voluntary action groups can work for sustainable development in various ways, e.g., by serving as watchdogs, conscientizing and organizing people against unsustainable projects, generating environmental awareness and literacy, and launching programmes of regenerating and environmental regeneration. For example, in India alone, over 900 voluntary groups are involved in various environmental movements and projects.

Raja Sekhar (1995) in his study on role of voluntary organizations in rural development found that Deccan Development Society, an NGO has been helpful to the public and it had created awareness amongst people about government schemes and there by became a bridge between the government and the people to champion rural development.

G.P. Pandey (1999) argued that in India with 50 per cent of the population unlettered and with the media's reach largely restricted to urban areas, information, education and entertainment do not reach a large majority of the people. The only meaningful access for such people is traditional folk media which have been informing, educating and entertaining them for centuries and have found roots in their culture.

I.P. Tewari (1997) contended that the object of communication activity in the process of development would be to make people accept and work for development. Communication can fulfil the task of mobilizing people for development, only if the communicator is clear about its objectives and does not operate on the periphery. According to him, communication is as much an input in total development activity as money is, as material, man, machines and methods are.

Arvind Singhal and Everett, M. Rogers (1989) observed that in 1980s the field of development communication was characterised by pluralism, a willingness to recognize that there can exist many pathways to development. According to them the key elements in this paradigm include: (a) Greater equality in the distribution of development investments, information and the consequent socio-economic benefits, by focusing developmental activities on the weaker sections of society, (b) Popular participation, knowledge sharing, and empowerment to facilitate self-development efforts by individuals, groups and communities, (c) Self-reliance and independence in development, emphasizing the potential of local resources and (d) Integration of traditional and modern communication system, self-reliance and the integration of traditional and modern communication systems. They felt that the social impact of new communication technologies like satellite based television broadcasting, long distance telephone, VCRs, and application of micro electronics in computers and telecommunications was generating optimism about the potential of development communication. Because communication via new technologies is interactive, demassified and asynchronous.

Ambekar Yadav (1992) contended that "Not only are communication and rural development interrelated to each other but both in turn are influenced by a number of other factors—social, economic, technological and ecological". He found in his study of a village in Karnataka that the communication and adoption of innovations through mass media as well as inter-personal communication has generally followed the trickle down pattern from the higher castes and classes to the lower castes and classes. Even at the adoption level there has been a time gap due to communication gaps and economic constraints. However, mass media can be effective only if coupled with the existing networks of interpersonal communication and support of technical, economic, or credit institutions. The village leaders and progressive farmers' 'activities' have helped to produce a demonstration effect on the people. The non-adopters in turn accept the innovations after personally seeing the concrete results. Thus, there is inequality in developmental communication, which is determined by economic and educational inequalities within the rural community.

Joni C. Joseph (1997) found in his study "Mass Media and Rural Development" that when a fair stage of development is achieved, the mass communication boosts it further. Until that stage is attained the media could prepare a socio-psychological ground for the take-off in development. He observed that the media communication is a better promoter of development for those sections of rural population who have attained a certain level of socio-economic advancement. That is, the less advanced categories are benefiting less by development communication. In this study the degree of awareness contributed by mass media was related to age, education, religious, caste affiliation and social overheads of the area of residence. The level of adoption was found to be associated with education, income, socio-economic status and the nature of main occupation. But age, religion, caste affiliation and social overheads of the area do not influence the level of adoption induced by the media persuasion.

Uma Narula (1994) did an analytical review of development

theories and practice both from international and Indian perspectives. She analyzed how globally the development communication scenario has changed in the first four development decades. According to her, there has been a four-pronged change—the focus of development, the availability of new communication channels, the characteristics of the audience and development demands. Presenting the Indian perspective of development communication, she maintained that the Indian development efforts since independence in 1947 through a series of five year national development plans have been based on specific development and development communication model. The mere publicity model of 50s has matured into development support models.

J.S. Yadava (2000) observed that there is a need for greater conscious efforts towards decentralization and participation at all levels. The new technologies offer the possibilities for greater decentralization and participatory communication and development. But the technological possibilities need to be backed by sound political will on the part of ruling elite and or pressure from below by the people.

Srinavas, R. Melkote (1991) dealt with the Dominant Paradigm of development, which consists of the analysis of post-World War-II development theories in sociology, rural sociology, social psychology, economics and communication approach of the Dominant Paradigm, critique of the dominant paradigm and its communication approach, alternative development approaches, and development support communication. He predicted that the idea of sustainable development will become an important conceptual and practical framework for all development activities in nineties and beyond.

Some scholars, viz., Juan Diaz Bordenave, Pradip Thomas, Thomas L. Jacobson, Keval J. Kumar, Robert White, Syed A. Rahim, K. Sadanandan Nair, Shirly A. White, Joseph Ascroft etc. (1994) focused the attention on participative communication, participatory decision-making, participatory development communication, role of communication in another development, cultural identity etc.

Significance of this Study

The foregoing review of literature shows that there have been studies carried out on development and communication, media and development, environment and media, environment and communication, rural development and communication media and rural development traditional folk media and development and participatory development communication. But, though sustainable development is the latest and present trend of development, so far, proper attention has not been paid to this area from communication point of view. Therefore, it has been felt worthwhile to study the 'Role of Communication in Sustainable Development'.

Research Questions

Sustainable development being the latest and the present trend of development, the broad aim of the present study is to analyze the role of communication in sustainable development and to recommend a communication strategy for sustainable development.

Specific objectives of this study are :

1. To find out the various implications of sustainable development.
2. To analyze the role of communication in sustainable development.
3. To identify the policies and programmes of Indian government towards sustainable development.
4. An empirical study has been intended to be carried out in a backward and environmentally affected district of Medak in Andhra Pradesh.
   (See chapter 5 for profile of Medak district). The following aspects were sought to be examined in Medak district :
   (a) Role of communication in the success or failure of poverty alleviation programmes.
   (b) Awareness about environment, family planning, and reflection of that awareness in the lifestyle.
   (c) Source of information to people and their media habits.
   (d) Role played by various communication media in relation to combating pollution and in connection with environmental movements.
5. To recommend a communication strategy for sustainable development.

Research Approach

This study is based on both secondary and primary data. The secondary data has been collected from the books, reports, journals, magazines, newspapers, dissertations, booklets, folders, government records, seminar papers (both published and unpublished) video films and internet. Also, informal interviews and discussions were held with government officers, such as, Project Director, District Rural Development Agency (DRDA), Medak district, Assistant Project Officers, DRDA, Village Development Officers (VDOs), Mandal Development Officers (MDOs), Superintendents and Village Administrative Officers (VAOs). Discussions were also held with Sarpanches, and Gram Sevaks (Village servants).

The primary data has been collected on two broad areas:

1. Communication and poverty alleviation programmes,
2. Environmental awareness and media habits among the people of Medak District.

For studying the role of communication, in the success or failure of the poverty alleviation programmes, two villages, viz., Uttarpalli and Pathuru were selected from two revenue divisions —Sangareddy and Medak of Medak district respectively. These villages were selected after having discussions with the officers in DRDA. In these two villages, information was collected from the target beneficiaries of IRDP and DWCRA. The respondents include both beneficiaries as well as non-beneficiaries of these schemes.

In selecting the beneficiaries of DWCRA, five DWCRA groups were selected from each of theses two villages—Uttarpalli and Pathuru. Again from each group every third person was selected as the respondent. Thus 25 respondents from each of these two villages, a total of 50 DWCRA beneficiaries were selected through systematic random sampling. Table 1.2 shows the composition of the respondents among DWCRA beneficiaries.

In selecting the respondents among DWCRA non-beneficiaries, the names of the non-beneficiaries were identified with the help of village sarpanches and gram sevaks (village servants) and 25 respondents from each of these two villages, a total of 50 respondents were selected in these villages through convenience sampling technique. Table 1.3 shows the composition of the DWCRA non-beneficiary respondents.

In Uttarpalli and Pathuru together 18 persons were covered under IRDP asset giving scheme (please see Annexures I and II for details).

Table 1.2 : Composition of Respondents Among the DWCRA Beneficiaries by Caste, Age and Village.

Name of the village and community of the respondents

Age	*Uttarpalli*				*Pathuru*				*Total*
	SC	*ST*	*BC*	*OC*	*SC*	*ST*	*BC*	*OC*	
21-30	8		5		5	1	5		24
31-40	5		3		2		2	1	13
41-50	2		1	1	6				10
51 and above					2		1		3
Total	15		9	1	15	1	8	1	50

Table 1.3 : Composition of Respondents Among DWCRA Non-beneficiaries by Caste, Age and Village.

Name of the village and community of the respondents

Age	*Uttarpalli*			*Pathuru*			*Total*
	SC	*ST*	*BC*	*SC*	*ST*	*BC*	
20 years and below	–	–	2	4	1	–	7
20-30	2	–	3	–	2	2	9
31-40	2	–	6	6	1	5	20
41-50	1	–	5	2	2	–	10
51 years and above	1	–	19	–	–	–	14
Total	6	–	17	12	6	7	60

Initially, this study aimed at covering all the respondents. But due to the non-availability of 4 beneficiaries in the villages, the remaining 14 respondents (78%) were covered in this study. Among the non-beneficiaries, 10 each from these two villages, a total of 20 respondents were selected through convenience sampling techniques.

In order to study the environmental awareness and media habits among the people of Medak district, a survey was conducted in the district. Information was collected from 200 respondents. The respondents were selected through multi-step stratified purposive sampling technique. Care was taken to include urban, rural, male and female respondents. Besides, educational background, income background and age were also taken as criteria while selecting the respondents. Out of these 200 respondents, 125 respondents belong to rural areas and 75 respondents belong to the urban areas. The rural respondents were selected from 3 villages, viz., Chitkul, Pathuru and Ponnala representing 3 revenue divisions of the districts, Sangareddy,

Medak and Siddipet, respectively. Urban respondents were selected from Sangareddy, Patancheru, Medak and Siddipet, the major urban areas in the district. Table 1.4 shows the composition of the respondents.

Table 1.4 : Profile of the Respondents by Age and Education

Education	*Urban*								*Rural*								
	Below 15		*16-30*		*31-40*		*41 and above*		*Below 15*		*16-30*		*31-40*		*41 and above*		
	M	*W*	*M*	*W*	*M*	*W*	*M*	*W*	*M*	*W*	*M*	*W*	*M*	*W*	*M*	*W*	
Illiterates	4	0	1	1	2	2	2	3	0	1	2	2	3	3	4	2	32
V Class & below	4	3	0	1	0	0	2	3	5	10	2	4	3	0	2	3	42
VI – X	2	5	2	2	0	2	0	1	11	12	10	14	2	2	1	0	66
XI to Graduation	0	0	4	5	3	2	1	1	0	1	12	5	1	0	3	2	40
PG & above	1	0	5	1	1	2	4	2	0	0	1	0	0	2	0	1	20
Total	11	8	12	10	6	8	9	10	16	24	27	25	9	7	10	8	200

M–Men W–Women

Tools of Data Collection

The data has been collected through interview schedules. Separate schedules were used to cover different subjects — IRDP, DWCRA and Environmental awareness. In case of the target beneficiaries of IRDP and DWCRA questions were asked in Telugu. With regard to environmental awareness, questions were asked in both Telugu and English as per the convenience of the respondents.

The variables studied are: In terms of communication and poverty alleviation programmes, the awareness about the scheme, sources of information about the scheme, sources of motivation to avail the scheme, improvement in the financial condition after availing the schemes, reasons for not availing the schemes in case of non-beneficiaries and the general impression of the respondents about the schemes: IRDP and DWCRA.

With regard to the environmental awareness and media habits, awareness about global, national and local environmental issues, life style of the respondents awareness about family planning, adoption of family planning, sources of information on environmental issues, and media habits have been broadly covered.

This book has been organized in the following manner:

The concept of development, development and communication,

emergence of the concept of sustainable development, review of literature, statement of the problem, aim, objectives and methodology and theoretical framework have been presented in the introduction, i.e., Chapter 1.

Various implications of sustainable development—poverty alleviation, environmental protection, population control, human rights, social welfare and women's upliftment, prevention and control of air, water and sound pollution; prevention and regeneration of deforestation, soil erosion, soil degradation, waste management, environment friendly lifestyle; have been dealt in Chapter 2.

The relationship between communication and sustainable development — role of communication in moulding a lifestyle, that is imperative for sustainable development, the role of communication in informing, educating, conscientizing, supporting various environmental, developmental activities; the specific roles of various communication channels, viz., mass media, traditional folk media, voluntary organizations, family, educational institutions, religious institutions, literature etc., have been analysed in Chapter 3.

Various policies and programmes of the government for sustainable development—poverty alleviation programmes, population control programmes, environmental protection programmes and the Acts which seek to promote the environment, have been discussed in Chapter 4.

A profile of Medak district with special reference to environment and development—poverty, literacy, environmental degradation, non-governmental organizations operating in the district, communication flow and communication facilities in the district as well as in the selected areas, have been presented in Chapter 5.

The role of communication in the success or failure of poverty alleviation programmes, viz., DWCRA and IRDP Asset giving schemes has been dealt in Chapter 6.

Awareness about environmental issues, family planning, life styles of the respondents, media habits of the respondents have been presented in Chapter 7. Besides Role of Communication in combating the Patancheru industrial pollution has also been presented in Chapter 7.

Summary, recommendations and the communication strategy formulated for promoting sustainable development; have been presented in Chapter 8.

REFERENCES

Agarwal, Anil (2000), "A Drought of the Mind, Not Water", *Times of India*, Calcutta, April 30, p. 11.

Akhileshwari, R. (1989), "Environment and the Media", *Vidura,* May-June, pp. 11-12.

Ascroft, Joseph and Sipho Masilela (1989) "From Top-Down to Co-equal Communication: Popular Participation in Development Decision Making" paper presented at the seminar on Participation: A Key Concept in Communication and Change, University of Poona, Poona, cited by Melkote (1991), *op. cit.*, p. 36.

Ascroft, Joseph and Sipho Masilela (1994), "Participatory Decision Making in Third World Development" in Shirly, A. White, Sadanandan Nair and Jeseph Ascroft (eds.) *Participatory Communication: Working for Change and Development*, Sage, New Delhi, pp. 259-292.

Bordenave, Juan Diaz (1994), "Participatory Communication as a Part of Building the Participative Society" in Shirly, A. White, *et al.* (eds.) 1994, *op. cit.* pp. 35-47.

Brookfield, H. (1975), *Interdependent Development,* Methuen, London Cited by B.S.S. Rao (1992) *op. cit.*, p. 21.

Brown, L.R., Flavin. C. and Postel, S. (1991), "From Growth to Sustainable Development" in cited by David Reid (1995), *op. cit.*, p. 4.

Chakrabarty, N.K. (1994) *Environmental Protection and the Law,* Ashish Publishing House, New Delhi, pp. 53-68.

Chapman Graham, Keval, J. Kumar, Cordine Fraser and Ivor Yaber (1997), *Environmentalism and the Mass Media: The North-South Devide,* Routledge, London, pp. 213-274.

Chitepo, Victorio (1986), quoted in WCED's (1987), *Our Common Future*, *op. cit.*, p. 34.

Dahlan, M. Alwi (1989), "The Environmental Approach to Mass Media Coverage", *Media Asia,* Vol.16, No.4, pp. 219-222.

Daniels, Walter, M. (1951), *The Point Four Programme, H.W. Wilson,* New York, P.11, cited by Melkote, S.R. (1991), p. 21.

Dissanayake, W. (1984), "A Buddhist Approach to Development: A Srilankan Endeavour" in Wang. G. and Dissanayake, W. (eds.,) *Continuity and Change in Communication Systems*, Cited by Melkote (1991), pp. 204-205.

Down to Earth (1999), "Cyberbabu of Hyderabad", February 15, Centre for Science and Environment, New Delhi, pp. 40-41.

Eddie, Girdner J. (1992), "In the Valley of Shadow of Death", *Third Concept, An International Journal of Ideas*, Vol.6, No.67, (Sept. '92) cited by Madhavi, C. (1993), *op. cit.*, pp. 14.

Fjes, Fred (1976), "Communication and Development" An unpublished paper, College of Communications, University of Illinois, Urbana-Campaign, cited by Melkote, S.R., (1991) *op. cit.*, p. 38.

Ganguly, J.B. (1996), *Sustainable Development in North-Eastern Region of India*, ICSSR, Shillong, pp. 11-15.

Goodland Robert and Ledec, George (1987), "Neo-Classical Economics and Principles of Sustainable Development", *Ecological Modeling*, Vol. 38, p. 36, cited by Akshay Jaitly (1993), *op. cit.* p. 29.

Govt. of A.P. (N.D.), Programmes of Poverty Alleviation in Andhra Pradesh, Panchayati Raj Rural Development and Relief Department, Hyderabad.

Gupta, V.S. (1989), "Environmental Reporting", *Vidura*, May-June, pp. 3.7.

Human Development Report (1994), United Nations Development Programme, Oxford University Press, New York, pp. 1-27.

IUCN-The World Conservation Union, United Nations Environment Programme and World Wide Fund for Nature, *Carrying for the Earth*, IUCN, UNEP and WWF, Switzerland 1991, cited by Akshay Jaitly (1991), *op. cit.*, p. 29.

Jacobson Thomas.L. (1994), "Modernization and Post-Modernization Approaches to Participatory Communication for Development in Shirly, A.White. *et al.*, (eds.) 1994, *op. cit.*, pp. 60-73.

Jaitly, Akshay (1993), *The Road from Rio*, Teri Publication, New Delhi, pp. 28-30.

James Gustore Speth (1989), "The Environment: The Greening of Technology", *Development*, Vol. 2, No. 3, cited by Akshay Jaitly (1993), *op. cit.*, p. 29.

James Sybil. L. (1994), "Facilitating Communication Within Rural and Marginal Communities: A Model for Development Support in Shirly. A. White *et al.* (eds)., *Participatory Communication: Working for Change and Development*, Sage, New Delhi, p. 332.

Joni, C. Joseph (1997), *Mass Media and Rural Development,* Rawat Publications, New Delhi, pp. 217-218.

Kantowski, D. (1980) *Sarvodaya: The Other Development,* Vikas Publishing House, New Delhi, cited by Melkote (1991) *op. cit.*, p. 204.

Kumar, Keval J. (1994), "Communication Approaches to Participation and Development: Challenging the Assumption and Perspectives" in Shirly A. White, *et al.* (eds), *Participatory Communication: Working for Change and Development*, *op. cit.*, pp. 76-80.

Lerner, Deniel (1958), *The Passing of Traditional Society,* Glencoe, Free Press, cited in Rao, BSS, *Television for Rural Development (1992), op. cit.*, p. 45.

Lutz, M. (1992), "Humanistic Economics: History and Basic Principles" in P.E. Kins and M. Max Neef (eds.) *Real Life Economics: Understanding Wealth Creation* Routledge, New York, p. 102.

Mac Neill, J. (1989), "Strategies for Sustainable Economic Development," *Scientific American*, pp. 105-113, cited by David Reid (1995), *op. cit.*, p. 4.

Manasa, N. (1995)'Global Fight Against the Hunger is Confined Only to the Lip Service', *Eenadu* (a Telugu Daily) March 13, Hyderabad.

Mcquil, Denis (1987) *Mass Communication Theory,* Sage Publication, New Delhi.

Melkote, Srinivas, R. *et al., op. cit.*, (1992), *Communication Gap in India,* Rawat Publications, New Delhi, pp. 59-60.

Melkote, Srinivas, R. (1991), *Communication for the Development in Third World Countries*, Sage, New Delhi, pp. 21-205.

Mukharjee, Amitava and Agnihothri, V.K. (1993), *Environment and Development: Views from the East and West,* Concept Publishing Company, New Delhi, pp. 574-577.

Narula, Uma (1994), *Development Communication: Theory and Practice*, Har-Anand Publications, New Delhi, p. 139.

Pandey, G.P. (1999), "Traditional Folk Media and Development: The Only Effective Way to Diffuse Messages", *Communicator*, New Delhi, July-September, pp. 35-36.

Pandey, K.N. Dubey, V.K. and Choubey, P.N. (1990), "Media and Environment: A Case Study of Doordarshan Kendra, Lucknow and All India Radio, Varanasi", *Media Asia*, Vol.7, No.1, pp. 40-42.

Parikh, Kirit, S. (1999-2000), *India Development Report*, Oxford University Press, New Delhi, p. 5.

Pearce, David, Anil Markandya and Edward B. Barbier (1989), *Blue Print for a Green Economy,* Earth Scan, London.

Pradeep Krishnathray (1989), "Environmental Journalism", *Vidura*, May-June, New Delhi, pp. 13-14.

Pradeep Thomas (1994), "Participatory Development Communication: Philosophical Premises" in Shirly. A. White, *et.al.*, (eds.) *Participatory Communication: Working for Change and Development, op. cit.*, pp. 49-59.

Prasad, Mani Shanker (1996), "Need for Environmental Awareness. *Third Concept*, January 1996.

Quebral, Nora C. (1975), "Development Communication; Where Does it Stand Today?" *Media Asia,* Vol.2 (4) 197-202.

Rahim, Syed (1994), "Participatory Development Communication as a Dialogical Process" in Shirly. A.White, *et al.* (eds.), 1994, pp. 117-136.

Rajasekhar, N. (1995), *Role of Voluntary Organisations in Rural Development: A Case Study of Deccan Development Society*, M.Phil. Dissertation, University of Hyderabad, Hyderabad, p. 134.

Rao, B.V.S., *et al.* (1990), *Status of Andhra Pradesh Environment*, Academy of Gandhian Studies, Hyderabad, p. 17.

Rao, B.S.S. (1992), *Television for Rural Development,* Concept, New Delhi, pp. 21-175.

Rao, Laxmana, Y.V. (1963), *Communication and Development: A Case Study of Two Indian Villages,* Ph.D. dissertation, University of Minnesota, cited by Melkote (1991), *op. cit.* pp. 84-85.

Recardo, Ramireg (1999) "Communication" a meeting ground for sustainable Development", A paper presented in University of Guelph, Ontario, Canada, pp. 1-2.

Reddy (1992) *Public Polity for Environmental Protection : A Study of Its Implementation in an Industrial Area,* M. Phil. dissertation, Dept. of Political Science, University of Hyderabad.

Reddy, Rammonhar C. (1995), "Towards a Better Life", *The Hindu*, Hyderabad, 5th March.

Reid, David (1995), *Sustainable Development: An Introductory Guide,* Earth Scan, London, pp. 9-175.

Rogers, Everett M. (1983) *Diffusion of Innovations*, The Free Press, New York, pp. 1-392.

Rogers, Everett M. (1976), 'The Passing of Dominant Paradigm—Reflections on Diffusion Research' in Schram and D. Learner (eds.) *Communication and Change*, University Press of Hawaii, Cited by Melkote (1991) *op. cit.*, pp. 56-57.

Rowe, Gerard C. (1991), 'International Environmental Sustainability Policy and Law', cited in Pradipto Ghosh and Akshay Jaitly (eds) *The Road from Rio* (1993, *op. cit.* p. 31.

Roy, Arundhati (1999) "The Greater Common Good", *Outlook*, New Delhi, May 24, pp. 54-72.

Sadanandan Nair, K. and Shirly. A. White (1994), "Participatory Development Communication : A Cultural Renewal", in Shirly A. White, *et al.* (eds.) (1994), pp. 138-189.

Schramm, Wilbur (1964), *Mass Media and National Development*, Stanford University Press, Stanford, California, cited by Ascrot and Masilila (1994) *op. cit.* pp. 271-272 and Melkote (1991) *op. cit.* p. 92.

Schumachar, E.F. (1973), *Small is Beautiful: A Study of Economic as if People Mattered*, Abacus edition, Sphore Books, London, p. 138.

Sharma, P.D. (1994), *Ecology and Environment,* Rastogi, New Delhi, pp. 369-467.

Sharma, S.L. (1996), "Towards Sustainable Development in India: Issues and Perspectives" a paper presented at ICSSR, North-Eastern Regional Centre, Shillong.

Sharma, S.L. (1998), "Sustainable Development: Socio-Cultural Imperatives" in Joshi. Y.G. and Verma, D.K. (eds.) *Social Environment for Sustainable Development,* Rawat Publications, Jayapur, p. 36.

Shiva Vandana (1991), *Ecology and the Politics of Survival,* Sage, New Delhi, p. 1.

Singhal Arvind and Rogers Everett M. (1989), *India's Information Revolution*, Sage, New Delhi, pp. 205-206.

Sixth Five Year Plan (1980), Planning Commission, New Delhi.

Subramanian, Meenakshi (1989), "Crusading Role of the Media", *Vidura,* May-June, pp. 1-10.

Tewari, I.P. (1997), *Communication Technology and Development*, Publications Division, New Delhi, pp. 96-100.

Vision 2020 (1998), *Pragathi Vijayalatho Swarnandhranu Nirmiddam* (with the Victories of Progress, Let us build the Golden Andhra Pradesh), Department of Information and Public Relations, Hyderabad, pp. 57-58.

White Robert (1994), "Participatory Development Communication as a Social Cultural Process" in Shirly A. White, *et al.* (eds.) (1994), *op. cit.*, pp. 95-114.

White, Shirly. A. (1994), Introduction – "The Concept of Participation: Translating Rhetoric to Reality in Shirly A.White, *et al.* (eds.) *Participatory Communication: Working for Change and Development,* Sage, New Delhi, pp. 15-31.

World Commission on Environment and Development (WCED) (1987), *Our Common Future*, Oxford University Press, New Delhi, pp. 3-141.

Yadav, Ambekar J.B. (1992), *Communication and Rural Development,* Mittal Publications, New Delhi, pp. 151-157.

Yadava J.S. (2000) "An Indian Perspective: Communication and Development" *Communicator,* MC, New Delhi, October-December 1999 and January-March 2000, pp. 30-33.

2 Sustainable Development

Implications for Communication

Introduction

The concept of sustainable development has occupied a central place in every aspect of human life today. It is a multi-dimensional and multi-disciplinary concept covering almost all spheres of human activity. Sustainable development has become the concern of economists, ecologists, administrators, lawyers, communication experts, environmentalists, human rights activists, feminists, scientists and NGOs. In other words, it has become everybody's cup of tea. Since the present study aims at studying the role of communication in sustainable development, it is not possible to study the role of communication in sustainable development without identifying the various implications of the concept. Therefore, an attempt has been made in the chapter to discuss the various implications of sustainable development.

As discussed in the first chapter, the report of World Commission on Environment and Development (WCED, 1987) *Our Common Future* is the key statement of sustainable development. Its definition of sustainable development is widely quoted, and effectively, the official one (Kirkby *et al.*, 1995). It defined sustainable development as the "development that meets the needs of the present without compromising the ability of future generations to meet their own needs" (WCED, 1987, p. 8). The United Nations Conference on Environment and Development (UNCED), commonly known as the Rio Conference of 1992, was the follow up to the Brundtland and sought to move towards the achievement of Brundtland's aims (Kirkby *et al.*, 1995). According to Holmberg and Sandbrook (1992), 70 definitions of sustainable development exist now. Many definitions are variants of Brundtland's reflecting the disciplinary standpoint of the particular author - many of them say the same thing at much greater length. Scholars from various disciplines concentrate on various dimensions of sustainable development in accordance with their discipline. For instance, while an economist pays attention to growth, a biologist pays attention to bio-diversity. Various dimensions of sustainable development are not contradictory but complementary, as the sustainable development is an integrated and holistic approach. There are some scholars who feel that the concern of sustainable development is ambiguous. For example, David Reid (1995) observed that the idea of sustainable development has attracted groups with different interests. He felt that the vagueness and ambiguity are also present in Brundtland's definition of sustainable development (Reid, 1995, p. XV). Such feelings were expressed by some others also. Daly (1992) fears that "the term is now in danger of becoming an empty Shibboleth". Similarly, Tim O' Riordan, has argued that its imprecision may lead to abuse. Both the environmentalist and the "developer" may invoke it in support of their own ends.

But actually, though the concept of sustainable development is broad, it is neither ambiguous nor its various facets or interests contradictory. It is true that the idea of sustainable development has attracted groups with different interests. But the interests of different groups cannot be seen separately. This is for coordinating and complementing the interests and activities of each other, towards meeting the common goal of sustainable development. For instance, while an economist pays attention to growth, a biologist pays attention to bio-diversity. All their efforts are towards meeting a common goal, i.e., sustainable development. In order to know the various implications of sustainable development, it is pertinent to examine the definition(s) of sustainable development. The World Commission on Environment and Development (WCED, 1987), which established the concept of sustainable development, defined it as the "development that meets the needs of the present without compromising the ability of future generations to meet their own needs". Though this definition sounds simple, it clearly describes the broad objectives of the sustainable development and though there are a number of other definitions, those definitions also corroborate the definition of WCED. Besides, there is a treasure of philosophy in this definition. Some of the implications of this definition are as follows:

Eradication of Poverty

Poverty eradication is seen as an indispensable requirement for sustainable development. Unless poverty is eradicated from the face of earth, the present generations cannot meet their needs and aspirations, which is an important component of WCED's definition of sustainable development. The most basic of all needs for a livelihood is employment (WCED, p. 54). Often, poverty is such that the people cannot satisfy their needs for survival and wellbeing even if goods and services are available. In the present world, out of 5.6 billion world population, more than one billion are living in extreme poverty. 1.3 billion people do not have access to clean drinking water and proper sanitation (Reddy, 1995). Every year, 1.8 crore people are dying due to the diseases caused by hunger. Owing to malnutrition every year 1.8 crore children are dying. Due to the deficiency of vitamin A, every year 25 lakh children are going blind. People are starving and dying due to diseases caused by hunger not because the food grains are not available. The overall availability of food in the world is not a problem. Even in developing countries per capita food production increased by 18 per cent average in the 1980s. There is enough food to offer every one in the world around 2,500 calories a day, 200 calories more than the basic minimum. People go hungry not because food is unavailable but they cannot afford it (Human Development Report, 1994).

Besides, it is often the poorest who suffer most from the consequences of pollution and environmental degradation. Unlike the rich, the poor cannot afford to protect themselves from contaminated water; in cities, they are more likely to spend much of their time on the streets, breathing polluted air; in rural areas they are more likely to cook on open fires of wood or dung inhaling dangerous fumes; their lands are most likely to suffer from soil erosion. The poor may also draw a large part of their livelihood from unmarked environmental resources, for example, common grazing lands of forests where food fuel and building materials have traditionally been gathered (World Development Report, 1992). As Mrs. Indira Gandhi observed in Stockholm Conference, poverty is a pollutant. Therefore, poverty eradication is indispensable to enable the present generations to meet their needs and to live healthy and harmonious life with nature.

Poverty is both relative and absolute. McNamara distinguished between relative and absolute poverty. While relative poverty underlined the inequity in the distribution and consumption of resources between and within nations, absolute poverty meant a life degraded by denial of basic human necessities. Developed countries generally suffered only small pockets of relative poverty whereas most of the population of Third World countries suffered absolute poverty (Ascroft and Masilela, 1994). He proposed reorientation of development policies from mere economic growth to suitable distribution of the fruits of economic growth. This calls for a switch from GNP targets to meeting basic needs of the poorest of the poor.

Some of the measures to meet this goal of basic needs were, acceleration of land and tenancy reform, better access to credit, assured availability of clean water, expansion of extension services and applied research, greater access to public services, organizational changes and new forms of rural institutions; popular participation in development decision-making; involvement of local leadership in programme planning, decentralization of authority to rural communities (Melkote, 1991, pp. 199-200). Development that is sustainable has to address the problem of the large number of people who live in absolute poverty, i.e. who are unable to satisfy even most of their basic needs (WCED, 1987, p. 49).

Change in the Quality of Growth

Sustainable development involves more than growth. It requires a change in the content of growth, to make it less material and energy-intensive and more equitable in its impact. These changes are required in all countries as part of a package of measures to maintain the stock of ecological capital, to improve the distribution of income, and to reduce the degree of vulnerability to economic crises (WCED, p. 52). In all countries—rich or poor—economic development must take full account in its measurements of growth of the improvement or deterioration in the stocks of natural resources.

Income distribution is another aspect of the quality of growth. A rapid growth combined with deteriorating income distribution may be worse than slower growth combined with redistribution in favour of the poor. For instance, in many developing countries, the introduction of large scale commercial agriculture may produce revenue rapidly, but at the same time, may also dispose a large number of small farmers and make income distribution more inequitable. In the long run, such a path may not be sustainable. It impoverishes many people and can increase pressures on the natural resource-base through over commercialized agriculture and through marginalization of subsistence farmer. Relying more on small holder cultivation may be slower at first, but more easily sustained in the long-term.

Economic development is unsustainable if it increases vulnerability to crises. A drought may force farmers to slaughter animals needed for sustaining production in future years. A drop in prices may cause farmers and other producers to over exploit natural resources to maintain incomes. But vulnerability can be reduced by using technologies that lower production risks, by choosing institutional option that reduces market fluctuations and by building up reserves, especially of food and foreign exchange.

Sustainability requires views of human needs and wellbeing that incorporate such non-economic variables as education and health, clean air and water, and the protection of natural beauty. It must also work to remove disabilities from disadvantaged groups, many of whom live in ecologically vulnerable areas such as many tribal groups in forests, deserts, nomad groups in remote hill areas etc.

Environmental Protection

Global awareness of environmental degradation has brought sustainability on the fore as an essential prerequisite of development (Bharara, *et al.*, 1998). Development that does not take into account environment is not sustainable. Sustainable development means that emphasis should not be placed only on accelerating the rate of economic development by excessive use of natural resources, but care should also be taken to protect environment and ecology so that the productive potential of natural resources remains intact for future generations (Singh, 1998). Of course, the meeting of basic human needs while sustaining the natural resource base, which supports these needs, is one of the major challenges mankind is facing in the contemporary society. But there is no alternative. Any form of social or economic development is, like life itself, ultimately dependent on the biosphere, a complex whole, which sustains a multitude of living species in a variety of media (Reid, 1995). Therefore, the protection of the environment is not merely for the sake of conservation: the quality and quantity of production depends upon the quality of environment. The degraded land, polluted water and air, desertification, Ozone layer depletion etc., not only affect production, but also affect survival itself. Hence, environment protection is an important dimension of sustainable development.

Environment protection is a broad area, which has a number of interrelated dimensions such as sustainable use of natural resources, conservation of biological diversity, prevention and control of pollution, land degradation, deforestation, etc.

Sustainable Use of Natural Resources

An economic definition of sustainable development places greater emphasis on the use of renewable natural resources in a manner that does not eliminate the future generations to meet their own needs (Goodland, *et al.*, 1987, p. 36). Economic growth primarily depends on the availability of resources, quality and productivity of resources, level of technology and utilization pattern of resources (Nanchariah, G. 1998). Nature is the base for any material resources. Natural resources are the raw materials obtained or derived from nature. They belong to two categories—renewable and non-renewable resources. The renewable resources are mostly biological in nature and include forestry, agriculture, animals (biomass-based), etc. These can be reproduced in nature and we may harvest them continuously through a sustained proper planning and management. Solar energy, wind energy, water energy, geothermal energy belong to this category and these are available in an inexhaustible form in nature. On the other hand non-renewable resources are physical resources like coal, oil deposits, natural gas, minerals, soils, metals etc. These are available in nature only in limited amount and cannot be reproduced. These account for 90 per cent of the world's production of commercial energy. Sustainable development calls for a shift in the use of natural resources, i.e. from non-renewable to renewable; and even when using the non-renewable resources, using them in a sustainable manner.

Energy being an important input in various walks of human life, covering household, agriculture, transport and industrial complexes, non-renewable sources of energy account for 90 per cent of the world's production of commercial energy. Hydroelectric and nuclear power are accounting for only 10 per cent. Countries all over the world have begun thinking about a policy on energy and looking into a possibility of having energy systems with no or very limited environmental impacts. The coal and oil deposits are to exhaust one day. Moreover, most of the non-renewable sources cause more pollution problems than the renewable sources of energy. The energy crisis has shown that for sustainable development in energy sector, we must conserve the non-renewable sources (Sharma P.D., 1994, p. 393). Therefore, energy is viewed as a means of contributing to the solution of major global problems. In fact, the global goal for energy can be stated very simply as sustainable development (Amulya, 1997).

Conservation of Biological Diversity

Conservation of biological diversity is an indispensable component of sustainable development. The human survival and wellbeing depends upon the entire life sustaining system. The biosphere constitutes a vital life support system for man. Its existence in a healthy and functional state is essential for the existence of human race. It is the complex collection of innumerable organisms (including seas, forests and sky birds) and it is the bio-diversity, which makes our lives both pleasant and possible. Scientists believe that the total number of species on earth is between 10 million and 80 million. We have been able to enlist only 1.4 million species so far. Nature has taken more than 600 million years to develop this exceedingly complex spectrum of life on this planet (Asthana and Asthana, 1998, p. 221). The existence of human race depends on health and wellbeing of other life forms in the biosphere. We are losing these accumulated heritages of millions of years at a very fast rate. An estimated 7.5 million hectares of tropical forests are cut down each year in developing countries and this pace is increasing (Jeffrey Leonard *et al.*,1990). Humans are causing the extinction of perhaps one species an hour (Kothari, 1997). It is estimated that about 25 per cent of the world's plant species might be lost by the year 2025 AD if the current rate of plant genetic erosion continues (Bharadwaj and Satyavathi, 1998).

The erosion of bio-diversity has serious repercussions on the health of the eco-systems on which we all depend, causing wide spread impoverishment, as rural populations lose their sources of livelihood, food and medicine as three-fourths of the worlds population still uses plants and animals for medicinal purposes, and eroding the genetic base of agriculture. Preservation of bio-diversity is essential for a successful food security and breeding programme. If we ignore plant genetic erosion, it may lead to losing sources of resistance to pests, diseases and climatic stress, leading eventually to crop failure and famine (Bharadwaj *et al.*, 1998). In fact, human survival itself is imperilled due to bio-diversity loss.

Recognizing the need of conserving bio-diversity, the Convention of Biological Diversity (CBD) was signed at the Earth Sumit in June 1992. By now, the CBD has been ratified by over 160 countries (Kothari, 1997, p. 41). The Biological Diversity Convention is fundamentally based on promoting the sustainable use of the components of biological diversity. This is defined as the use of the components of biological diversity in a manner at a rate that does not lead to the long-term decline of biological diversity, thereby meeting its potential to meet the needs of present and future generations.

Thus, the conservation of biological diversity is an important implication of sustainable development for communication. Various media of communication have a potential role to play in conserving biological diversity. The conservation of biological diversity is not possible unless the people are aware of the importance of conserving biological diversity. Therefore, in creating awareness and in conscientizing people about the sustainable development, various channels of communication are of crucial importance.

Prevention and Control of Pollution

The environmental pollution is posing a serious threat to the survival of not only human beings, but also other living beings and life sustaining system from local level to global level. The natural environmental resources of air, water, soil, plant and animal life constitute the natural capital on which man depends for his survival and to meet the developmental needs and aspirations. Since the dawn of industrial era man started over-exploiting the natural resources, which resulted in disturbing the delicate ecological balance between living and non-living components of biosphere. The earth planet along with the atmosphere (air, land and water) that sustains life is called biosphere. It extends into about 7 kms. of the earth surface itself, downward into the ocean depths of about 10.67 kms. and vertically into the air to about to 10 kms., where life is found to exist (P.D. Sharma, 1994).

Pollution is an undesirable change in the physical, chemical or biological characteristics of air, water and soil that affect the life or create a potential health hazard to any living organism. Pollution thus brings about direct or indirect change in any component of biosphere that is harmful to the living component(s), and in particular undesirable for man, affecting adversely the agricultural, industrial and other kinds of progress.

Since the dawn of industrial era, owing to the over-exploitation of natural resources, industrialization, urbanization, population explosion, overuse of fertilizers, pesticides, herbicides and deforestation (various ingredients of natural environment have been contaminated), air, water, soil which are basic requirements for survival and productivity have been contaminated. Environmental pollution can be broadly classified into: (a) air pollution, (b) water pollution, (c) soil pollution, and (d) noise pollution.

Air Pollution

Air is a mixture of different gases, which produce equilibrium. When this equilibrium of gases is disturbed beyond the limits fixed by environment itself, air pollution occurs (Singh & Aggarwal, 1998). The industries, thermal power stations, automobiles and domestic emissions are the common sources of air pollution causing health hazards like respiratory problems and related lung and heart diseases, apart from leading to the ozone layer depletion and global warming. That is why, it has become a local as well as a global concern.

Ozone Layer Depletion

The planet earth is surrounded by a thin ozone layer, which actually protects the planet from biologically active ultraviolet radiation. Since the discovery of the ozone hole over Antarctica in 1985, the hole has been continuously increasing. Preliminary data from the satellites show that ozone depletion reached a record size of 10.5 million square miles (27.3 million square kilometers) on September 19, 1998. The previous record of 10.0 million square miles was set on September 7, 1996 (Chemistry and Environment, 1998, p. 55). It now measures 28.3 sq. kms. (*Down to Earth,* November 2000).

Therefore, the ozone depletion would imply an increase in UV radiation, which could lead to an increase in skin cancer and cataract. The UV radiation breaks the photosynthesis of plants, which leads to tremendous agricultural losses. By affecting the cellular membranes, it is also capable of annihilating animals and can also adversely affect crop yields. Enhanced UV-B rays have reportedly been damaging aquatic and marine food chain. This has heavily decreased fishery stocks and affected the growth and reproduction of organisms like zooplankton, harvel crabs, shrimps and juvenile fishes, which form foods for bigger sea creatures (Ninawe, 1995). There was a 70-fold increase in Chlorofluorocarbons between 1950 and 1980, which is causing the ozone layer depletion. Experts suggest that a 60 per cent cut is necessary to stabilize concentration at the present level. If this is not taken care of, the global mean temperature would go up b y 3 degrees before 2100 A.D., leading to catastrophic changes, including the extinction of species, especially animals and plants with chain effects, rising of sea levels, shortage of drinking water and expansion of deserts, etc. Therefore, controlling of CFCs accumulation is inevitable for the healthy and productive living of present and future generations.

Global Warming

Another grave problem posing threat to the globe is greenhouse effect or global warming. Under normal conditions (with normal CO_2 concentration), the temperature at the surface of the earth is maintained by the energy balance of the sun rays that strike the planet and the heat is radiated back into space. However, when there is an increase in CO_2 concentration, the thick layer of this gas prevents the heat from being re-radiated. This thick CO_2 layer thus functions like the glass panel of a greenhouse (or the glass windows of a motorcar) allowing the sunlight to filter through by preventing the heat from being re-radiated in outer space. This is called greenhouse effect. Thus, most heat is absorbed by CO_2 layer and water vapours in the atmosphere, which adds to the heat that is already present. The increasing CO_2 levels tend to warm the air in the lower layers of atmosphere on a global scale.

Some analysts believe that changes in the earth's mean temperature will be apparent by 2050, when the temperature would increase by 1.5 to 4.5°C. According to one projection, changes will be the least in the tropics and the most at the poles. So, Greenland, Iceland, Norway, Sweden, Finland, Siberia and Alaska will be among the most affected. The polar icecaps would melt. The Floating Western Antarctica ice sheet could begin to melt. A rise of temperature by five degrees would raise the sea level by five meters within a few decades, threatening all the densely populated coast cities from Shanghai to San Francisco. It is suggested that North America would be warmer and drier. The U.S. would produce less grains. On the other hand, North and East Africa, the Middle East, India, West Australia and Mexico would be warmer and wetter, enabling them to produce more grain. Rice-growing season as well as area under rice cultivation could increase. However, this may not happen, as higher surface temperature will increase the evaporation of water. Thus, it reduces grain yield. According to U.S. scientist, George Woodwell, India's annual monsoon rains may even cease altogether.

According to an estimation, if all the ice on the earth melts 200 feet of water would be added to the surface of all oceans and low-lying coastal cities such as Bangkok and Venice would be inundated. A rise in sea level of 50-100 feet, caused by ocean warming, would flood low-lying Bangladesh and West Bengal. Due to greenhouse effect, there may occur more hurricanes and cyclones and early snow melts in mountains causing more floods during monsoon. According to some, within the next 25 years or so, there will be a rise in sea level by 1.5 to 3.5 meters, and in Bangladesh alone, 15 million people will have to move out or drown. Low-lying cities of Dhaka and Calcutta may be inundated (P.D. Sharma, 1994). A study by the National Oceanic and Atmospheric Administration shows that 1998 was likely to be the warmest year in the last 1200 years. Scientists believe that the heat wave was due to Carbon dioxide and emissions from the burning of fossil fuels like coal and oil (*Down to Earth*, January 1999).

Thus, air pollution encompasses problems, posing a threat to the life sustaining system from local level to global level. Therefore, controlling air pollution is imperative for the healthy living of not only human beings, but also all living beings. In order to control the pollution, various communication channels have a vital role to play; in focusing the attention of the government, and in educating and conscientizing the people about various types of air pollution.

Water Pollution

Another important basic requirement for the survival and healthy living of any living being is water. It is essential for various purposes, from drinking to cultivation. Survival, health and productivity of not only human beings, but also animals, plants, crops and land depends upon the availability and quality of water.

Such precious water is polluted by dumping of domestic wastes like sewage and industrial wastes in rivers, lakes or in open places; excessive use of fertilizers and pesticides in agricultural practices, the greenhouse effluents changed into acids and bathing of human beings and animals, cleaning of utensils and throwing of half burnt or unburned corpses into lakes, rivers and ponds, etc. (Singh and Aggarwal, 1998). Water pollution results in causing water-borne diseases such as Cholera, stomach diseases and skin diseases, and also in the killing of plants and animals inside and outside the water. For example, in Patancheru area near Hyderabad, owing to water pollution caused by industrial effluents, the health of nearly 50,000 people was affected. Moreover, crops, cattle and other living beings were also severely affected (Reddy, 1994). Therefore, prevention and controlling of water pollution is essential not only for the healthy and productive living of the present generations but also future generations.

Noise Pollution

Another pollutant, causing irritation, annoyance and other disorder is noise. The word 'noise' is usually defined as unwanted or unpleasant sound that causes discomfort. Noise is also defined as wrong sound, in the wrong place, at the wrong time. Noise pollution means the unwanted sound dumped into the atmosphere, leading to health hazards (Sharma, P.D., 1994, p. 350).

Formerly noise was limited only to the industry. This too was not much, as there were only few industries. But now, due to rapid industrial growth, population explosion and urbanization, it is caused by other factors too such as traffic, loud-speakers, etc. The effect of noise on human beings and other organisms depends upon its intensity, frequency and duration. Noise can be measured in units called 'decibel' (dB). 85 decibels is considered as the tolerance limit of noise. When noise level crosses this limit, noise pollution takes place. It causes threat to our physiological wellbeing by causing deafness, neurosis, disturbing sleep thus affecting mental health etc. Therefore, reducing and controlling noise pollution is also imperative to provide a healthy environment for living.

Prevention, Control and Countering Deforestation, Dessertification and Soil Erosion

Deforestation, dessertification, soil erosion and soil degradation are a chain of interrelated problems leading to adverse effects on agricultural production. Forests are crucial for maintaining and improving the productivity of agricultural land. Yet agricultural expansion, a growing world timber trade and fuel wood demand have destroyed much forest cover. Although this destruction has occurred worldwide, today the greatest challenge faced in developing countries particularly in tropical forests (WECD, 1987).

Deforestation most severely disrupts mountainous areas and upland watersheds and the eco-systems that depend on them. The uplands influence precipitation, and the state of their soil and vegetation systems influence how this precipitation is released into the streams and rivers and onto the croplands of the plains below. The growing severity of both floods and droughts in many parts of the world have been linked to the deforestation of upland watersheds.

Dissertification is another problem that affects the production. Land permanently degraded to desert-like conditions continue to grow at an annual rate of 6 million hectares. Each year 21 million additional hectares provide no economic return because of the spread of dessertification (WECD, 1987). It is caused by a complex mix of climatic and human effects. The human effects, over which we have more control, include the rapid growth of both human and animal populations, detrimental land use practices (especially deforestation), adverse terms of trade and civil strike. The cultivation of cash crops on unsustainable range lands has forced the herders and their cattle move on to marginal lands, which is resulting in desertification.

Soil erosion is another interrelated problem the world is facing today. Erosion makes soil less able to retain water, depletes it of nutrients, and reduces the depth available for the roots to take hold. Land productivity declines. Eroded top soil is carried to rivers, lakes and reservoirs; silts up ports and waterways reduces reservoir storage capacity; and increases the incidence and severity of floods.

Soil Pollution (Degradation)

Increased use of chemical fertilizers, flood watering, pesticides, insecticides and herbicides and excessive use of soils (multiple cropping) have changed the soil ecology and have degraded it so much that it has lost the basic elements which maintain the soil fertility and natural soil structure. This phenomenon is known as soil pollution (Yeshpal *et al.*, 1998). The extent of degraded land varies from country to country. For instance, degraded land in Myanmar is 35 per cent while in India it is over 50 per cent (Mukherjee, 1999). Therefore, controlling soil degradation and upgrading the degraded land is essential for the sustainable use of land, which is the source of livelihood for the survival and wellbeing. Soil degradation has many adverse effects on agriculture. For example: In Canada, soil degradation has been costing farmers $ 1 billion a year.

Therefore, there is a great need to prevent and control the deforestation, dessertification and soil degradation through afforestation, tree plantation and through proper crop, land and water management methods to meet the goals of sustainable development. Different communication channels have a catalytic role to play in educating and motivating people about afforestation, proper crop, land and water management, to control the land degradation.

Waste Management

Wastes are created by human population, science and technology and industry. There are mainly three types of wastes—solid, liquid and nuclear wastes. Bulky solid wastes can be again classified into two categories—biodegradable and non-biodegradable wastes. The latter ones are causing a serious threat. The main methods followed for disposal of solid garbage are burning, and recycling. The only cost effective, environment friendly method is recycling. Liquid wastes like dissolved pesticides; chemicals and nuclear wastes, such as radioactive gases are also posing threat to the existence and health of not only human beings but also other species. Therefore, it is essential to device various means of waste management to protect the environment and the lives of human beings and other species. A slogan of today's world is reduce, reuse and recycle. In making the slogan meaningful, and in educating and conscientizing the people about the disadvantages of materials such as carry bags. Various communication channels are of crucial importance.

Using Appropriate Technologies

As the tremendous developments in science and technology led to the deterioration of environment over a period of time, again for solving such problems also using appropriate technologies is the solution. For example, water is polluted by the chemicals and other effluents. By using appropriate technologies, such polluted water can be treated.

Similarly for saving energy, production, recycling too using appropriate technologies is essential to make development sustainable. Russian scientists have found a method of regenerating Ozone in the earth's atmosphere using Laser radiation. Similarly, even though the plastic waste is difficult to recycle, a German company has now come forward and started producing a recyclable plastic called 'recycloner' with the waste materials (*Technorama*, 1998). Thus, with regard to every environmentally counterproductive technology, we need to find out environment-friendly alternative technologies, and different media have a crucial role in disseminating information about these technologies.

Land Reforms

Every human being has, for that matter every living being, has the right to live on this earth and to avail the natural resources of the earth for survival. Land is the source from which human beings derive their food for living. Possession of large areas of land by a few deprived the rights of the millions of people from meeting their basic needs. There can be no justification to the fact that millions of people in some parts of this world go hungry while their productive talents and energies are being wasted. At the same time, large areas of uninhabited land, controlled by a few, is lying uncultivated or cultivated quite below its productive capacity by poor and inefficient management (Singh, D.V., Jagdish Chanda and *Tulsiram*, 1989). In many countries where land is very unequally distributed, land reform is a basic requirement. Without it, institutional and policy changes meant to protect the resource base can actually promote inequalities by shutting the poor off from resources and by favouring those with large forms, who are better able to obtain the limited credit and services available. By leaving hundreds of millions without options, such changes will have the opposite of their intended effect, ensuring the confirmed violation of ecological imperatives. Dandekar and Neelakantha Rath's study (1971) reveals that landlessness was one of the main reasons for poverty in India. From 1956-57 to 1963-64, about 60 per cent of the labour households had no land and hence they depended almost entirely on the personal labour of their members. The remaining 40 per cent cultivated small pieces of land; nevertheless, their main dependence was on wage employment in agriculture or outside agriculture. Nearly three-fourths of the labour households worked as casual labourers, i.e. they worked if and when work was available otherwise they were unemployed (Dandekar and Rath, 1971).

Therefore, to correct the unequal and inequitable distribution of land, and for efficient land management as well as to provide employment and livelihood to the deprived sections, land reforms in this direction are essential to enable the people to meet their needs and aspirations. Thus sustainable development implies and calls for land reforms as well. Media have a crusading role to play in supporting the movement for land reforms and in focusing the attention of the government for the implementation of land reforms.

Population Control and Stabilization

In the past five decades more people have been added to the globe than in all history before the middle of the 20th century. The growth continues unabated. The world population is growing by 92 million people annually and in India, every second, a member is added in the population (Singh *et al.*, 1998). Rapid population growth exacerbates the mutually reinforcing effects of poverty and environmental damage. There is a direct relationship between increase in population and environmental impact as well as in aggravating poverty conditions. More people require more food utilizing more land for cultivation, more housing, and utilizing more land for buildings, more minerals, more water, more energy and more employment. The side effects include enhanced use of chemicals, chemical fertilizers, insecticides, pesticides, deforestation, increased pollution, and heavy load on transportation, unemployment, poverty etc. Countries like India are caught in a vicious cycle of poverty, rapid population growth, environmental deterioration and more poverty. The major challenge to environmental crisis in India is the rapid growth of population. Its population has already crossed one billion mark. Therefore, population stabilization (reducing birth rate so as to keep it at par with death rate, i.e., population growth rate) is inevitable for improving the condition of poor, as well as to protect the environment, which constitute precisely the meaning of sustainable development. Since the change in the attitudes of people is essential for adopting family planning, various communication media have a potential role in changing the attitudes of people in favour of adopting the family planning.

Sustainable Development and Human Rights

Sustainable development involves human rights and responsibilities in many folds to exercise at different levels. To meet the needs and aspirations of people, states have right to exploit the natural resources within those boundaries. The principles of Stockholm Conference on Human Environment declared that states have the sovereign right to exploit their own resources, pursuant to their own environmental policies and the responsibility to ensure that activity within their own jurisdiction or control do not cause damage to the environment of other states or of areas beyond the limits of national jurisdiction (Jaitly, 1993). This principle also is clearly acknowledged in the Rio declaration. Similarly at local and individual levels people, for that matter other living beings also have the right to live on this earth and beyond the earth, as well as to avail the natural resources weather economic or free goods for their survival and well being. As Justice Bhagavathi observed the so-called development strategies which pollute the air, water and soil; endangering the survival of people by making even free air and water scarce, are affecting the peoples right to live (Uma Rao, 1992). Therefore, the strategies should not be based on merely development, but sustainable development.

Interpreting Article 21, i.e. 'Right to Life a Fundamental Right' guaranteed by the Constitution of India, Supreme Court of India held that the right to livelihood is an integral part of the right to life (Narendra Kumar *vs.* State of Haryana, 1994). Certain directions regarding hazardous chemicals were given by the Supreme Court in another case (M.C. Mehta *vs.* Union of India, 1987). Relying partly on Article 21, in the above judgment, there are dicta that life, public health and ecology have priority over unemployment and loss of revenue. Right to pollution free air falls within Article 21 (Subhash *vs.* State of Bihar, 1991). Various recent environmental movements also reflect the endeavour of environmentalists to protect the right to life.

At international level, in 1986 the UN had adopted a Declaration on the Right to Development based as the report of the Commission on Human Rights of the Economic and Social Council. The December 1986 United Nations General Assembly resolution contained an annexure with a 'Declaration on the Right to Development' which spelt out the details of the content of the right to development. Elements of the right were held to be the following: the right of peoples to self-disarmament, the right of peoples to full sovereignty over their natural wealth and resources, an element of international economic justice, people-oriented development, development assistance and consequently the flow of funds from richer to poorer nations, international cooperation, discernment and popular participation in the decision-making process. The process of global environmental governance may be altering the content of the right to development. In stressing sustainability and intergenerational equity, the focus seems to be shifting from equity between present people (in different nations or in different parts of individuals nation) to include intergenerational equity (Jaitly, 1993).

Equity

Two kinds of equity are embodied in the WCED's definition of sustainable development. The first one is intergenerational equity, i.e. equity for people living now who do not have access to natural resources or social and economic goods, and the second one is intergenerational equity. The former is important because, unequal distribution of resources has resulted in unequal patterns of consumption within and across the nations leaving one section of people in utter miserable conditions and another section with over consumption and opulent lifestyle. For instance, 86 per cent of the world industries, 78 per cent of trade, 85 per cent of chemical products, 90 per cent of motor vehicles belong to developed countries (Manasa, 1995). In this back drop, some analysts point out that environmental issues in developing countries can not be resolved without alleviating poverty, and call for redistribution of wealth and incomes spatially, both within countries and between rich and poor nations (Jaitly, 1993).

The latter (intergenerational equity) is the obligation of current generation to future generations. To define the notion of intergenerational equity, it is helpful to view the human community as a continuous partnership across all generations, whose purpose is to realize and protect the well being of every generation and to conserve the resources of the planet for this purpose (Jaitly, 1993).

Many recent efforts to guard and maintain human progress, to meet human needs, and to realize human ambitions are simply unsustainable in both the rich and poor nations (WCED, 1987). For instance, every year more than 11 million hectares of forests are destroyed. Over three decades, this would equal to an area about the size of India. Each year another 6 million hectares of productive dry land turns into worthless desert. Over three decades this would amount to an area roughly as large as Saudi Arabia (WCED, 1987). If we observe today's consumption patterns, the north has roughly one-fifth of the world's population and four-fifths of its income. It consumes 70 per cent of the world's energy, 75 per cent of its metal and 85 per cent of its wood. Replacing the patterns of the North in the South would require ten times the present amount of fossil fuels and roughly 200 times of mineral wealth. And in another 40 years, these requirements would double again as the world population doubles (Human Development Report, 1994). This situation implies the need to change the consumption pattern of north and control the population of the south to provide for investments that build up and maintain resources for the future. According to Akshay Jaitly, despite the fact that sustainable development implies, primarily, intergenerational equity, it is necessary to be aware that where spatial inequities are not prevented, or at least compensated for, societies tend to be unaware of possible intertemporal inequities and the capacity of institutional structures to prevent them are likely to be absent.

Social Welfare and Women's Upliftment

In a welfare state perspective, sustainable development has been described as development that improves healthcare, education and social wellbeing (Human Development Report, 1991). An important dimension of sustainable development is concern for the status, entitlements, and say in family and society and decision-making of women. It has been realized that neglect of women at the stage of formulation and implementation of various policies has adverse impact on women. Women are the worst affected by the environmental degradation. Environmental degradation in developing countries is now believed to have significant unfavourable impact on women. Because of the increasing difficulty of collecting fuel, drawing water, and grazing livestock, there is increase in drudgery. Time spent on infant and childcare is also reduced, adversely affecting the health and prospects of the literacy of the next generation (Ghosh and Malhothra, 1993).

In the backdrop of environment *versus* women's problems, in fact, the concept of eco-feminism also emerged (*Technorama*, 1999).

Therefore, the sustainable development paradigm makes it an imperative to conduct gender impact analysis of projects and programs, so that the woman dimension in development is fully taken account of in the policy making process.

Proposals in Agenda 21 on actions for women's status and welfare recognize that their education and empowerment, in the family, in society generally and politically can have deep impacts on population growth, schooling, infant mortality, sanitation, nutrition and resource conservation. The proposals accordingly focus on these two objectives i.e. women's education and empowerment (Ghosh and Malhothra, 1993). Already media have played a significant role in promoting the sustainable development.

Local to Global Participation

Sustainable development endeavour is not confined to one locality or region or nation, but it calls for the involvement and conscious effort of people at individual, local, regional, national and international levels. It is like 'think globally and act locally' (White, 1994). Until recently, the planet was a large world in which human activities and their effects were neatly compartmentalized within nations, within sectors (energy, agriculture, trade) and within broad areas of concern (environmental economic, social). These compartments have begun to dissolve. We are now forced to be accustomed ourselves to an accelerating ecological interdependence among nations. Ecology and economy are becoming evermore inter-woven—locally, regionally, nationally and globally into a seamless net of causes and effects (WECD, 1987). We came to see that a new development path was required, one that sustained human progress not just in a few places for a few years, but for the entire planet into the distant future. Thus sustainable development becomes a goal not just for the developing nations, but for industrial ones as well (WCED, 1987).

It is the concern of all global people that they should protect the mother planet earth and its life-sustaining system. This concern has been reflective in the Earth Summit at Rio De Janeiro and in its Agenda 21 in 1992. Different channels of communication, mass media, NGOs, educational institutions, etc. have a vital role to play in promoting the global thinking and local actions which would lead to the fulfillment of the various goals of sustainable development.

Equitable and Environment-Friendly Lifestyle

Sustainable development calls for a lifestyle that is in harmony with nature, aims at meeting the need, but not greed; and which maintains certain ethical values towards not only fellow human beings, but also towards other living beings as well as the future generations (Rao, *et al.,* 1990). The science that produced space travel and nuclear weapons should be able to create an environment friendly alternative lifestyle. When such lifestyle emerges overlooking the national boundaries and other differences, when all people of the world feel that they are the children of mother earth and they should protect her, it resembles the ultimate stage of communism where state will wither and everyone will work according to the ability and consume, according to the need, as well as the Indian concept of *Vasudhaiva Kutumbakam* (universal family). The mass media which influence our life styles to a great extent, have the potentialities and the responsibility of moulding such equitable and environment-friendly lifestyle. The heroes, heroins and other actors or characters, who are role models to the common people need to become the 'green' role models to the people.

Conclusion

The foregoing discussion shows that though there are many definitions and multiple dimensions to sustainable development, these definitions and dimensions are not contradictory to each other but they corroborate each other. Broadly, the sustainable development can be described as the poverty alleviation, i.e. to enable the present generations to meet their needs (providing intragenerational equity) and environmental protection to enable the future generations to meet their needs. In relation to communication, it implies that communication in general and various communication channels in particular have a vital role to play in creating awareness about the various poverty alleviation programmes initiated by the government; in the problem articulation by poor, and thus, in bridging the gap between the planner and the beneficiary.

Environmental protection and promotion and population control being the other broad dimensions of sustainable development, various communication channels have a responsible role to play in informing, educating and conscientizing the people about various environmental issues and promotional programmes sustainable use of natural resources, using renewable sources of energy, conservation of biological diversity, waste management, prevention and control of pollution, family planning, etc. Besides, communication is of vital importance in promoting human rights, gender equality, social welfare and peace. Since the sustainable development calls for the participation of people —individuals, communities, organizations and governments at individual, local, regional, national and international levels, various communication channels are of great importance in facilitating the participation of people from individual, local levels to global level. Besides, since sustainable development calls for a lifestyle that is equitable and environment-friendly in moulding such lifestyle throughout the globe, communication has a potential role to play, as discussed in detail in the next chapter.

REFERENCES

Amulya Reddy, K.N. (1997), "Energy Sustainable Strategies", *The Hindu Survey of the Environment*, Chennai, p. 27.

Ascroft, Joseph and Sipho Masilela (1994) "Participatory Decision Making in Third World Development" in Shirly A.White *et al.* (eds.) *Participatory Communication: Working for Change and Development*. Sage, New Delhi, pp. 259-311.

Asthana, D.K. and Meera Asthana (1998), *Environment Problems and Solutions*, S.Chand and Company, New Delhi, p. 221.

Bharadwaj, C. and C. Tara Satyavathi (1998), "Bio-diversity: Key to Food Security Ahead", *Employment News,* 30 May-5 June, 1998, New Delhi, pp. 1-2.

Bharara, L.P and S.K. Verma (1998), "Social issue of Environment for Sustainable Development" in Joshi, Y.G. and D.K. Verma (eds.) *Social Environment for Sustainable Development,* Jaipur & New Delhi, Rawat Publications, p. 109.

Daly (1992), *Steady-State Economics, Earth Scan,* London cited by David Reid (1995) *op. cit.* p. xvii.

Dandekar, V.M. and Nilakantha Rath (1971), *Poverty in India*, Sangam Press, Pune, p. 15.

Down to Earth (1999), January 15, 1999, New Delhi, pp. 16-17.

Down to Earth (2000). "The Hole Truth November", Centre for Science and Environment.

Ghosh, Pradito and Akshay Jaitly (1993), *The Road from Rio*, TERI, New Delhi.

Ghosh and Malhothra (1993), "Implications of Agenda 21 – An Overview" in Pradipto Ghosh and Akshay Jaitly (eds.) *The Road from Rio,* TERI, New Delhi, p. 80.

Goodland Robert and George Lede (1987), "New Classical Economics and Principles of Sustainable Development", *Ecological Modelling* Vol. 38, p. 36. Quoted by Pradipto Ghosh and Akshay Jaitly *op. cit.*, p. 29.

Holmberg, J. and R. Sandbrook "Sustainable Development: What is to be done?", in J. Holmberg (ed) *Policies for a Small Planet*, Earth Scan, London 1992, pp. 19-38.

Human Development Report (1991), UNDP, Oxford University Press, New York.

Human Development Report UNDP, Oxford University Press, New York.

Jaitly Akshay (1993), "An Overview of Post-Rio Political Economy Issues", in Pradipto Ghosh and Kirkby, John, *et al.*, "The Earth Scan Reader in Sustainable Development, *Earth Scan*, London, p. 1.

Jeffrey Leonard H. and Katrina Edie Brandon (1990), "Biological Wealth and Human Poverty: A Tragic Embrace?", *Media Asia*, Vol. 17, No.1, p. 44.

Kirkby John, *et al.* (1995) The Earth Scan Reader is Sustainable Development, *The Earth Scan,* London, p. 1.

Kothari, Ashish (1997), "Bio-diversity in India, Deep Slumber", *The Hindu Survey of the Environment*, Chennai, 1997, p. 41.

Manasa, N. (1995), "Global Fight Against the Hunger is Confined Only to the Lip Service", *Eenadu* (a Telugu Daily), 13th March, Ushodaya Publications.

Martin, P. (1998), "River Pollution in India: An Overview", *Employment News*, New Delhi, 28 March-3 April, p. 1.

Mehta, M.C. *vs.* Union of India, (1987) Supp SCC 131: AIR 1987 SC 1086. Cited by Bhakshi, P.M. (1997), *op. cit.*, pp. 35-45.

Melkote, Srinivas R. (1991), *Communication for Development in Third World Countries,* Sage, New Delhi.

Mukharjee, A.K. (1999) "Environment and Sustainable Development", *Technorama*, January, Vol. 48, Institution of Engineers India, Calcutta, pp. 4-6.

New Records in Ozone Depletion, *Research Journal of Chemistry and Environment*, September, 1998, Vol. 2(3) Indore, p. 55.

Nanchariah, G. (1998), "Social Environment and Economic Develoment" in Joshi, Y.G and D.K. Verma (eds.) *Social Environment for Sustainable Development* op. cit. p. 87.

Narendra Kumar vs. State of Haryana LJT (1994) 2SC 94 Quoted in The Constitution of India: With Selective Comments by Bakshi, P.M. (1997), Universal Law Publishing Co. p. 40, New Delhi.

Ninawe, A.S. (1995), "Environment and Ozone Depletion", *Employment News*, New Delhi, 16-22 December 1995, p. 1.

Rao, B.V.S. (*et al.*) 1990, "Andhra Pradesh Paryavarana Paristhithi : Praja Nivedika (Status of Andhra Pradesh Environment: A Citizens Report) Academy of Gandhian Studies, Hyderabad, p. 285.

Reddy, C.R.M.(1995), 'Towards a Better Life', *The Hindu,* Hyderabad, 5th March.

Reddy, D. N. (1994), "Patancheru Industrial Pollution", *Paryavarana Bharati* (Telugu), Society for Information and Dissemination on Environment, Hyderabad, March-June, pp. 8-9.

Reid, David (1995), Sustainable Development: An Introductory Guide, *Earth Scan*, London, pp. XV-XVI 89.

Rowe, Gerard C. (1991), "International Environmental Sustainability: Policy and Law", The Science of the Total Environment, 108. Cited in Pradipto Ghosh and Akshay Jaitly (eds.), *Road from Rio* (1993), *op. cit.*, p. 31.

Sharma, P.D. (1994), *Ecology and Environment*, Rastogi Publications, Meerut, pp. 340-346.

Singh Yeshpal and Anju Aggarwal (1998), "Environment Crisis: A Challenge Ahead", *Employment News,* 30 May, 5th June, New Delhi, pp. 1-2.

Singh, D.V., Jagadish Chand and Tulsiram (1989), "Impact of Land Reforms on the Socio-Economic Structure of farming families —A Case Study in Himachal Pradesh" M.L. Sharma and R.K. Punia, (e d.) in *Land Reforms in India*, Ajanta Publication, New Delhi, pp. 12-18.

Subhash *vs.* State of Bihar, AIR 1991 SC 420. cited by Bhakshi, P.M. (1997), *op. cit.*, pp. 35-45.

Technorama (1999), January, Vol. 48, p. 41.

Uma Rao, Sunil (1992), Patancheru Pollution (Documentary Film) Produced by University of Hyderabad.

United Nations Development Programme (1991), Human Development Report, Oxford University Press, New York, cited by Akshay Jaitly (1993), p. 29.

Verma, Jag Mohan Singh (1998), "Bio-Socio-centric Model for Sustainable Development" in Joshi, Y.G. and DK Verma (eds.) *Social Environment for Sustainable Development*, Jaipur & New Delhi, Rawat Publications, p. 97.

World Commission on Environment and Development (WCED), (1987). *Our Common Future*, Oxford University Press, New York, pp. 2-141.

World Development Report (1992), Oxford University Press, New Delhi, p. 2.

3 Communication and Sustainable Development

Introduction

As discussed in the previous chapter, sustainable development is an integrated and holistic approach that calls for the participation of individuals, groups, organizations, public and governments at individual, local, regional, national and global levels. The goal of sustainable development is not confined to one locality or region or nation but embraces the entire globe. It extends not for a few years, but for the distant future too. Thus spatially and temporally its scope is very wide. It requires people to think globally and act locally. Informed and conscious citizens can utilize poverty alleviation programmes effectively, and successfully. Informed and conscious citizens can also play a responsible role in promoting environmental protection in various walks of their lives. In fact, to fulfill the goals of sustainable development, there is an indispensable need to mould a life style that is environment friendly and equitable, all over the world. Communication in general and various communication channels in particular, have a potential role to play in moulding such a lifestyle. In this chapter an attempt has been made to identify and delineate the role of communication in general and specific roles of various communication channels in meeting the goals of sustainable development in particular. In case of generality, the potentialities of communication, and in case of specificity, the manner in which communication plays its role is discussed in detail.

SECTION A

ROLE OF COMMUNICATION IN SUSTAINABLE DEVELOPMENT

Communication

Communication is a basic instinct of man like hunger, thirst and sleep. It is the fact of life of not only human beings, but also of animals, birds and other living beings. Communication maintains and animates life. It is also the motor and expression of social activity and civilization. It leads people and peoples from instinct to inspiration, through various processes and systems of enquiry, command and control. It creates a common pool of ideas, strengthens the feeling of togetherness through exchange of messages and translates thought into action, reflecting every emotion and need from the humblest task of human survival to supreme manifestations of creativity or destruction. Communication integrates knowledge, organization and power and runs a thread linking the earliest memory of man to his noblest aspirations through constant thriving for a better life. As the world has advanced, the task of communication has become ever more complex and subtle to liberate mankind from want, oppression and fear and to unite it in community and communion, solidarity and understanding (Mac Bride, *et al.*, 1980, p. 3).

Meaning and Definitions of Communication

The word 'communication' is derived from the Latin word 'Communis', which means establishment of commonness of experience, sharing (Tewari, 1997). Communication has been defined in a number of ways. Theodorson and Theodorson (1969) defined it as the transmission of information, ideas, attitudes, or emotion from one person or group to another (or others) primarily through symbols. According to Gerbner (1967) communication may be defined as social interaction through messages. In the most general sense, we have communication wherever one system or a source influences another, its destination, by manipulation of alternative symbols, which can be transmitted over the channel connecting them (Osgood, *et al.,* 1957). Herald D. Lasswell maintained that a convenient way to describe an act of communication is to answer the following question :

Who
Says what
In which channel
To whom with what effect?

This is known as the Lasswell formula, and if transformed to a graphic model it gives the diagram 3.1.

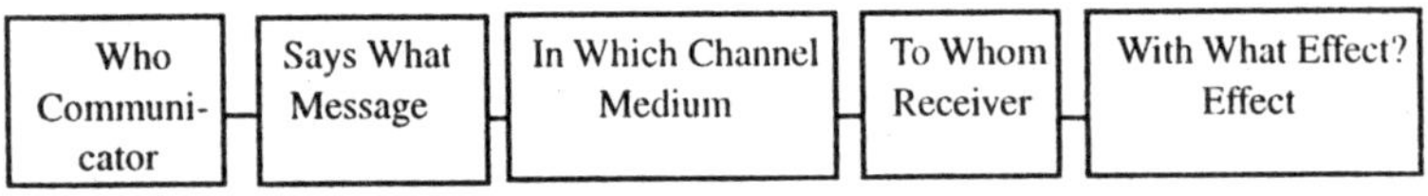

Fig. 3.1 : Lasswell's Model of Communication

Thus, in the most general terms, communication implies a sender, a channel, a message, a receiver, a relationship between sender and receiver, an effect, a context in which communication occurs and a range of things to which messages refer. Some times but not always, there is an intention, or purpose to communicate or to receive. Communication can be any or all of the following: an action on others, an interaction with others, and a reaction to others (Mcquail and Sven Windal 1981).

Communication is a Transactional Process

While Lasswell's model describes communication as a liner process,

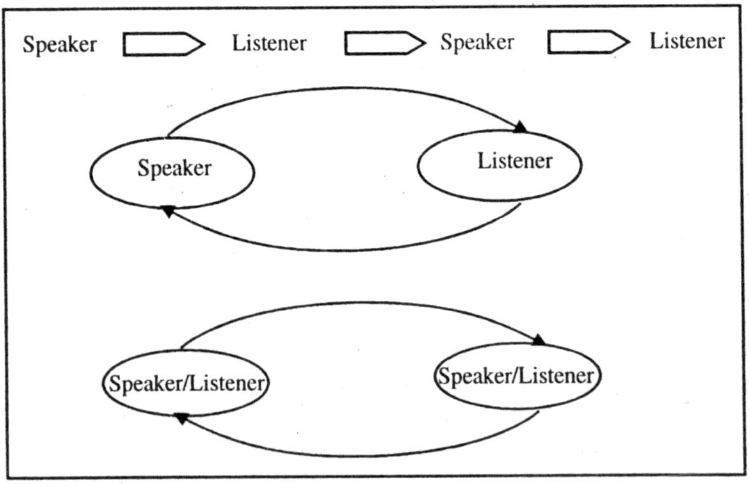

Fig. 3.2 : Transactional Model of Communication

Branland (1970), Watzlawick (1971) etc. described communication as a transaction (Devito, 1994). The implication of viewing communication as transactional is that each person is seen as both speaker and listener, as simultaneously communicating and receiving messages. Fig. 3.2 illustrates this transactional view and compares it with other views of communication.

Fig. 3.2 represents a linear view of communication in which the speaker speaks and the listener listens. The middle figure represents an interaction, in which speaker and listener take turns speaking and listening. A speaks while B listens and B speaks while A listens. The bottom figure represents a transactional view in which each person serves simultaneously as speaker and listener, at the same time sending message as well as receiving messages (Devito, 1994).

Types of Communication

Communication is both direct and indirect. Direct communication is achieved without the help of the technical medium. A person talking to another is direct communication (Rao, 1994). This type of communication also includes, verbal communication, non-verbal communication, organizational communication, public communication etc. The communication is intimate and complete and feed back is immediate. Depending on the number and nature of the patterns involved in communication process, communication of different types.

Intra-Personal Communication

This type of communication takes place within oneself. Inner thoughts, impressions, memories interact with external stimuli—the door of a room, a row of slum houses etc., to create a silent discourse, continuously changing and renewing itself and influencing one's perceptions of self and the world (Waston and Hill, 1991).

Inter-Personal Communication

Any mode of communication, verbal or non-verbal, between two or more people (Waston and Hill, 1991).

Group Communication

This is communication among relatively small collection of individuals who are related to each other by some common purpose and have some degree of organization among them (Devito, 1994).

Mass Communication

Mass communication comprise the institutions and technology by which specialized groups employ technological devices (Press, radio, films, etc.) to disseminate symbolic content to large, heterogeneous and widely dispersed audiences (Janowitz,1968).

Communication in Sustainable Development

Poverty eradication, protecting the environment, reducing the consumption of non-renewable resources and increasing the use of renewable resources, conservation of biological diversity; controlling various types of pollution, land degradation and deforestation, waste management, using appropriate technologies, land reforms, population control and stabilization, upholding basic human rights, social welfare and women's upliftment, promoting intra-generational and intergenerational equity; and participation of people from individual, local levels to global level, being the various important objectives of sustainable development, different communication channels have a potential role to play in fulfilling these objectives. Though communication alone is not sufficient to meet these objectives, it is a crucial element in facilitating the fulfillment of these objectives.

Sustainable Development: Need for Evolving a New Lifestyle

As a result of a trend spreading in the west, in other parts of the world also there is a need to adopt a new lifestyle, i.e. productive, equitable and environment friendly style. In the west hundreds of thousands of people belong to organizations, such as, the National Wild Life Federation, Sierra Club, Audubon Society and Wilderners Society. The environmental movements exist as one of the most important social movements of the 20th century. Environmental movements are not confined to the West. In developing countries also such movements are gaining significance. In India Mrs. Medha Phatkar, Mr. Sundarlal Bahuguna are known for spearheading such environmental movements as *Narmada Bachavo Andolon, Chipko* Movement etc. In the West, in addition to joining national organizations, individual and family lifestyles have changed including behaviours such as recycling aluminium cans, increasing visits to national parks and purchasing environmentally friendly products. Manufacturers have responded by featuring green themes in advertising campaigns (Neuzil, *et al.*, 1996). More bio-degradable, compostable and recyclable materials are incorporated in packaging to meet consumer demand. Neighbourhood clean up programmes enjoy wide participation in all sizes of communities.

Role of Individuals

Every individual influences and is influenced by the environment. An individual can contribute for the degradation or up-gradation of environment depending upon how one moulds one's lifestyle. For instance, by throwing the garbage in streets, cutting trees, by over consuming or wasting water, power fuel, one can contribute for the environmental degradation. On the other hand by keeping surroundings neat by planting trees, by recycling wastes, by adopting family planning, and by consciously using and minimizing the use of water, power and fuel, one can contribute to the upgradation of environment. If every individual grows a tree at his or her house automatically that village or colony looks like a beautiful garden. Thus individuals and their lifestyles have a responsible role to play in making sustainable development a reality.

In the erstwhile West Germany, Green Peace Movement was started and gradually it was supported by people all over the world. Today while purchasing any item in the market, every one thinks about the effects of such items on environment. If the products are not environment-friendly people reject them. Therefore, manufacturers are also taking care to manufacture the products which are not harmful to environment. In western countries, for promoting environmental protection, people are trying to use bicycles instead of motor vehicles and gradually shifting from non-vegetarian to vegetarian food (Rao, *et al.*, 1990). Such environment-friendly life style has to be adopted all over the world including India. Environmental awareness, consciousness and sensitivity towards environmental problems as well as commitment for its preservation and promotion should be part of each and every culture and sub-culture on the planet earth.

Development projects aiming at improving the standards of living of the poor must enlist the active participation of the intended beneficiaries so as to achieve the desired results. Every plan document from a district five year plan to that of a state expresses the importance of public participation in schemes and programes (Rao, 1993). If people are to participate in development, they must be aware of the issues. Schemes are complex and intricate. The entire complexity and intricacy is to be brought out to the people, so that they may understand and benefit from the Plans for their development. This should be more in the nature of education than publicity. In return, the response of people to a programme is also to be conveyed to those who administer in order that they may take it into account during administration. Such a process ensures that the view point of the people is always reflected in a scheme.

Thus, for the success of poverty alleviation programmes and for environmental protection, communication is an essential ingredient. It plays a key role in preparing people to make various programmes relating to sustainable development success in the following manner.

Creating Awareness

Awareness among people is one of the primary requirements for the success of any programme relating to sustainable development whether it is a poverty alleviation programme or family planning programme or afforestation programme, people should be aware of it, its importance and its utility. When people are aware of AIDS disease, its dangerous consequences, how it spreads and precautions to be taken to prevent it, then they can take such precautions and help in preventing the spread of AIDS. Here, information and awareness are very crucial in averting diffusing danger to human beings. Similarly to improve the quality of life of people, especially those who are living in poverty, and to conserve the life sustaining system on planet earth, all the peoples of the world should be aware of various environmental problems from local to global levels. Besides, they should also be aware of the causes, solutions and their role to be played relating to such problems.

Communication has a great role to play in creating awareness pertaining to various aspects of sustainable development. Different communication channels can create awareness at different levels. As Ramanamma (1997) observed, in the global context mass media have a greater role to play in bringing about environmental awareness. At national and regional levels also mass media have a vital role to play in creating awareness. At local levels various governmentaland non-governmental organizations (NGOs), institutions and interpersonal channels have a significant role in creating awareness among people.

Educating Masses

Communication has a potent role to play in sustainable development by educating people, providing more details and explaining complexities. The most relevant in this context is the Chinese perception about education which says "if you plan for one year, plant rice, if you plan for ten years, plant trees, if you plan for one hundred years, educate the people" (Sharma, 1994). The issue of environmental education has been thoroughly discussed at several national and international seminars, workshops and conferences after the deliberations at Fourex in 1971 and at Stockholm in 1972. There was held an international conference on Environmental Education at Tbilisi, USSR in 1977.

The chief objective of environmental education is that individual and social groups should acquire awareness and knowledge, develop attitudes, skills and abilities and participate in solving real life environmental problems. As P.D. Sharma (1994) observed the perspective of environmental education should be integrated, interdisciplinary and holistic in character. The lay public in rural, tribal, slum and urban areas, women, students and teachers in schools, colleges and universities as well as planners and policy makers, programme implementors and Research and Development Workers need to be educated about environment.

Environment Education in India

The environmental scenario in India is very wide and diversified. India has a high diversity in terms of climate, geology, geography, flora, fauna, languages and economic and social status of people. Therefore, environmental education has to be essentially location specific. At the first level special attention must be paid to school going children and women. They are to be educated about health, family planning, nutrition, slum improvement, sanitation, water and food contamination, conservation of environment etc. Formal and non-formal (e.g. Adult-education) educational institutions, mass media, governmental and non-governmental organizations have a significant role as channels of communication in educating people. The Centre for Environmental

Education (CEE), Ahmedabad, under the Ministry of Environment and forests is carrying on such a task with its nation wide network and integrated communication approach (CEE Annual Report, 1993-94). There are over 150 NGOs which are working in the area of environmental education and awareness.

Translating Technical Knowledge into Peoples Language

For creating awareness among people and for their effective participation in various programmes aiming at sustainable development, complexities, technical knowledge and different aspects of international conventions have to be translated into peoples' languages. For instance, for successful conservation and proper utilization of biological diversity, involvement of local communities and social activists working with them and effective functioning of various communication channels are essential. Therefore, as Asish Kothari (1997) observed, since India is a signatory of Convention on Bio-diversity (CBD) this and other relevant documents need to be translated into Indian languages. The development support communicator has the job of bridging the gap between the technical specialists with expertise in specific areas of knowledge, such as, health matters and agriculture, and the users who may need such knowledge and its specific applications. The development support communicator is expected to translate technical knowledge and ideas into messages that would be comprehensible to users (Melkote, 1991).

Conscientization

To achieve the goals of sustainable development, active involvement and commitment of every individual in relation to their decisions and acts is inevitable. To achieve this, mere awareness is not sufficient, people have to be actively conscious. For instance, many people are aware of saving power by putting off lights when they are not needed, using water economically, opting public transport instead of using personal vehicles. But some people fail to do so because of the lack of such consciousness and commitment. As Mani Shankar Prasad (1996) pointed out, the extent to which individuals and groups are conscious of their life surroundings forms the basis of their response and responsibility to the demands of those surroundings for their sustenance and longevity. Majority of our people are unconcerned of their surroundings. Many of us restrict our awareness to individual activities.

Freire's concept of conscientization is central to the theme of participation. To activate consciousness and critical awareness of one's situation and environment, one's identity, one's talents and one's alternatives for freedom of action is an imperative to participatory action (White, 1994). Conscientizing people about their problems, and also about environmental problems at national and global levels, their solutions, their involvement and responsibilities is very crucial for sustainable development. Communication has this crucial role of conscientizing people. Different communication channels have to be used to meet different target groups in different situations Ramanamma (1997) observed that mass media are the best instruments to create environmental consciousness, which is a constitutional mandate, while S.L. Sharma (1995) emphasized the role of NGOs in conscientizing the people. Mani Shankar Prasad (1996) contended that environmental education as part of both formal and non-formal education makes one conscious of the need to understand the consequences of such human activities which cause harm to environment and the manner in which the degree of harm can be reduced.

Facilitating People's Expression and Interaction at Grassroots Level

People's participation being crucial for the success of any programme, a basic factor in participation is self expression. Participation is a process of empowering the people. By doing so the individuals are made active in the development programmes and processes; they contribute ideas, take initiatives, articulate their needs and problems and assert their autonomy (Ascroft and Masilea, 1989). Media, as extensions of man, should be natural channels for citizens to express their views and feelings. They should not be reserved to communication professionals, but be the authentic voice of the people.

Communication media can act as tools for diagnosis. When a communication problem is an ingrained part of people's life they tend to ignore the existence of such a problem. Media can dramatize its manifestations and help the community become aware of it. In doing so, media induce community's reflection on important issues. They provide case studies that provoke discussion and questioning. Media facilitate problem articulation among persons, groups, and communities (Juan Diaz Bordenave, 1994). A video cassette or audio programme can enable several communities perceive that they have common problems so that joining the force would be desirable. Where various communities are facing some common environmental problems, such as water contamination and soil erosion, communication channels should facilitate the horizontal communication among people. Besides, people's articulation about their problems and needs are also to be facilitated by the communication channels.

Such an effort is going on as a part of *Janma Bhoomi* Programme of Andhra Pradesh which was launched in May 1997. In this, people identify their problems in *Gram Sabhas*, which are conducted by the nodal officers of the particular region and send project proposals to the government. This programme is highly people's participation oriented. In 1997-98, the government planted nearly 46 million trees under the 'Clean and Green' campaign, which is a part of the *Janma Bhoomi* Programme (*Down to Earth,* Feb.,1999).

Changing Attitudes and Behaviour

Various communication channels have a catalistic role to play in changing attitudes of people, by creating awareness, educating and conscientizing. Environment-friendly growth, equity oriented attitudes and behaviours are essential among all people to translate the concept of sustainable development into a reality. There is a close connection between attitudes and behaviour, (Severin and James, 1988). One's attitude influence one's behaviour. Attitude is basically an internal state, whereas behaviour is overt. Attitude is primarily a way of being 'set' towards or against certain things (Murphy *et al.*, 1937). Attitude refers to one's tendency to act for or against a person, object, or position (Devito, 1994). There is an indispensable need to mould the attitudes and behaviour of people towards family planning, wildlife, falling trees, energy use etc., to establish a life style and culture that will be productive and harmonious with nature. Various communication channels all over the world have to play the role of change agents to carry on this task.

Supporting Organizations and Movements for Environmental Protection

Communication media, mainly, mass communication media and traditional folk media have a stimulating, inspiring and supporting role to play pertaining to organizations and movements for protecting environment and people's rights. The media played a notable part in carrying forward the message inherent in the Chipko Movement, which is basically a movement for protecting environment (Gupta, 1989). Chipko activities have attracted the attention of environmentalists, Gandhians, various people interested in the process of social change and the media personnel throughout the world.

The media have helped to project the cause of organizations like the Prakriti Samrakshana Samithi comprising students and intellectuals which protested against the Pooyamkutty Project in Idduki district, Kerala. Under this ecologically disastrous project 12,800 hectares of natural forests are to be cleared, which provide 50,000 tonnes of reed per year and livelihood to 1,00,000 people (Meenakshi, 1989).

In Andhra Pradesh too, media played the role of a supporting ally with regard to environmentalists, organizations and environmental movements. Media played active role in Patancheru Anti-pollution agitation. As a result of massive public campaign by the environmentalists and support from the press, the setting up of a nuclear power plant at the mouth of the Nagarjuna Sagar irrigation project was withdrawn (Akhileshwari, 1989).

For the success of any movement, people have to be well informed. Information and its dissemination through the media should form a major activity of the activists. One commendable aspect of mass media in this respect is that they have moved far beyond their traditional bounds of informing, educating and entertaining the people. They are playing the role of activists, crusading for a cause, whether of environment, in its myriad aspects, or human rights.

Focusing Attention of the Government

Communication media, especially mass media have a constructive role to play by focusing attention of the government on various problems by offering constructive suggestions, and by criticizing the government whenever it seeks to push through unproductive decisions and harmful environmental projects. For instance, media focused attention of the government on threat to the Taj Mahal because of the oils refinery at Mathura at a distance of barely 40 km. from Agra. Immediately after the foundation stone of the refinery was laid by the then Prime Minister in October, 1973, protest letters were written to the newspapers. Questions were raised in the Indian Parliament and public opinion was sought for the safety of Taj and other historical monuments at Agra. The awareness created due to sustained efforts through the press and a spate of articles and editorials that appeared in leading newspapers made the government appoint an expert committee to examine the dangers to Taj Mahal. These sustained efforts resulted in the government closing down the two thermal power stations located at Agra and shifting the existing small scale industries and foundries to an area beyond the Taj, apart from the provision for establishing a green belt between Agra and Mathura (Gupta, 1989). The Silent Valley Hydro-electric Project which raised a storm of protest at home and abroad for ten years was scrapped on November 5, 1983, entirely because of media outbrust (Meenakshi, 1989). Mass media also have to play a watch dog role in monitoring the progress of various projects promised or started by the government.

Supporting Development

Governments have been initiating various programmes and projects aiming at poverty alleviation, employment generation, conserving and protecting environment etc., IRDP, TRYSEM, DWCRA, Clean and Green are this kind of programmes. For the effective implementation and good results of such programmes, target groups or beneficiaries have to be well informed and thorough awareness has to be created about the programmes meant for them. Thus communication has a gap filling role between benefactor and beneficiary or the planner and the target group.

Creating Consensus Among Global Countries

Communication media, especially, mass media, computer networks, books and research journals have a vital role to play in creating consensus and cooperation among global countries by motivating them to work for a common cause, that is, betterment of human life and environment by sharing responsibilities, resources and technologies etc. International seminars, conferences and summits, such as Stockholm Conference on Environment (1972), Earth Summit in Rio De Jeneiro (1992), Kyoto Summit (1997), Johannesburg Summit (2002) are of great importance in this respect.

SECTION B

SPECIFIC ROLES OF VARIOUS COMMUNICATION CHANNELS IN SUSTAINABLE DEVELOPMENT

Communication is an important ingredient in sustainable development. It is very crucial in creating awareness, educating, conscientizing, facilitating peoples, expression, changing attitudes and behaviour of people and in moulding a new lifestyle and culture for the next millennium. On the other hand it is also of vital importance in supporting the programmes and projects of the government, criticizing government whenever it takes unproductive decisions, supporting productive movements and organizations and in offering constructive suggestions to the government.

As people, problems, programmes and purposes of communication are diverse, there is a great need to use different types of communication and various channels of communication so as to suit to communicate to different types of people in different situations, different types of messages and for different purposes, sustainable development being the overall goal. In this section an attempt has been made to show how different channels of communication have been used in various environment concerns. Such an exercise would help to realize the role of communication in sustainable development which may be further strengthened.

Channel

Each message carrying signal requires its route along which it is transmitted from the sender to the receiver and along which feedback may be obtained. Channels may be physical (our voices or bodies), technical (the telephone) or social (our school, media etc.). In business organizations or institutions they may be vertical, hierarchical, formal and predominantly one way from the boss down towards or horizontal, democratic, informal and two way as between workmates and groups with common tasks, interests and sympathies (Waston and Hill, 1989).

Mass Media

A medium is any object or device used for communicating a message; that is, for moving information over a distance or preserving it through time (Defleur and Dennis, 1991). All media are not necessarily mass media. Media represent the channel in communication process. Generally in our day- to - day life different communication channels are used depending on the type of communication and purpose of communication. For effectiveness and to achieve desirable change, often multimedia communication approach is adopted. Considering the vast task of communication in meeting the goal of sustainable development, that is from creating awareness and educating to moulding a life style, an integrated and multimedia communication approach is inevitable. Therefore, along with interpersonal and group communication channels, mass media have a vital role to play in accomplishing the goals of sustainable development.

Mass media are the technical devices that multiply and disseminate the messages to masses (large, heterogeneous and anonymous audiences). For instance, press, television, radio and cinema make the mass media. Mass media have excellent potentiality of reaching large number of people at a time. They play a vital role in society and influence society by informing, entertaining and educating. In moulding a new lifestyle which is imperative for sustainable development from individual to global level, different mass media have specific roles to play.

Press

Newspapers, magazines and journals being the conventional channels of communication to the large number of people and scholars respectively and the press being the fourth estate and the channel of communication between people and government, they have a vital role to play in fulfilling the goals of sustainable development. By popularizing various issues, creating awareness and through constructive criticism and suggestions, the Press can play a catalystic role in sustainable development. Constant campaign of the media can influence the government and public to a great extent. Graham Chapman, *et al.* (1997) found the press the main source of information, especially in imparting technical knowledge about the environment. In Andhra Pradesh, *Eenadu*, a popular Telugu daily set apart two pages, one in the state edition and another in the local edition to give news about the arrack agitation during the anti-arrack movement in 1992-93. It stimulated and strengthened the movement, which resulted in total prohibition of liquor in the state (Ramudu, 1996).

Environment and Press in India

The Conference on Human Environment at Stockholm in 1972 evolved the concept of eco-development—that is development based on sustainable resource utilization and not exploitation—which would benefit a very wide cross-section of society (Akhileshwari, 1989). This resulted in some articles being published in Indian newspapers. One of the foremost issues that the press took up was the threat to the Taj Mahal because of the oil refinery (Meenakshi, 1989). The Bhopal Catastrophic could be considered as a watershed for awakening both media persons and lay people to the question of environmental degradation and the havoc it can and has brought on people, their land, their environment and ultimately on the quality of their lives. The upcoming journalists and writers promptly identified a highly potential area to work on. A healthy relationship was established between the media and the environmental activists who supported each other in their common objectives of creating environmental consciousness (Akhileshwari, 1989).

The environment has taken an interesting turn over the past few years, solely because of the media, which provide the mental plane for it (Meenakshi, 1989). Slogans such as 'save the tigers' and 'save the trees' are giving way to save the people. Newspapers and magazines have done their bit in highlighting such issues in their columns (Akhileshwari, 1989). New environmental journalism is developing as a specialized area. Newspapers and magazines, such as *Times of India, The Hindu, The Statesman, Eenadu (Telugu), India Today, Outlook, Frontline*, etc., are paying due attention to various aspects of sustainable development from time-to-time. Every year *The Hindu* is publishing a special issue, 'Survey of the Environment', which throws light on different facets of sustainable development.

Publication of some specialized magazines and journals promoting the cause of sustainable development, has also started. For example, as Graham Chapman *et al.* (1997, 21) observed, in environmental topics excellent magazines, such as, *Down to Earth*, published by Centre for Science and Environment, New Delhi; *Sanctury*, published from Bombay and *Science*, published by Publications and Information Directorate (New Delhi) exemplify this particular trend.

Journals being the channels of communication, carrying the research results and advancements in various disciplines, journals of various disciplines are of crucial importance in strengthening and promoting the cause of sustainable development. They enlighten and enrich the intellectuals, who in turn play an influential role in society.

Television

Television has emerged as a dominant medium with its excellent combination of the characteristics: audio-visual, ubiquity, intimacy and immediacy. Indeed, it has made the concept of global village a reality. With its distinct nature, it has assumed great significance in terms of providing information, education and entertainment to the people. Being an audio-visual medium, it has an excellent educational and instructional potentiality, unique informative ability of taking the viewer to the spots where various events are taking place and wonderful entertainment capacity.

In India, television was introduced as an educational media (Chatterjee, P.C., 1991). It introduced various programmes in the direction of education and development, such as, Delhi School Project, *Krishi Darshan* (1967), SITE (Satellite Instructional Television Experiment: 1975-76), Kheda etc., aiming at supporting the formal and informal education, family planning and rural development. On July 7, 1984 Doordarshan introduced a pro-development soap opera, *Hum Log*. Pro-development soap operas represent a unique combination of education and entertainment style programming that one can call it 'enter-education' or 'edu-tainment' (Singhal and Rogers, 1989). *Hum Log* began as a family planning soap opera and gradually drifted away from the family planning theme and address a variety of other social problems, such as, the unequal status of women, family disharmony, lack of national integration, dowry and alcoholism *(Ibid.)*. It was highly popular with its audience. Most viewers reported learning positive attitudes and behaviours about family harmony, equal status for women, smaller family norms and imitating the positive role models in the television soap operas more than they imitated the negative role models (*Ibid.* p. 208). Thus television has a vital role to play in sustainable development through pro-development themes. Stories and characters of role models in programmes which can contribute in promoting various aspects of sustainable development such as small family, status of women, social evils and inequalities, environmental protection etc., are essential to mould a new life style for sustainable development.

Magazines or documentary kind of educational programmes in

TV are of immense value in creating awareness, educating and conscientizing the people relating to various aspects of sustainable development. For example, programmes like *Living on the Edge, Heads and Tails, Turning Point,* and programmes relating to various schemes of poverty alleviation, such as, IRDP, TRYSEM, DWCRA. Without a large measure of concientization of the poor resulting in a strong and vibrant group or collective action by them, they would not be able to extract any gain from programmes or to retain it. The TV has an important task in creating awareness among the poor at the ground level about what gains are available to them from integrated Rural Development Programme, National Rural Employment Programme etc. (Joshi, 1985).

As sustainable development calls for the involvement of people at individual, local, regional, national and global levels, the television as a medium of communication is capable of disseminating messages at local, regional, national and global levels. It is the responsibility of broadcasters to see that every message that is broadcast is relevant to its viewer. It was found with regard to satellite Instrumental Television Experiment (SITE) that each language programme was common to a vast area. Thus a programme on cotton cultivation would have little relevance to viewers near Jaipur, though it would be of considerable interest to audiences in Kota, both in Rajasthan (Chatterjee, 1991). What the people need is that programmes should meet their local requirements. Therefore, as P.C. Joshi Committee (1985) recommended area specificity in development programmes, localization of development communication is essential.

Television has the ability to take the viewer to various situations to show the realities. Documentaries on various aspects of sustainable development can create awareness and mould the attitudes and behaviour. For instance, the environment documentary, *A Matter of Life and Death*, shows water is a source of life and how that water is being polluted by various sources (Chapman, *et al.*, 1997). Similarly, the discovery channel is quite effective in showing the various aspects of wildlife.

Television being an educational medium, in its educational programmes also, such as, Country-wide Class Room, Tarang, Indira Gandhi National Open University telecast etc., it can disseminate information on various facets of sustainable development.

Video and Tele Conference

By facilitating video or television conferences also television helps the speedy and effective decision making, planning and implementation. For example, the video conferencing enabled the Andhra Pradesh former Chief Minister Mr. Chandra Babu Naidu to have an emergency meeting with various district authorities to take precautions at the time of Super Cyclone in November, 1999. Thus, television has a prominent role to play in fulfilling the goals of sustainable development.

VCRs and VCD Players

Video Cassette Recorders (VCRs) provide users with a greater control over their television consumption. They provide greater control to users in three ways : (1) time shifting, (2) zipping (or video speeding), and (3) zapping (elemination of certain broadcast content). In India, the use of VCRs for time shifting is less frequent than the use of VCRs for rented video cassettes. Now gradually VCDs and VCD players are replacing the video cassettes and VCRs though they are not completely alternative. In India, VCRs are used mostly to view movies (Singhal and Rogers, 1989). But VCRs have got potentialities to be used for development. For example, video helped the Manekchowk women of Ahmedabad to reach policy makers, politicians and bureaucrats, who seldom come into direct contact with the poor people. Video allowed the Manekchowk women to air their grievances freely providing the Municipal Commissioner with an 'unobtrusive' measure of their feelings (Singhal and Rogers, 1989).

As Singhal and Rogers (1989) observed, the decentralized and demassified nature of video technology can provide villagers a direct contact with government policy makers about development programmes. Such feedback may be much more impactful than the formal evaluations of these development programmes by social scientists. The people actually affected by a development programme can convey their experiences, positive or negative to top leaders via video. Similar cases of how video technology brought the poor into direct communication with policy makers have occurred in Nepal, Tanzania and other nations. In creating awareness about various poverty alleviation programmes, environment, family planning etc. VCRs or VCDs players can be highly useful.

Radio

Deniel Learner and Wilbur Schramm argued that the mass media, especially radio could play an important role in development by conveying useful information, changing attitudes, encouraging nationalism and by facilitation in school instruction (Singhal and Rogers, 1989). Radio has certain unique advantages under Indian conditions. Unlike the press, it can get through to illiterates. Compared to television or film, it is relatively cheap, making it possible for radio broadcasts to be localized to each community. This localization allows radio broadcasts to deal with topics that are of special interest to local people. Radio being informative entertainment and educational tool, it can be used to educate and motivate people to act locally on various aspects relating to sustainable development in specific localities.

Besides, with its unique nature of simplicity and immediacy, it has a pivotal role to play at regional, national and global level in creating consensus and marching towards the goal of sustainable development by creating awareness, educating, motivating and convincing the people and governments. Radio has a responsible role to play on its part in moulding a new lifestyle that will be in tune with sustainable development through its variety of programmes. In this respect, there is a need, while applying news values, selecting themes, stories, characters, for development angle being given importance. In radio news bulletins, like business news, sports news there should be a section, specially devoted to environment and development news.

Films

Films have become an inseparable part of our lives. Whether in movie halls or in television, films, film songs and scenes are primary entertainment to many people from illiterate villagers to elite and urbanites. Perhaps, the cinema hall is the only place where mass and class people sit together and enjoy. Film being the audio, visual, intimate and ubiquitous medium, it can communicate effectively. India has the largest film industry in the world (*Times of India,* 1998). India as a developing country where less than five per cent of the population buy or read newspapers and books, the talkie film is perhaps the only popular form of culture available to a large number of the common people. The contact of most of the people with spoken prose is the dialogue that they hear in pictures. The only poetry that enriches their lives is the poetry of film lyrics and their models for style, fashion and mannerisms being the celluloid heroes (Malhan, 1985). Therefore, experts think that the film can educate, inspire, motivate people and change their attitudes and behaviours. Film being such an influential mass communication medium, it has its due role to play in sustainable development, by depicting, exposing, criticizing, advising, inspiring conscientising, sensitizing, changing the counter productive social relations and in moulding a life style that is essential for sustainable development.

Almost every developing country produces films, mostly short films in the form of news reels or documentaries for the purpose of making the people know, understand and appreciate its development projects. However, these films, by and large, fail either to enthuse or motivate the people. Because they adopt a Public Relations approach where by the achievement alone is highlighted and credit for the achievement is given to an individual, group, organization or government (Srinivasan, 1979). Therefore, instead of publicity nature, films aiming at development should be of educative nature with entertainment.

Development films should always portray identifiable local environment, local characters, local problems and locally tried solutions. They should invariably be made in consultation with the film users and where possible, material should be pre-tested in the field at the various stages of scripting and production. Post production evaluation should be a standard professional practice. Depending on the audience composition, programmes relevant to such audiences should be screened. For instance, before the commencement of an adult movie an educative short film on AIDS or contraceptives can be shown.

Feature Films

As feature films command great influence over people, the film makers, producers, directors, script writers and actors should be concerned not only about entertaining the people for profits, should also be concerned about creating awareness, educating, conscientizing, sensitizing and promoting certain values through their themes, stories, characters, dialogues, ideology etc. They should make films in such a way that they would reflect the society. Some film makers tried to project the social realities and incorporated development angle in films like *Atchuta Kanya, Manthan, Maa Bhoomi etc.*

In recent years, *Hindustani* (1996) which was made in three languages (Hindi, Tamil, and Telugu) is a notable picture for its crusading nature over corruption. This film was made when the corruption reached peak stage from bottom to top. It was directed by Shankar, staring Kamal Hasan, Urmila and Manisha Koerala. In this film *Senapathi* (Kamal Hasan) a veteran freedom fighter wages a fight against the corruption prevailing in the various departments of government and hospitals. This film has been quite empathetic in exposing corruption. In such films where natural and real problems are projected, unfortunately unnatural solutions are offered. Hindustani is not an exception. While offering solutions to the problems projected also, the film makers should be realistic. To encourage and motivate people for utilization of poverty alleviation programmes, adoption of family planning and to create environmental consciousness and sensitivity, film makers can motivate the people through such stories and characters, which can be the role models for others.

For example, environmental concerns are the theme of Jahnu Barua's *Banani* (Forest, 1989) in which an idealistic forest officer runs fight against of powerful timber merchants and smugglers, who manage to have him constantly transferred from place to place. When offered bribes, he refuses to compromise. His wife fails to understand her husbands obsession with forest preservation, which leads to tension in their family life. Finally, through his example, he is able to make the villagers aware of their exploitation. Though the action is specific to Assam where the rampant large scale timber smuggling is rapidly destroying forests, it has significance for other parts of the country also (Garga, B.D., 1996). Similarly, Kannada film maker and environmentalist Suresh Hebilkar made award wining movies, set amidst the Western ghats and forests in an attempt to combine his twin interests in cinema and environmentalism (Riti, 1998). As films are expected to reflect the society, there is a need for more and more films portraying the growing environmentalism in the society. Film makers should not ignore the importance of adding environment and developmental angle in their films. Film personalities can influence people to a great extent. As Heblikar admitted, the recognition value he has as a film actor helps him greatly in his attempt to conscientize the people about the need to protect their environment (Riti, 1998).

Films have a great responsibility in changing the attitude of people towards the girl child, encouraging the education of the girl child and eliminating the social evils like dowry system, as these are inseparably connected with health and family planning. Film makers should be more empathetic towards women. There is a need to depict the woman roles beyond the stereo type way of showing them as erotic objects or/and as obedient and dutiful wives, sisters etc., as the feminist film theory describes (Prince, 1997).

Computers

Computers are playing very important role in various walks of life. They are accelerating man's progress in multiple ways. They are serving the mass media in various ways and they are also providing the services of mass media to people through internet and CDs. They are accelerating the development in various fields by computing, interpreting and quickly transmitting the information. In monitoring the quality of environment also computers are being used. For example as part of a comprehensive forestry project funded by the World Bank, the Andhra Pradesh Government has installed computers to interpret the data supplied by the satellite of the National Remote Sensing Agency, which circles the earth ones in 22 days. The data beamed by the satellite as it moves over the forest zones of the state, if interpreted properly, can tell the planner the changes in the use of forest land taking place every year. It can correctly estimate the area under teak, timber fuel wood and the open land (Prasad, 1994). The data can be used to plan for the afforestation of degraded land, and for the involvement of poor people living on the fringe so that they are motivated to protect the forests and derive advantage from the forest produce. Thus computers and Space Application Technologists have a pivotal role to play in sustainable development.

Computers being the sources of information reception, storage and transmission through various net works and Internet, have a pivotal role to play in providing library information, mass media information etc., to the researchers and other activists involved in sustainable development.

Traditional Folk Media

Traditional folk media are the various arts (Drama, songs, puppetry etc.) of the illiterates, villagers, tribals, artisans, seamen, pasturalists and non-elites, which are an inseparable part of their lifestyle. On various occasions—such as rituals and festivals they serve as means of communication and entertainment. In a country like India, where nearly half of the population constitute the illiterate the poor and as a majority live in rural areas, mass media have many limitations. On the other hand there are innumerable folk forms which are integral part of people's lives. Their cost is low, easily available and above all they are in tune with peoples language's, culture and tastes. The greatest advantage of the traditional media over electronic media is their flexibility in accommodating new themes (Sasireha, 1995). They cater to small audiences at a time, but these audiences are soon completely caught up in the folk forms, that the impact on them is at a much deeper level. Traditional media, unlike the conventional modern mass media, involve and often invite audience participation.

The traditional folk art forms play a major role in creating awareness among rural people about child rearing, education, science and modern technology in agriculture, environment pollution, health, family planning etc. Traditional folk media can also be used in modern mass media to disseminate messages on various aspects of sustainable development. Besides, this also helps in highlighting and preserving national cultures, which is a tenet of development media theory (Mcquail, 1987).

Extension Communication

There is a need to bridge the gap between planner and beneficiary and lab to land from time-to-time. This calls for a two way communication process. Extension workers, such as demonstrators, who can function as channels of communication between planner and beneficiary, lab and land to be given orientation by organizing orientation classes on latest developments. From time-to-time such extension workers also should give a feedback from farmers, side areas of sustainable development like sustainable agricultural practices. This is to carry on various tasks in accordance with the goals of sustainable development.

Non-Governmental Organizations (NGOs)

In meeting the audience-specific needs of communication, mass media channels have certain limitations. Therefore, to trigger the developmental activities and to facilitate the effective communication at grassroots level, there is need for communication channels operating in specific local areas. Such need is fulfilled by various NGOs operating at specific local areas. Voluntary organizations facilitate direct, face-to-face and group communication. Therefore, as S.L. Sharma (1995) pointed out, NGOs have a vital role to play in creating awareness and in conscientizing. For example, Deccan Development Society, operating in over 60 villages of Medak district of Andhra Pradesh is creating awareness, conscientizing the rural women and encouraging the savings and various development as well as environment protection activities.

Display Calendars

In addition to displaying the dates, holidays and important occasions, calendars also convey various messages through pictures and slogans. To popularize organizations, calendars are also used as a means of communication by organizations like Life Insurance Corporation of India, Power Grid Corporation of India etc. Some Christian Organizations are also using calendars as a means of communication to convey certain religious messages to make the users to follow the meaning of such messages in everyday life.

Similarly, Power Grid Corporation of India also through its calendar (1999) conveyed green messages and messages about recycling and clean technologies which would contribute for environmental sustainability. There is a need that more and more organizations, through the pictures and messages, in their calendars should convey various messages relating to sustainable development, so as to persuade the users to follow those messages in their day-to-day activities.

Posters

Posters being an important means of communication have to be used for creating awareness. Especially for creating environmental awareness, posters are used as a means of communication. For instance, the Department of Ecology, Assam University, is seeking to create environmental awareness and consciousness through posters. In Andhra Pradesh awareness is sought to be created through posters about clean and green programme.

Educational Institutions

Sustainable development requires changes in values and attitudes towards environment and development—indeed, towards society and work at home and in factories (WCED, 1987). There is an urgent need to bring about desirable change in the attitudes and behaviour of children, youth and adults pertaining to proper sanitation, pollution, love for plants, animals and other natural resources; family planning etc. All education is communication (Mulay, 1979). Educational institutes being the communicating institutions to the students of different levels and ages, aiming at bringing about a desirable change in them, have a vital role to play in imparting knowledge about various aspects of environment and development; and in moulding the attitudes and behaviour so as to be in tune with the goal of sustainable development. It is only through a proper and sustained environmental education we can transmit the relevant messages of environmental protection to our general mass. They have to be taught not only to stop such activities which are likely to produce injurious effects on environment, but also to engage themselves in a set of activities which result in regeneration of natural resources (Prasad, 1996).

Education

Education whether formal or informal is a powerful means of promoting changes in awareness and attitude (Reid, 1995). Education and communication are important in changing both attitudes and behaviour (WECD, 1987). Educational institutions, therefore, should provide comprehensive knowledge, encompassing and cutting across the social and natural sciences and the humanities, providing insights on the interaction between natural and human resources, between development and environment. Both formal and non-formal educational institutions are of vital importance in preparing people for sustainable development.

Formal Education

As sustainable development is a broad one, encompassing almost all spheres of human activity, there is adequate scope to include it in all disciplines. Environmental education should be included in all disciplines of the formal education curriculum at all levels to foster a sense of responsibility for the state of the environment and to teach students how to monitor, protect and improve it. These objectives cannot be achieved without the involvement of students in the movement for a better environment (WCED, 1987). For example, school children in Andhra Pradesh are involved in planting trees as part of 'Clean and Green' programme (Ganesh and Mohan, 1998).

A critical point of intervention is needed during Teacher's training. The attitudes of teachers will play the key role in increasing understanding of the environment and its links with development. To enhance the awareness and capabilities of teachers in this area, multi-level and bilateral agencies must provide support for the relevant curriculum development in teacher training institutions for the preparation of teaching aids and for other similar activities (WCED, 1987, p.114). For instance, in India, Centre for Environment Education (CEE) is one such organization involved in curriculum development. Global awareness could be fostered by encouraging contacts among teachers from different countries, for instance, in specialized centres, set up for this purpose.

In extra curricular activities such as group discussions, debating competitions, essay writing, drawing etc., sustainable development related aspects should be given importance.

Non-formal Education

Adult education, on the job training, mass media and other less formal methods also must be used to educate as wide group of individuals as possible (WCED, 1987, p.113). Persons involved in the National Adult Education Programme can be the best agency of environmental education (Prasad, 1996). They can easily bring their influence to bear on people, particularly the rural community and teach them the need and urgency of environmental education in their curriculum. They have done a remarkable job in this direction.

The young instructors of the rural adult education centres can involve people in environmental activities by exercises like cleaning wells and streets, planting trees at public places, watering the growing plants etc. To create awareness and to motivate people about various poverty alleviation programmes and family planning programmes also adult education is an effective means of facilitating (Group) communication.

Literature

Literature is also a form of communication between writer (communicator) and reader (receiver). Here various literary forms, such as, poems, novels, short stories are the channels through which writers communicate their ideas and feelings in a creative manner to the people. Literature holds the mirror to the society. It reflects changing trends and values and aspirations of people in society. Literature has been the inspiring force behind many movements. For example, Dalit Literature, Feminist Literature etc. Literature plays a vital role in moulding values and lifestyle. As S.V. Satyanarayana, pointed out depicting the changes that are taking place in the lives of people today is the obligation of writers, contributing to the progress of the country (Satyanarayana, 1998).

For a long time, poets and other writers have been fascinated by the environment. Nature's environment has been reflected in literature, cutting across the regions and languages. Of course it is a fact that we cannot imagine the survival or happiness of man without environment. Wordsworth, T.S. Eliot, Omar Quayyam, Kali Das, Peddana etc., depicted the beauty of the environment in their works. Indeed, environment has been an inspiration for many writers. Like the liveliness and beauty of the environment giving pleasure to man, its destruction gives misery to man. Writers described in literature, the beauty of nature, and melodious sounds of rivers and streams make deers, greenery and flowers etc.

When such a beautiful environment is being destroyed in the name of development, jeopardizing the survival of life itself, there is a need that poets and other writers should reflect this situation in their writings. Like Dalit literature, Feminist literature, there should emerge environment literature and development literature. This trend has already started. It has to gain a momentum and it should become a movement. Environmental literature should aim at promoting the cause of environment. For example, Oddi Raju Praveen Kumar's (1998) following poem aims at creating awareness about the importance of growing trees and motivating them to plant a sapling at every house.

పచ్చగా మొలకెత్తుదాం

జీవితాలను కూల్చుకుంటున్నాం
మనం మన పచ్చని దారుల్లో
మంటలను ఎగదోసుకుంటున్నాం
సంపాదనే ధ్యేయంగా
పరిమళాల ప్రకృతి రమణీయతపై
విష జ్వాలలను చిమ్ముతూ
మన జీవనాలకు వికృతులను లిఖించుకుంటున్నాం
మనల్ని నాగరికత మెట్టెక్కించిన చెట్టునే
మరచి పోతూ
చెట్టంత ఆదర్శన్ని చెట్టు సాక్షిగా నరుక్కుంటున్నాం
రహదారి మీద దారి తెలియక నిలుచున్న నన్ను
చెట్లు చేతులూపుతూ
స్తబ్ధతా లోగిళ్ళలోంచి చలన గవాక్షంలోకి లాక్కు
వచ్చేవి
చిగురు గుబురులు
పూల కుదురులు పచ్చని గాలివీస్తూ
చెదిరిన నా గుండె చుట్టూ చెలిమెలను పారించేవి
చెట్ల కళ్ళలో ఆకురాలిన నేలమీద నడచినప్పుడల్లా
అమ్మ పొత్తిళ్ళలో కదులుతున్నట్టే ఉండేది
పూల మొగ్గలు గుబాళిస్తూ
నేల కౌగిళ్ళలో వికసించుకుంటున్నప్పుడు
నా మనసు తేనెటీగై
ఒక అమ్మాయి జడలో వికసించుకునేది
అంతా సవ్యంగానే జరుగుతుందను కున్నంతలోనే.

నాగరికతల అభివృద్ధి దారుల్లో
మట్టి రేణువులను
బురద మరకలను అసహ్యించుకుంటూ
చెట్ల ఉనికినే మరచిపోయాం
కాలుష్యం కోరల నీడల్లో
విషతుల్యమైన జీవితాలను మోస్తూ
మృత్యు కుహరంలో కూరుకుపోయాం
ఇక ఇప్పుడు
బతుకు బండిని చావు పారలు కొప్పేయక ముందే
ఇంటింటికో మొక్కను నాటుదాం

పచ్చని దారై చల్లగా సాగుదాం

-ఒద్దిరాజు ప్రవీణ్ కుమార్

LET US GERMINATE IN GREEN

We are destroying our lives
By putting fire in our green ways
Being greedy for wealth
We are destroying the beauty of nature

Spewing the poison, we are inviting the
Havocs into our lives
Forgetting the tree that brought us
Into civilization,
We are slashing our humanity
For which the tree itself is a witness

When I stood as an aimless person
On the road, a tree called by
Sending the breezes with its green branches

It pulled me from apathy into dynamism
Tree has filled my disturbed heart
With a feeling of friendship
When I walk on the fallen
Leaves of trees, I remember my
Childhood days in which I was in my mother's lap.

When the fragrance is spread by the flower,
My heartfelt feelings
Would bloom in the ponytail of
A beautiful girl
When I felt that every thing was alright,
In the development ways of civilization disliking the soil and mud
We have forgetten even the existence of trees

Bearing our lives prone to the poison
In the shades of pollution
We are entangled in the death trap
Now before our lives are encompassed by death
Let us plant a sapling at every house
Let us transform our lives into a green way
And live more peacefully

— Praveen Kumar Oddi Raju (1998)

దీనబంధు

అలసిన కూలీలకు ఆ చెట్టు తన కొమ్మల చేతులు చాపి
సాదరంగా ఆహ్వానం పలుకుతుంది!
సుగంధాలు విరజిమ్ముతూ పూల రెమ్మలతో
వింజామరలు వీస్తుంది!
ప్రకృతికి పక్షపాతం లేదనుకుంటారు
తల్లికి తన అర్భకపు జబ్బు పిల్లవాడిమీద లాగ
చెట్టుకి రాజు కంటె పేదమీదే మక్కువ ఎక్కువ!
ఇపుడు ఎక్కడ చూసినా 'చెట్లు' నరికి
'కాంక్రీటు చెట్లు' నాటుతున్నారు!
ఈరకం చెట్లు వేలాది ప్రజలకు ఆశ్రయం ఇస్తాయి.
రాళ్ళెత్తిన కూలీలకు తప్ప!
శ్రమజీవన సౌభాగ్యానికి ఆటపట్టు "పల్లెపట్టు"!
ఈనాడు పల్లెల్లో కూడా కాంక్రీటు చెట్లు మొలుచుకొచ్చి
పంటపొలాల్నీ, పాటిమట్టి దిబ్బలనీ ఆక్రమించుకున్నాక
పొట్టచేత పట్టుకుని పట్నం వలస వచ్చిన రైతన్న
ఇక్కడ రోజువారీ కూలీగా రూపాంతరం చెందాడు!
వేకువ ఝామున రోడ్డు వార మంట పెట్టి, ఆత్రంగా గంజికాచుకుని
పెద్ద పెద్ద భవంతులు మొలిచే చోటుకి పోటీపడిపరుగులు పెడతాడు!
క్షణం ఆలస్యం అయితే ఆ రోజుకి ఇహ పని లేదు!
కాలే కడుపుకి మండే గంజి కూడా దక్కదు!
ప్రమాదాల మెట్లమీద, అకాశమంత ఎత్తు
పదే పదే ఎక్కిదిగి, అలసిసొలసి సొమ్మసిల్లే
ఆ శ్రమజీవులకి, చీకటి పడితే తలదాచుకోడానికి గూడు లేదు!
రోడ్డువార కునికి పాట్లుపడే నిరుపేద జీవులని
తల్లిలా కడుపులో పెట్టుకుని కాపాడుతుందిపచ్చని ఆ చెట్టు!
చల్లచల్లగా జోకొట్టి
కలతలు లేని కమ్మని నిద్ర ప్రసాదిస్తుంది!
తెల్లవారితే పీడకలలాంటి పగలు
కాకలు పుట్టిస్తూ కాచుకుని వుంటుందని తెలుసు!
చెట్టుకి తెలియందల్లా ఒక్కటే
రేపు తనని వధిస్తారని!
తన అర్భకపు పేద సంతానానికి
కలత నిద్ర కూడా కరువు చేస్తారని!
అక్కడ, ఒక కాంక్రీటు వృక్షాన్ని నాటుతారని!

- డాక్టర్ మానుకొండ సూర్యకుమారి

Dr. Manu Konda Suryakumari's (1998) following poem also focuses attention of the reader on the importance of trees and how such trees are being cut mercilessly.

DEENA BANDHU
(The Friend of meek/helpless)

The tree stretches the hands of its branches for the tired labourers
and invites them
Spreading the fragrance with flowers it blows the breezes
People think that nature does not show any discrimination
But like mother loving more the weak children
Tree also loves the poor more than loving others
Now-a-days wherever we the see trees are cut and the
concrete trees are planted

This kind of trees provide shelter to
A number of people
But not to the labourers who laid the foundation stones
Village is the reflection of the beauty in labour
Today in villages also the concrete trees are germinating
Occupying the croplands and heaps
With this, the farmer who came to city with a starving belly has
Become a daily wage labourer.

In the wee hours after preparing his gravel
He rushes to the places whereby buildings
Are coming up with competition.

If he is late by one minute
For that day he will not have work
Nor the gravel to his starving belli.

On the steps of danger the labourers
Climb into sky and get tired
They do not find a shelter to stay in the night

The green tree like a mother
Provides shelter and comfortable sleep to the poor people
Tree knows when the night passes off the day
enters like a nightmare.

But it does not know only one thing
Tomorrow it is going to be cut
A concrete tree is going to be brought
And its poor children are not going to have the comfortable sleep.

—Dr. Suryakumari Manukonda (1998)

Pran Rao's novel *Neelipapa* (1995) in Telugu has depicted the plight of the people who became the victims of Patancheru Industrial Pollution. It is a healthy trend that popular writers like Arundhati Roy, have become staunch environmental activists and they are also writing for this cause. Like Sri Sri's "Keka" (Scream) (1939) which depicted the intensity of hunger, Pedalu (Paupers) (1939), which depicted the plight of poor, Gaddar's Bhopal (1985) which depicted the Bhopal gas tragedy, literature should emerge and it should create a movement for alleviating poverty, hunger, misery and equity from the face of this earth, and also to promote the cause of environment.

Thus literature as a channel of communication plays a vital role in meeting the goals of sustainable development by depicting environment and development related themes and aspects, and by projecting in stories and novels environment friendly and equitable life styles as role models to be followed by others.

Religion

Religion being an important institution in human life, directing the values and lifestyles, it has a remarkable role to play in moulding the attitudes and lifestyles so as to be in consonance with the goals of sustainable development. Religious leaders, priests and organizations being communicators to their religious groups, should also contribute through their messages to promote the various aspects of sustainable development, keeping in view, the wellbeing of the present and future generations. As WCED (1987) observed, the world's religions could provide direction and motivation informing new values that would stress individual and joint responsibility towards the environment and towards nurturing harmony between humanity and environment (WCED, 1987, p. 111).

For example, in ancient India, religion was quite harmonious with nature and it promoted the sense of preserving environment. While Vedic people worshipped nature as they found it, the *Itihasic* age had learned to set aside certain clearly demarcated pieces of land as sacred and these were full of Guarded trees (Ahana, 1995). The first sacred grove in ancient Sanskrit literature is Ashoka grove in *Ramayana* which concerns Sita.

While in the earlier *Puranas* and other literatures, the sanctity associated with trees was positive, the latter texts are full of admonishment against the misuse of environment. For instance, cutting down a particular tree was believed to provoke retribution. Indeed, cutting down a healthy green tree (Pacchaimaram) was considered a heinous sin (Ahana, 1995).

Like this, today also there is a great need of all religions playing a due role in moulding a way of life that facilitates sustainable development. A four days Peace Summit held in New York between 28th August to 31st August, 2000, 2000 religious heads and spiritual leaders drawn from all faiths gathered together. Among the resolutions taken on this occasion, an important one is ending the violence of poverty and environmental degradation (Sudha, 2000). All the religious leaders and priests have a responsible role to play in materializing this objective.

Legislators

As it was envisaged by the people affected by Patancheru industrial pollution, legislators also, whether Assembly or Parliament are the effective communication channels between people and government. Especially, in conveying the grievances, needs, and aspirations of people to the government and seeking proper action from the government. Being the representatives of people they have also a vital role to play in mobilizing the public opinion by issuing press statements, organizing and addressing public meetings in support of sustainable development.

Family

The family being the primary social unit and an important institution, to a great extent it influences one's lifestyle through interpersonal communication and group communication among its members. Attitudes and behaviour of children and younger members are moulded depending upon the orientation given to them by the elder members and the interaction between various members. For instance, in terms of maintaining neatness in the surroundings, power use, water use, loving plants, animals etc. Family members should give proper orientation to the children right from their childhood to make them competent and responsible citizens to cope up with various aspects of sustainable development. Parents and other family members can be of great help while teaching the infants the basic things about environment. Thus family members have a responsible role in communicating various aspects of environment and development with other members to mould a conducive lifestyle for sustainable development.

Conclusion

In order to meet the goals of sustainable development, there is an indispensable need to mould a lifestyle that is productive, equitable and environment friendly, all over the world. In carrying out this uphill task, communication in general and various types and channels of communication in particular have specific roles to play. As Wolfenson (1998) observed "economics are built not merely through the accumulation of physical capital and human skill, but on a foundation of information, learning and adaptation." Since every individual has a responsible role to play in protecting and promoting environment from local to global levels, communication is of immense value in making people informed, educated, sensitized and concientized. For the success of poverty alleviation and family planning programmes also, communication is an important element. Communication is crucial in bridging the gap between planner and beneficiary. Various communication media—press, television, radio, cinema, computers, traditional folk media, NGOs, educational institutions, literature, posters, etc., have a specific role to play in meeting specific audiences. Already these media are being used for the purposes of promoting sustainable development at a limited scale. They are to be more effectively used to shape a lifestyle that is productive, harmonious with nature and fellow human beings to protect the globe with its life sustaining system into a distant future. Since various communication channels have an important and specific roles to play in this regard, the sustainable development calls for an integrated communication approach.

REFERENCES

Ahana (1995), "How forests were once Conserved", *The Hindu*, Hyderabad, March 4.

Akhileshwari, R. (1989), "Environment and the Media" *Vidura*, May-June, pp. 11-12.

Ascroft, Joseph and Sipho Masilela (1989), "From Top–Down to Co-Equal Communication: Popular Participation in Development Decision Making. A paper presented at University of Poona, Pune, 1989, as quoted by Srinivas R. Melkote, 1991.

Calendar (1999), Power Grid Corporation of India Ltd., North Eastern Region, Shillong.

Centre for Environment Education (CEE) Annual Report, 1993-94, Nehru Foundation for Development, Ahmedabad.

Chapman, Graham, *et al.* (1997), *Environmentalism and the Mass Media: The North-South Devide,* Indian Institute of Advanced Study, Shimla, pp. 21-197.

Chatterjee, P.C. (1991), *Broadcasting in India,* Sage, New Delhi, pp. 51-130.

Defleur, Melvin L. and Dennis, Everett E. (1991), Understanding Mass Communication, Goyl Saab, New Delhi, p. 8.

Devito, Joseph A.(1994), *Human Communication: The Basic Course*, Harper Collins College Publishers, New York, pp. 32-389.

Down to Earth (1999) "Cyber Babu of Hyderabad", February 15, pp. 40-44.

Gaddar (1992), Bhopal, *Gaddar Kavithalu*, Jana Natyamandali Publications, Hyderabad, 1992, p. 49.

Ganesh, E.V. and Mohan, V.V.K. (1998) "Paripurnatha Saadhinchina Proja Udyamam" (People's movement that achieved perfection) Andhra Pradesh, January, p. 7.

Garga, B.D. (1996), *So Many Cinemas: The Motion Picture in India,* Eminence Designs Pvt. Ltd., Mumbai, p. 307.

Gerbner, G. (1967), 'Mass media and human communication theory' in Dance, E.F.X. (ed.) *Haman Communication Theory*. cited by Denis Mcquil and Sven Windahl (1982), *op. cit.* p. 3.

Gupta, V.S. (1989), "Environmental Reporting Some Issues", *Vidura*, New Delhi, May-June 1989, p. 3.

Janowitz, M. (1968), The Study of Mass Communication in Sills, D.E.(ed.)
International Encyclopedia of the Social Sciences, New York, McMillan and Free Press, Vol. 3, p. 41. As quoted in Communication Models. *op. cit.* p. 4.

Joshi, P.C. *et al.* (1985), *An Indian Personality for Television*, Vol.1, Publications Division, New Delhi, pp. 42-43.

Juan Diaz Bordenave (1994), "Participative Communication as a Part of Building the Participative Society", *Participatory Communication : Working for Change and Development* (ed) by K. Sadanandan Nair, *et al.*, Sage, New Delhi, p. 44.

Kothari, Asish (1997) Biodiversity in India: Deep Slumber, *Survey of the Environment,* The National Press, Chennai.

Mac Bride, Sean, *et al.*, *Many Voices One World*, UNESCO, London, 1980, p. 3.

Malhan, P.N. (1985), *Communication Media: Yesterday, Today and Tomorrow*, Publications Division, New Delhi, p. 156.

Manukunda, Suryakumari (1998), "Deenabandhu", *Andhra Pradesh*, Department of Information and Public Relations, Hyderabad, November, p. 23.

Mcquail, Denis and Sven Windahl (1982), *Communication Models,* Longman.

Mcquail, Denis (1987), *Mass Communication Theory*, Sage, New Delhi.

Meenakshi Subramaniam (1989), "Crusading Role of the Media", *Vidura*, New Delhi, May-June 1989, p. 9.

Melkote, Srinivas, R. (1991), *Communication for the Development in Third World: Theory and Practice*, Sage, New Delhi, pp. 262-263.

Mulay, Vijaya (1979), "Films for Development and Education" *Symposium on Cinema in Developing Countries*, Publications Division, pp. 142-149.

Murphy, G., L.B. Murphy and T.M. Newcomb (1937) *Experimental Social*

Psychology: An Interpretation of Research upon the Socialization of Individual, Harper and Row, New York, p. 889 as quoted by Severin, *et al.* (1988). *op. cit.*

Neuzil, Mark and Willam Kovarik, (1996) *Mass Media and Environmental Conflict: America's Green Crusade,* Sage, New Delhi, pp. 9-10.

Osgood, C.E., Suci, G.J. and Tannenbaum, P.H. (1957), The Measurement of Meanings. Urbana : University of Illinois Press cited by Denis Mcquil and Sven Widahl (1982). *op. cit.* p. 3.

Prasad, Mani Shankar (1996), Need for Environmental Awareness, *Third Concept,* New Delhi, January, 1996.

Praveen Kumar Oddi Raju (1998), "Pachaga Molakethudam", (Let us germinate in green) *Andhra Pradesh* (Telugu), Department of Information and Public Relations, Hyderabad, November 1998, p. 13.

Prince Stephen (1997), *Movies and Meaning : An Introduction to Film,* Allyn and Bacon, London, pp. 362-363.

Rajendra Prasad, R.J. (1994), "Computers to Assess Forest Wealth", *The Hindu,* Hyderabad, December 17, 1994.

Ramanamma, M.V. (1997), "Green Journalism: A Social Imperative", *Comunicator,* Indian Institute of Mass Communication, October-December, 1997, pp. 17-18.

Ramudu, Sripathi (1996), Anti-Arrack Movement in Andhra Pradesh (1992), M.Phil. Dissertation, Department of Political Science, University of Hyderabad, p. 44.

Rao, B.V.S. *et al.* (1990), Andhra Pradesh Paryavarana Parishithi (the Status of Andhra Pradesh Environment), Academy of Gandhian Studies, Hyderabad, p. 138.

Rao, Pran S.M. (1995), *Neelipapa,* Visalandhra Publishing House, Hyderabad.

Rao, P.L.V. (1994), Principles of Communication and Public Relation, Dr. B.R. Ambedkar University, Hyderabad, p. 53.

Rao, P.L.V., (1993) 'Public Relations as a Two Way Communication Process', *Public Relations and Development,* in Abdur Rahim, *et al.* (eds.) Dr. B.R. Ambedkar Open University, p. 9.

Reid David (1995), Sustainable Development : An Introductory Guide. *Earth Scan,* London, pp. xy-175.

Riti, M.D. (1998), "Doing What Comes Naturally", *The Times of India,* Sunday Review, New Delhi, October 18.

Sasireha, S. (1995), Contribution of Traditional Media in Creating Awareness, *Communicator,* Indian Institute of Mass Communication, July-September, 1995, p. 29.

Satyanarayana, S.V. (1998), *Telugu Saahityamlo Abhyudayam Velugulu,* (Telugu) (The Light of Progress in Telugu Literature), *Andhra Pradesh* (Telugu Monthly), Department of Information and Public Relations, Hyderabad, May, p. 31.

Severin, Warner J. and James W. Tankard Jr. (1988), *Communication Theories: Origin, Methods and Uses,* Longman, New York, p. 458.

Sharma, P.D. (1994), *Ecology and Environment,* Rastogi Publications, New Delhi, 1994, p. 467.

Sharma, S.L. (1995, "Towards Sustainable Development in India : Issues and

Perspectives" a paper presented at ICSSR, North Eastern Regional Centre, Shillong.

Singhal, Arvind and Rogers, Everett, M.(1989), *India's Information Revolution,* Sage, New Delhi, p. 17.

Sri Sri (1939), Keka and Pedalu, *Maha Prasthanam,* Visalandhra Publishing House, Hyderabad, 1950, pp. 82-84.

Srinivasan, C.(1979), "Search for Identity", *Symposium on Cinema in Developing Countries,* Publications Division, New Delhi, p. 91.

Stephen Prince (1997), *Movies and Meaning : An Introduction to Film,* Allyn and Bacon, London, pp. 362-3.

Sudha Prasad (2000) – "World Religions Summit: A Confluence of All Faiths", Civil Services Chronicle, New Delhi, November, p. 28.

Tewari, I.P. (1997), *Communication, Technology and Development,* Publications Division, New Delhi, p. 2.

Theodorson, S.A. and Theodorson, A.G. (1969), *A Moden Dictionary of Sociology,* New York, Cassell. Cited by Denis Mcquil oud Sven Windahl (1982) *op.cit.* p. 3.

Times of India (1998), "Shooting Stars" (Editorial), New Delhi, October 14, p. 12.

Waston James and Hill Anne (1989), *A Dictionary of Communication and Media Studies,* Universal Book Stall, New Delhi, 1989, pp. 32-40.

WCED (1987), *Our Common Future,* Oxford University Press, New Delhi.

White Robert (1994), "Participatory Development Communication as a Social Cultural Process" in Shirly, A. White *et al.* (eds.) *Participatory Communication for Development and Change. op. cit.* pp. 95-114.

White, Shirly, A. (1994), "The Concept of Participation: Transforming Rhetoric to Reality" *Participatory Communication: Working for Change and Development* (ed.) by Shirly.A.White, K. Sadanandan Nair and Joseph Ascroft, Sage, New Delhi, p. 25.

Wolfenson, James, D, (1998), Preface, World Development Report, Oxford University Press, New York, pp. iii-iv.

4 Policies and Programmes of Government for Sustainable Development

Introduction

As it has been discussed in foregoing chapters, the concept of sustainable development was established by the Bruntland Commission (WCED) in 1987 and strengthened by Earth Summit in 1992, and it still continues to be a solution to balance the economy and environment. Even though the idea of sustainable development and sustainable lifestyle started catching on around the world from 1987 onwards, various policies and programmes, which contribute towards its fulfillment were initiated by various nations even before the emergence of this concept. For instance, various programmes were initiated by the governments for poverty alleviation, population control, forest conservation, etc. In this chapter, policies and programmes of the Indian Government since independence towards fulfilling the goals of sustainable development have been examined. This chapter is divided into two parts—Part I and Part II. In Part I, poverty alleviation programmes and population control programmes have been examined, and in Part II, environmental protection programmes have been discussed with a view to realize the significance of communication component in sustainable development.

PART I
POVERTY ALLEVIATION AND POPULATION CONTROL PROGRAMMES OF THE INDIAN GOVERNMENT

Section A

Sustainable Development and Poverty Alleviation

For the last five decades, the major objective of the governments, especially in developing countries, has been the removal of poverty. Poverty alleviation is an essential component of sustainable development. Because, every year, 1.8 crore people are dying due to the diseases caused by hunger (Manasa, 1995). The overall availability of food in the world is not a problem. Even in developing countries, per capita food production increased by 18 per cent on an average in the 1980s. There is enough food to offer to every one in the world-around 2,500 calories a day—200 calories more than the basic minimum. People go hungry not because food is unavailable, but because they cannot afford it (Human Development Report, 1994). As our late Prime Minister, Mrs. Indira Gandhi, focused the attention at Stockholm Conference in 1972, poverty was the worst form of pollution (Dilli, K.T., 1996). Besides, the worst sufferers of environmental degradation are the poor (Madhavi, 1993). Therefore, alleviation of poverty is inevitable for improving the condition of these people to enable them to meet their needs and aspirations, which is a broad goal of sustainable development.

Poverty Alleviation and Intervention of the State

The state seeks to intervene positively in the development process through a number of public policies by stimulating production and ensuring distributive justice. The entire thrust appears to be on improving the quality of life of all the citizens. The policies are broadly of two types: one, the policies, which might be called comprehensive and lead to structural transformation, and two, incremental policies, which are of a reformative type. Policies like land reforms, ceilings on property and wealth belong to the former category, as they touch the ownership of the means of production, and policies like reservations, public distribution system, subsidized anti-poverty schemes fall in the latter category. The incremental policies are intended to provide some relief to the poorer sections without affecting the basic socio-economic structure of the society. The modern state pursues both types of policies and covers a wide range of socio-economic process touching the life of the community at various points (Reddy Ram and Haragopal, 1985). India has also followed both comprehensive and incremental policies.

Public Policy for Alleviation of Poverty in India

Long before the World Bank and other international agencies discovered poverty, India had started paying attention for alleviating it. As far back as in 1938, Jawaharlal Nehru's National Planning Committee stated that getting rid of appalling poverty and providing people with food, clothing, housing and every other essential requirement of human existence was India's primary goal. The Directive Principles of State Policy of the Indian Constitution, although not enforceable by any Court, urge the State to strive to secure "a social order in which justice—social, economic and political—shall inform all the institutions of the national life and to minimize inequality of income" [Article 38(1) and (2)]. The principles also assign the raising level of nutrition and the standard of living of the people and the improvement of public health as some of the primary duties of the State (Article 47). The development of agriculture and animal husbandry along modern scientific lines is also assigned to the State (Article 48). The provision of free and compulsory education for all children under the age of fourteen years in a period of ten years from the commencement of constitution (Article 45), and equal pay for equal work for both men and women (Article 39D) are other notable goals the state should achieve (Laskar, 1988).

The evolution of government policy in India passed through different phases. Aiming at the rapid development of the country, five year plans started from 1st April 1951. Alleviation of poverty in one form or the other has always occupied an important place in the list of stated objectives of all the five year plans in the country.

Poverty Alleviation in Five Year Plans

The First Five Year Plan declares that the central objective of planning in India is to raise the standard of living of the people and to open to them opportunities for a richer and more varied life (First Five Year Plan). And it took the stand that in the initial stage, the accent of endeavour must be on increased production—because without this, no advancement is possible at all. The Second Five Pear plan was formulated in the wake of the government decision to adopt a socialist pattern of society and a pronounced egalitarian thrust in the direction of the economy. It gave priority to provide equity for. Along with rapid growth, it also evinced concern for less privileged sections, equity and reduction of inequalities between rich and poor. It can be understood from the plan document declared that the pattern of development and the structure of socio-economic relations should be so planned that they result not only in appreciable increases in national income and employment but also in greater equality in incomes and wealth. The benefits of economic development must accrue more and more to the relatively less privileged classes of society, and there should be a progressive reduction of the concentration of incomes, wealth and economic power (Second Five Year Plan). As Kamta Prasad (1985) observed, this plan contained the conflict between the objectives of growth and equity, and at operational level, emphasis was on increasing the role of public sector without caring much as to how this alone would help in raising the living standards of the masses.

In the third plan also, growth continued to have an important position. But in this plan, special attention was also paid to poverty. It was stated in the plan that "the principal aim of the third plan is to secure a marked advance towards self-sustaining growth" (Third Five Year Plan). Besides, it also stated that the plan seeks to provide basic necessities to all citizens, more specifically food, supply of drinking water, clothing, elementary education, health and sanitation, housing and progressively also work for all. Thus, as Morley Mohanlal observed (1988), during the first two decades of economic planning, emphasis was laid on the need to maximize the rate of growth of the GNP mostly in conformity with the conventional approach, through stepping up the rate of investment in the economy, the goal being increased production. It was considered that automatically public investment would stimulate induced investment by private sector, which, in turn, would push the GNP. It was assumed that increased productivity would contribute significantly to poverty alleviation and employment generation through trickledown effect.

Though poverty is prevalent both in rural and urban areas, since more than 80 per cent of people lived in rural areas, by and large, government concentrated on the eradication of rural poverty. During the fifties and sixties, emphasis was on community development, Panchayat Raj, Intensive Area Development, Development of Backward Regions, modernization of agriculture, and so on. In this direction, the following were the major programmes initiated during this period:

(a) The Community Development Programme was introduced in 1952.

(b) The Intensive Agricultural District Programme started in 1960-61.
(c) The Intensive Agricultural Area Programme (IAAP) was introduced in 1964.
(d) High Yielding Varieties Programme (HYVP) was introduced in 1966-67.

Morley (1988) felt that community development programme succeeded to some extent increasing a viable infrastructure in the rural areas, including the extension machinery. It was observed that in the selection of works, the village leaders were often able to influence decisions favouring them. The better-off villages became better and those which badly needed improvement in the living conditions came to be left out. The neglect of the weaker sections continued during the Intensive Agricultural Development Programme (IADP) strategy, which followed the Community Development Programme. In times of scarcities, the supplies of inputs like fertilizers and improved seeds are pre-emptied by larger farmers who generally dominate the cooperative structure. Further, in the name of progressive farmers, it is the farms of large farmers, which are usually selected by the agriculture department as Seed Centres for multiplication of better quality seed.

The above-mentioned programmes contributed in bringing about a sizeable increase in agricultural production and ushering in the Green Revolution. However, studies undertaken to assess the consequences of this Green Revolution revealed the gap between the rich and the poor, more particularly, small farming communities who were left out of the productive process (Morley, 1988).

Thus, even though government initiated some programmes for the alleviation of poverty in fifties and sixties, they could not yield good results. And even though per capita national consumer expenditure increased from Rs. 276.2 in 1960-61 to Rs. 287.0 in 1967-68, i.e. by 3.9 per cent, the small gains were not equitably distributed among all sections of the population. Consequently, the condition of the bottom 20 per cent of urban poor has deteriorated, and for another 20 per cent of the urban population, bottom 20 per cent of rural people has remained more or less stagnant (Dandekar and Rath, 1971). Thus, while the character of rural poverty has remained the same as before, the character of the urban poverty has deepened further.

Directly Beneficiary Oriented Programmes

In the late 1960s, it was realized that any indirect policy measure would not be of much help to the rural poor (Ram Reddy and Haragopal, 1985). Development with social justice involving the large sections of the small farming communities was considered to be important for the alleviation of poverty. So, it was thought necessary to provide them a separate institutional base to speed up the required help to improve their level of productivity and living. Implementation of Land Reforms, Nationalization of Banks for the service of the farming communities and other weaker sections, drought-prone area programme were the other activities that government undertook at the macro level for poverty eradication. Therefore, in this direction, the following are the directly beneficiary oriented programmes:

Small Farmers Development Agency (SFDA) (1969-80)

Target group approach was adopted from the Fourth Plan. The objective was to produce a direct impact on the status of the rural poor. It started with the Small Farmers Development Agency (SFDA) and Marginal Farmers and Agricultural Labourers Development Agency (MFALDA) were introduced on the recommendations of the Rural Credit Review Committee in 1969 with a view to improving the economic conditions of small and marginal farmers and agricultural labourers. In the case of small and marginal farmers, this was sought to be done by developing the capacity of their land through additional capital. For, most of them hardly have any surplus income to spare for investment to improve their production. The high incidence of indebtedness among the group confirms this assumption (Chakravarty, 1980). In the case of agricultural labourers, who are paid low wages and have no other avenues of income, the need for assistance is all the greater. Added to it, the number of days for which employment was available for rural labourers declined by 10 per cent for men, 7.5 per cent for women and 5 per cent for children (Labour Enquiry Report, 1974-75). Therefore, SFDA and MFAL agencies were expected to offer schemes, which can generate additional income and these agencies were expected to bring the benefits of modern technology to the small and marginal farmers and agricultural labourers and raise their standards of living by improved agriculture, subsidiary occupations and supplementary employment (Compendium, 1975).

These agencies were started in 1969-70 on a pilot basis in 87 project areas throughout the country. These 87 projects include 46 SFDA projects and 41 MFAL projects. However, it did take some time to get the whole scheme implemented, 1971-72 was the first full year of working for most of the projects. The projects were to continue till 1975-76 to complete five years, duration. In the year 1973, the National Commission on Agriculture recommended that "the artificial distinction between SFDA programmes and MFAL programmes be given up" and asked for considerable expansion of these programmes. Accordingly, during the first year of the Fifth Five Year Plan, these programmes were brought under a single agency, namely, SFDA. And the total number of the projects was raised from 87 to 168, which included eight projects of Command Area Development Authority.

Each SFDA was expected to cover 50,000 families of small and marginal farmers and agricultural labourers. The main objectives of the SFDA were :

1. To identify the members of the target groups (small farmers, marginal farmers and agricultural labouers) and their problems;
2. To draw up and execute plans (schemes) for investment and production in respect of activities, which might be taken up by them for their own benefit;
3. To review the progress and effectiveness thereof, a budget of Rs. 1.5 crore was allowed for each SFDA for five years and the entire amount was provided by the Government of India. Financial assistance to beneficiaries included a subsidy of 25 per cent of the cost in the case of small farmers and $33^1/_3$ per cent in the case of marginal farmers and agricultural labourers subject to a maximum limit of Rs.3,000. The balance amount was supposed to come as a loan from banks. Apart from providing subsidies and arranging for loans, the SFDA was required to organize and arrange for supplies of inputs such as fertilizers, seeds and pesticides, agricultural implements, marketing services and other facilities to small and marginal farmers. The households were expected to cross the poverty line through its developmental schemes.

The SFDA: The Impact on Target Group

Several studies were conducted on the impact of SFDA in different

States. About the coverage of the target groups, the studies from Bihar, Kerala, Karnataka, Rajasthan, Madhya Pradesh and Uttar Pradesh point out that it was very low and fell short of the targets awfully. The cases of wrong identification of the beneficiaries have been pointed out. Most of these studies maintain that the benefits did not percolate to the target groups. Ineffectiveness of the agency is traced to lack of awareness about the agency on the part of target groups to take government loans, misutilization of the loan amount and cornering of the benefits by richer sections (Ram Reddy and Haragopal, 1985).

However, certain successful schemes were reported from Karnataka, Haryana and Himachal Pradesh. Karnataka study reveals that households under sheep rearing category derived the benefit. The studies from Haryana report that the agency has left a favourable impact on the employment conditions of the beneficiaries, since a rise in both the man-days of work and wages were noticed. The dairy development programme was pointed out, attained marked progress crossing the set targets more than $2^1/_2$ times.

In their classic study on SFDA in Andhra Pradesh, Prof. Ram Reddy and Haragopal (1985), found that in a target of 10 lakh households, the total number of members covered accounted for 4.18 lakh, i.e. 48 per cent. Of the households covered, the small farmers constitute 1.67 lakh, the marginal farmers 2.32 lakh, and agricultural labourers 81.5 thousands. Among the farmers covered, the target number is that of marginal farmers followed by small farmers. Agricultural labourers constitute 17 per cent in which scheduled castes were 28 per cent. Out of the total of 56 lakh small and marginal farmers in Andhra Pradesh, the target covered was seven per cent. From the 83 lakh agricultural labourers, the target covered was less than one per cent.

An analysis of income on account of the scheme shows that the schemes hardly had shown any impact on the target groups. Category-wise, the impact on small farmers was very little and on marginal farmers, negligible. In the case of agricultural labourers, it resulted in further impoverishment of this class. For, the number that could cross the poverty line was absolutely negligible. A comparison between the income levels of beneficiaries and those of non-beneficiaries further confirmed that the scheme had an impact on the target groups (Ram Reddy and Haragopal, 1985).

Thus, though SFDA occupied a place of pride for about 10 years during the Fourth and Fifth Plans, the amount sanctioned under this has been very meagre by all standards and the impact on the poorest of the rural poor even in areas having best performance was, therefore, not likely to be significant. The SFDA has merged with the IRDP in October 1980.

Rural Works Programme

Considering under-employment and unemployment as one of the basic problems of the rural poor, the Third Five Year Plan had proposed to organize a rural works programme on a mass scale to provide employment for about 1,00,000 persons in the first year, about 4,00,000 to 5,00,000 in the second year, about a million in the third year, rising to about 2.5 million in the last year of the plan at an estimated total cost of Rs.150 crores during the plan period at the then prevailing prices (Third Five Year Plan, p. 165). The plan had also indicated the possibility of considering ways of paying wages in part in the form of food grains. But the scheme did not gain much ground because only Rs.19 crore could be made available for such programmes.

Food for Works Programme (April 1977—October 1980)

The Maharashtra Government introduced the Employment Guarantee Scheme in 1972-73. Karnataka Government also initiated a similar scheme. In April 1977, the Central Government launched a nationwide 'Food for Work Programme' to enlarge employment opportunities for rural poor. The basic objectives of the programme were :

1. To generate additional gainful employment to a large number of unemployed and under-employed persons both men and women, in rural areas for raising their incomes and consequently their nutritional levels;
2. To create durable community assets and strengthening the rural infrastructure; and
3. To utilize surplus food grains for the development of human resources.

Performance

This programme was based on the pattern of the rural works or crash employment programmes. But unlike them, a massive effort was made for the first time. As much as 56 lakh metric tonnes of food grains were released under this programme till October 1980, of which 46.5 lakh metric tonnes were utilized. Employment generated since the inception of this programme in 1977 to 1979-80 is reported to be 8,686 lakh man-days (Prasad, Kamta, 1985).

National Rural Employment Programme (NREP) (1980 October to 1989)

Since October 1980, the Food for Work Programme was renamed as the National Rural Employment Programme (NREP) and made a part of Sixth Five Year Plan. It was a centrally sponsored programme with equal contributions of the central and state governments. Like food for work programme, it provided supplementary employment opportunities to work seekers during the lean period of the year. Apart from FWP objectives, it aimed at social forestry.

For implementing NREP, there was a total outlay of Rs.1,620 crore for both central and state sectors during the sixth plan. However, a total amount of Rs. 1,873 crore (Rs. 1,079 crore on central share and Rs. 794 crore on state share) was actually made available and an amount of Rs. 1,834 crore was utilized under the programme during the Sixth Plan period.

Impact on the Beneficiaries

Against the target of generation of 1,500-2,000 million man-days, 1,775 million man-days were generated during the Sixth Plan period. The target of generating more than 300 million man-days were achieved during each year of the Sixth Plan period. Moreover, employment generated for SC/ST during the Sixth Plan period accounted for roughly 42 per cent of the total employment generation, which indicated that the programme catered to the needs of the weaker sections, particularly SC/STs, to a great extent (Morley, 1988).

Under social forestry sector, for which 10 per cent of the funds were earmarked from 1981-82 onwards, Rs. 152.61 crore were utilized during the year 1981-82 to 1984-85. During the Sixth Plan period, 4.69 lakh hectares have been brought under plantation and about 596.99 trees have been planted. NREP merged with Jawahar Rozgar Yojana (JRY) in April 1989.

Rural Landless Employment Guarantee Programme (RLEGP) (August 1983-April 1989)

It was felt that hardcore of rural poverty, particularly pertaining to employment opportunities for the landless during the lean agricultural periods, when work is scarce, has to be tackled in a more direct and specific manner. Accordingly, a new scheme called Rural Landless Employment Guarantee Programme (RLEGP) was launched in August 1983 (Morley, 1988). The basic objectives of this programme were (1) to improve and expand employment opportunities for rural landless with a view to providing employment for at least one member of every landless labour household up to 100 days in a year, and (2) to create durable assets for strengthening rural infrastructure, which will lead to rapid growth of rural economy.

Under the programme, the State/UT governments were required to prepare specific projects relevant to the 20 points programmes and the minimum needs programmes such as:

(a) Construction of rural link roads;
(b) Construction/renovation of field channels to maximize the utilization of potential created by existing irrigation projects;
(c) Land development and reclamation of waste land or degraded land with special emphasis on ecological improvement in hill and desert areas;
(d) Social forestry; and
(e) Soil and water conservation works including the improvement of minor irrigation works (Morley, 1988).

The programme was fully funded by the central government. During the Sixth Plan, Rs. 600 crore was provided (Rs. 100 crore for 1983-84 and Rs. 500 crore for 1984-85). Employment generation to the extent of 360 million man-days was expected during the Sixth Plan. In April 1989, RLEGP merged with Jawahar Rozgar Yojana (JRY).

Integrated Rural Development Programme

The 20-point programme, which is an important dimension of the National Development Strategy, includes as many as seven aspects, which are directly related to rural development. The IRDP is also an important component of it.

The Integrated Rural Development Programme (IRDP) represents a combination of schemes in different sectors of rural economy, i.e. in the primary sector, such as crop production and minor irrigation in agriculture, animal husbandry, development of women and children in rural areas (DWCRA), social forestry, and also a number of self-employment programmes in secondary and tertiary sectors through Training of Rural Youth for Self-Employment (TRYSEM) and developing industry service and business (ISB) activities in rural areas.

IRDP, in its present form, was introduced in 1978-79 with the objective of reducing poverty through generation of employment and income and also achieving a balanced development of rural sector in a coherent manner. Prevalence of widespread unemployment and under-employment and the fact that almost 50 per cent of the households fell below poverty line provided the backdrop in which IRDP was conceived as a strategy to combat rural poverty. In a nutshell, the programme envisages a direct attack on rural poverty by providing viable income generation assets to the identified target groups and also to enable them through training extension and supportive infrastructure facilities to maintain and manage the assets provided (Morley, Mohan Lal, 1988). This programme envisages that 600 poorest families shall be assisted in each of the 5,011 development blocks in the country every year to improve their income. It is a centrally sponsored programme funded by the centre and the states on 50 : 50 basis. In the Sixth Plan, in each of the 5,011 blocks in the country, the poorest were targeted to be identified. Thus the Sixth Plan aimed at assisting 15 million families. At the beginning of the Sixth Plan, approximately, 46 million households in rural India were poor.

Target Group

IRDP has the target group, the weaker sections of the rural population, which includes Schedule Castes and Scheduled Tribes, agricultural and non-agricultural labourers, rural artisans, marginal and small marginal farmer and those who are living below the poverty line.

Development of Women and Children in Rural Areas (DWCRA)

Women constitute nearly 50 per cent of population in India. But it is a historical reality that women have been neglected. Their contribution to the national economy as well as to the wellbeing of their families is well known. It is observed that in the whole process of implementation of IRDP, women have been, by and large, overlooked. Family approach, in a way, ignored the economic potential of women workforce. Therefore, to cure the situation to some extent, a women component of IRDP has been designed, which is called the "Development of Women and Children in Rural Areas" (DWCRA), was launched in September 1982 with the objective of focusing attention on women below the poverty line so as to improve their income generation activities. Since individual ventures may not be effective due to the existing socio-economic constraints operating in regard to rural women, the scheme was designed to operate through groups. Hence, homogeneous groups are formed with a membership of 15-12 in order to facilitate and promote activities. A provision was made for childcare facilities.

Economic Activities under DWCRA

Tailoring, knitting, embroidery, weaving, readymade garments, carpet weaving, khadi spinning, fibre-making, hand-printing, bread-making, palmleaf mat-making, bamboo basket-making, pickles-making, food processing, bakery, vegetable growing, fishnet making, fishery, poultry, goat rearing, duckery, dairying, piggery, bee-keeping, paddy pounding, brush making, book binding, handmade paper-making, candle-making, chalk-making, match-making, paper bag-making, envelop-making, basket-making, soap-making, fruit and vegetables/fish preservation, decoration pieces or toys and wood works.

Training of Rural Youth for Self-Employment (TRYSEM)

Training of Rural Youth for Self-Employment (TRYSEM) was launched on 15th August 1979 as a centrally sponsored scheme. The scheme is an integral part of the Integrated Rural Development Programme (IRDP). The objective of TRYSEM is to provide technical skills to the rural youth from families below poverty line to enable them to take up self-employment. The target group under this scheme comprises rural youth between the age group 18-35. In certain conditions, wage employment can also be taken up under the scheme.

The identified youth are put through a properly designed training courses either with a training institution or a master craftsman to provide them necessary technical and entrepreneurial skills. Training is to be provided on the basis of actual needs, and therefore, it has been decided not to have separate targets at macro level under TRYSEM. On successful completion of training, the trained youth are assisted under IRDP through subsidy and loan for acquiring income-generating asset(s).

Identification and Selection of Trainees

According to the guidelines, the Block Development Officer (BDO) will invite applications from youth belonging to the target group in his area. There are no educational qualifications prescribed for selection of trainees. Once an exhaustive list of potential trainees is available, a committee presided over by the BDO and including members from the training institutions of the area, Panchayati Raj Institutions, and any other, which it may wish to co-opt, finalizes selection on the basis of the following criteria :

(i) Members of the poorest families should be selected first;
(ii) At least one-third of the candidates should be women;
(iii) Priority should be given to members of scheduled castes and tribes—a minimum of 30 per cent of the trained youth should belong to the SC/ST; and
(iv) Some consideration should be given to persons who have completed the nine-month course under the National Adult Education Programme.

Impact of IRDP on Poor

Impact of IRDP on poor is not in a uniform way in all the states. In his comparative study of IRDP performance in West Bengal and Gujarat, Ray found that in West Bengal, there was a sharp decline of percentage of income in low categories and all respondents were in the income categories of Rs. 4,801 and above. But a similar trend was not observed in Gujarat villages, where there was only a 3 per cent decline in the very poor category. Taking Rs. 6,400 as the poverty level, about 57 per cent of the respondents have come out of poverty level in the study area of West Bengal compared to 17 per cent in Gujarat (Ray, C.N., 1992). Giriappa's study in Karnataka reveals that on the whole, about 15 per cent of the beneficiaries have crossed the poverty line of

Rs. 6,400 (Giriappa, S., 1992, JRD). As per the official estimates, IRDP has been "exceptionally" successful in Jammu and Kashmir. In most of the districts, achievements had exceeded the targets (Mahammad Sultan Bhat and Jatinder Kaur Badshi, 1992, JRD).

B.P. Maithani and Haloi's study (1988) agrees with the statement contained in the volume, 'Nagaland's Rural Development in Action', which reads thus: "though we have made commendable success in achieving the (IRDP) target fixed for the plan period, a random survey of the programme so far implemented shows that the assistance extended to the families is negligible and in many cases, it does not help their economic progress".

Jawahar Rozgar Yojana

With the objectives of providing employment and alleviating poverty in rural areas, the Government of India launched the biggest wage employment scheme 'Jawahar Rozgar Yojana' (JRY) in April 1989. The existing schemes, known as National Rural Employment Programme (NREP) and Rural Landless Employment Guarantee Programme (RLEGP), have been merged with this new Yojana (JRY), which is now being implemented and administered by the village panchayats all over the country. Over 440 lakh families, which are below the poverty line, are intended to benefit from this scheme. It provides employment to at least one member of each poor family for 50 to 100 days in a year in the vicinity of their residence. Of the total expenditure incurred, 15 per cent will be transferred to village panchayats to be used exclusively for the benefit of scheduled castes and scheduled tribes. Of the beneficiaries under the JRY, 30 per cent will be women. Broadly, the objectives of JRY are :

A. Generation of additional gainful employment for the unemployed and underemployed persons, both men and women in rural areas;
B. Creation of productive community assets for direct and continuing benefits to the poverty groups and for strengthening rural, economic and social infrastructure that will lead to rapid growth of the rural economy along with a steady rise in the income levels of the rural poor and to bring about improvement in the overall quality of life in the rural areas.

The expenditure on JRY is being shared on 80 : 20 basis between the centre and the states. The funds are made available by the DRDA of each district from the centre and distributed to the village panchayats on the basis of the SC/ST population. The village panchayats have the power to plan and execute the works as per the guidelines of JRY (Jos, *et al.,* 1995). The criteria for the distribution of resources to village panchayats from the districts are on the basis of population of the village panchayat. If the population of village is less than 1000, then it is assumed 1000 for the allocation of funds. Panchayats, with a population of 3000 to 4000, would receive funds of the order of Rs. 80,000 to Rs. 1,00,000.

Now, the JRY aims at strengthening the planning process at the village level by involving village panchayats in planning and implementation of projects. A sum of Rs. 2,600 crore will be spent in the central sector on JRY. As such, it becomes the biggest employment programme in the world. The use of funds will be decided solely by the Gram Panchayat on the basis of the felt needs of the local people.

It is pertinent to observe that of the total allocation at the district level, 6 per cent will be earmarked for Indira Awas Yojana (IAY) for scheduled castes and scheduled tribes. Of the 80 per cent amount to be given to village panchayats, 20 per cent will be used at the district level. DRDA/ZP will use 5 per cent of their funds for administrative expenditure, while up to 10 per cent can be spent for maintenance of the assets created under JRY. The rest will be distributed on economically productive assets (35 per cent), social forestry work (25 per cent), individual beneficiaries of SCs/STs (15 per cent) and on other works, including roads and buildings (25 per cent). Gram panchayats have, however, the freedom to change the sectoral allocations.

Impact of Economic Reforms and Poor

The present economic reform in India was initiated in July 1991 to improve efficiency and growth through free competition in an open market economy so that the country become one of the strongest economies in the world by the end of this century. Generation of industrial production, trade, foreign exchange and foreign investment is the important feature of new economic policy. It provides new opportunities to industrialists, big farmers and the business community. It does not have any direct relationship with poverty eradication except creating new job opportunities. According to G.V. Rajeev "Indian government invites foreign investment because not only investment but foreign technology also will flow into the country and consequently exports of industrial products and employment opportunities will be generated". But as Satish Sarangi and Gary Cohen (1995) observed, most of this industrial investment is 'capital intensive' instead of 'labour intensive', which means that even on economic grounds, these large-scale industrial projects do not solve the unemployment problem in India. For example, the Dabhol Power Plant outside Bombay, which will cost Rs. 90,530 million on construction, will provide only 2000 permanent jobs, while directly displacing 2000 villagers. The Thapur-Dupont Nylon Factory, recently rejected in Goa, would have only provided 650 jobs, while depriving thousands of people of their traditional livelihood. In fact, the official unemployment rate has risen by 6 per cent since liberalization took effect (Satish Sarangi & Gary Cohen, 1995).

Though economic reforms do not have any direct relationship with poverty eradication, as S.P. Gupta observed, every economic unit has role either as a consumer or producer or both. The impact of economic reforms work via income and price changes (Gupta, 1995). In this regard, economic reforms can show their impact in two ways. The first one being the employment generation, second one is prices. But for last four years, they could not have any positive effects on poor, instead, they adversely affected the poor by rising/increasing unemployment and the prices of essential commodities (Balakrishna, 1995).

Presenting his first budget of 1991-92, Dr. Manmohan Singh, had promised that structural reform would have a 'human face'. Presenting his 1993-94 Budget, he had to warn, "there can be no adjustment without pain". But he once again promised that "it shall be our endeavour to minimize the burden of adjustment on the poor" (Tandon, 1995). To continue economic reforms on the one hand and to minimize their burden on the poor and to uplift the poor on the other hand, the outlay for rural development has been enhanced to Rs. 30,000 crore in the Eighth Five Year Plan and for the year 1995-96, it has been fixed at Rs. 7,700 crore to implement the poverty eradication programmes like JRY, IJRY, IRDP, DWCRA and TRYSEM (Upadhyaya, 1995). Therefore, in the light of economic reforms, poverty eradication programmes can be seen as concomitants of structural adjustment. This is called the two-track strategy of accelerating growth and strengthening anti-poverty programmes.

During the period of structural adjustment, the key aspect eradicating poverty lies in the effective implementation and utilization of anti-poverty programmes.

Swarnjayanti Gram Swarozgar Yojana (SGSY)

The multiplicity of programmes such as IRDP, TRYSEM, DWCRA, etc., being viewed as separate programmes in themselves, resulted in a lack of proper social intermediation, absence of desired linkages among these programme *inter se* and the implementation being more concerned with achieving individual programme targets rather than focusing on the substantive issue of sustainable income generation (SGSY Guidelines). To rectify the situation, government has decided restructuring the self-employment programmes. A new programme, known as Swarnjayanti Gram Swarozgar Yojana (SGSY), has been launched from April 1999. This is a holistic programme, covering all aspects of self-employment such as organization of poor into self-help groups, training, credit, technology, infrastructure and marketing. SGSY will be funded by the centre and the states in the ratio of 75:25.

With the coming into force of SGSY, the earlier programmes, IRDP, TRYSEM, DWCRA, SITRA, GKY and MWS are no longer in operation (Rao, 2000). SGSY aims at establishing a large number of micro-enterprises in the rural areas, building upon the potential of the rural poor. It is rooted in the belief that rural poor in India have competencies, and given the right support, can be successful producers of valuable goods and services. The people benefited by this scheme are not called as beneficiaries, but as *Swarozgaries*.

The objective of SGSY is to bring the assisted poor families (*Swarozgaries*) above the poverty line in three years by providing them income generating assets through a mix of bank credit and government subsidy. It would mean ensuring that the family has a monthly net income of at least Rs. 2,000. Subject to availability of funds, the effort will be to cover 30 per cent of the poor families in each block during the first five years.

Section B

Land Reforms

Every human being has, for that matter, every living being, the right to live on this earth and to avail the natural resources of the earth for survival. Land is the source from which human beings derive their food for living. In a predominantly agrarian economy, access to land is more relevant in determining relative economic position of different categories of people as land is a symbol of security, the principal source of income and wealth as well as of social, political and economic power. Similarly, the access to land also determines the poverty and deprivation. Possession of large areas of land by a few deprived the rights of the millions of people from meeting their basic needs. There can be no justification to the fact that millions of people in some parts of this world go hungry while their productive talents and energies in growing their own food supplies are being wasted, while at the same time, large areas of uninvited land, controlled by a few, is lying uncultivated or cultivated quite below its productive capacity by poor and inefficient management (Singh, D.V. *et al.*, 1989). Dandekar and Neelakantha Rath's study (1971) reveals that landlessness was one of the main reasons for poverty in India. In both the periods (from 1956-57 to1963-64), about 60 per cent of the labour households had no land, hence they depended almost entirely on the personal labour of their members. The remaining 40 per cent cultivated small pieces of land, nevertheless, their main dependence was on wage employment in agriculture or outside agriculture. Nearly three-fourths of the labour households worked as casual labourers, i.e. they worked if and when work was available, otherwise, they were unemployed. Therefore, to correct the unequal and unequitable distribution of land and to provide employment and livelihood to the deprived sections. Land reforms are inevitable.

Land Ceiling and Redistribution

Since land is an important source of income and wealth, it was thought that poverty alleviation would be easier if implementation of land reforms related to ceiling on holdings is speeded up. The Congress Agrarian Reform Committee (1949) presided by J.C. Kumarappa spelled out that "all intermediatory interests should be abolished and land should belong to the tiller". According to a government report (1977-80), land ceiling measures were initiated in 1950s and early 1960s, which resulted in distribution of 8.10 lakh hectares of ceiling surplus land among 10.60 lakh rural landless families. However, ceilings set under these laws were very high and in many cases, exemptions provided were too many. A new national policy of land ceiling was, therefore, evolved in July 1972, which removed these deficiencies and suggested a certain degree of uniformity in the laws of different states and union territories. Accordingly, laws on ceilings of agriculture lands have been enacted and are being implemented in all the states of the country, particularly where land ceiling is relevant.

The available figures show that with the revised ceiling, 29.40 lakh hectare area of land has been declared surplus up to February 1986. Out of this, 23.19 lakh hectares have been taken over by the state and 17.52 lakh hectares of land have been distributed among 33.76 lakh allottees. This shows that about 1.8 per cent area has been declared surplus and the area actually distributed has been about 1.1 per cent of the cultivated area in the country. This shows that the average amount of land obtained by each beneficiary has been 0.52 hectare (Savita Varmani, 1989). This small portion of land cannot make the required dent on the poverty of the weaker sections of the society.

New Economic Policies and Land Reforms

In 1990, an attempt was made by some state governments to relax the Land Reform Act. The Karnataka government moved to bring about amendments in the Karnataka Land Reforms Act to relax the ceiling on agricultural land and to dilute the basic tenet of land to tiller. Already legislation from West Bengal and Maharashtra are pending with the centre for Presidential assent. The former Chief Minister of Punjab, Beant Singh, had also raised the issue before his assassination, and in Kerala, the High Court had quashed a state law to revise the land ceiling laws (Prasad, Gargi, 1995). In the light of these legislations of various state governments, it is obvious that in the wake of the liberalization of the economy, a powerful, moneyed lobby of realtors, Multi-National Corporations (MNCs) and Non-Resident Indians (NRIs) gained ground against the peasants, the poor and the landless and marginal farmers in the country.

Section C

Population Control

In the past four decades, more people have been added to the globe than in all of history before the middle of this century. And growth continues unabatedly. The world's population is now expanding at the unprecedented rate of nearly 1 billion per decade and the United Nations and the World Bank project an additional six billion inhabitants by the end of the next century. Virtually, all this growth is expected to occur in Africa, Asia and Latin America.

Rapid population growth exacerbates the mutually reinforcing effects of poverty and environmental damage, increased population adds pressure on the natural resources. As Cynthia Green (1992) puts it, "rapid population growth burns nature's candle at both ends generating more consumers, while reducing natural resources". The poor are both victims and agents of environmental damage, because they lack resources and technology. It is often the poorest who suffer most from the consequences of pollution and environmental degradation. Unlike the rich, the poor cannot afford to protect themselves from contaminated water. According to World Development Report (1992, p. 2), in cities, the people are more likely to spend much of their time on the streets, breathing polluted air; in rural areas; they are more likely to cook on open fires of wood or dung, inhaling dangerous fumes; their lands are more likely to suffer from soil erosion.

Despite the disagreements about future prospects, there is broad agreement that a reduction in rapid population growth in the developing world will enhance the prospects for improved standards of additional billions in the decades ahead (John Bongarts, 1994). The World Bank (1993) estimated \$4 to 5 billion per year is now spent in Africa, Asia and Latin America.

Population Policy and Programmes in India

Realizing the adverse effects of an expansion of the human population, organizations such as the International Planned Parenthood Federation (to link family planning programmes appearing in many countries) and the population council (to serve as a scientific resource for the field) were created in 1952. India became the first country to adopt an official policy to reduce population growth by promoting family planning (John Bongarts, 1994). India's concern for controlling its population is reflected in its five year plans. It was stated in the First Five Year Plan that "the recent increase in the population of India and the pressure exercised on the limited resources of the country have brought to the forefront the urgency of the problem of family planning and population control (First Five Year Plan). In this plan, importance was given to changing the attitudes of people in favour of using the contraceptives, spacing between child to child and to adopt family planning. A sum of Rs. 65 lakh was allocated by the central government in this plan.

During the second plan, a sum of Rs. 5 crore was allocated to family planning. During this period, Action-*cum*-Research Programme was initiated. The plan envisaged to set up 300 urban, 2000 rural clinics, which would aim at creating the general awareness about the problem and provide advice and service (Second Five Year Plan, p. 554). 1694 family planning centres (549 in urban areas and 1100 in rural areas) were opened. Research in the field of demography, reproduction physiology, motivation and communication was undertaken. Centres to study the usefulness of family planning were established at Delhi, Calcutta and Trivandrum.

1961 census marked higher rate of growth of population than expected. Therefore, urgency with regard to implementation of family planning was felt. Hence, the third plan (1961- 66) clearly stated that stabilizing the growth of population should be the central feature of planning and family pianning programme. An amount of Rs. 24.86 crore was allocated to family planning during this period. Cafeteria approach, i.e., freedom to the family planning acceptor to choose any of the contraceptive methods was pursued by providing a series of service points, aided by an extension system of male and female family planning workers. Distribution of condoms through distributors of commercial goods was also taken up. In 1966, a full-fledged Department of Family Planning was created in the Ministry of Health, Family Planning and Urban Development.

During the Fourth Five Year Plan (1969-74), high priority was accorded to family planning. Rs. 315 crore was allocated to this programme in this plan. Reduction of crude birth rate from 39 per thousand to 32 per thousand by 1973-74 was aimed at. Its emphasis was on group acceptance of family planning, personal knowledge of family planning methods and ensuring availability of family planning supplies and services. In 1971, Medical Termination of Pregnancy Act was enacted.

During the Fourth Five Year Plan (1969-74), an integrated approach, i.e. integrating family planning with health, maternity, child healthcare and nutrition services at all levels was adopted. And on

April 16, 1976, a New Population Policy was announced. This policy aimed at direct assault on the problem, i.e. pressurizing the people to adopt family planning. As a part of this policy, minimum marriageable age for girls was raised from 15 to 18 years and for boys from 18 to 21. Population values were included in education through NCERT. Activities of Voluntary Organizations, especially of women and youth organizations, were intensified. Income Tax was exempted for amounts given as donations for family planning programmes. Research was increased in reproductive biology and contraceptives.

During the emergency period, coercive methods like forcing unwilling people to go in for family planning, insistence of sterilization certificate for various government benefits were adopted. To achieve targets, overzealous officials harassed the people. As people were not mentally prepared for family planning, they developed revulsion. As a result, the programme suffered a severe jolt, and it contributed a great deal to the fall of the Congress Government in 1977 elections. During 1977-80, the Janata Government gave up coercive methods and adopted persuasive methods. The Department of Family Planning was renamed as Department of Family Welfare Programme.

The Sixth Five Year Plan (1980-85) aimed at developing confidence among people in the Family Planning Programme. Coercive methods were discarded. Reducing the average size of the family from 4.2 children to 2.3 children, birth rate from 33 per thousand to 31 per thousand and death rate from 14 to 9 per thousand were fixed as goals of this plan (Sixth Five Year Plan). Rs. 1,010 crore was allocated to this programme during this period. Education was given more importance in this plan to make the family planning programme a success.

During the Seventh Five Year Plan (1985-90), emphasis was laid on improving the efficiency of family planning, infrastructure and family education. An important role was assigned to non-governmental organizations like *mahila mandals* and youth clubs in making family planing activities popular. An amount of Rs. 3,256 crore was allocated to family planning during this plan. For achievement of the two children norm, it was considered essential to enhance the child survival rate (Seventh Five Year Plan).

During the Eighth Five Year Plan (1992-97), emphasis was laid on improving the efficiency of Family Planning infrastructure and family education. An important role was assigned to non-governmental organizations like Mahila Mandals, Youth Clubs in making family planning activities popular. Rs. 6,500 crore was allocated to Family Planning during this plan. In the subsequent plans and policies also, concern has been shown by the government to control the population, aiming at materializing the goals of sustainable development. Yet, the population of India has crossed 1 billion mark. If the same growth rate continues, India's population is estimated to be more than the population of China by 2045 (Reddy, Sphurthi, 2001). Therefore, it is inevitable at this juncture to adopt one child per a couple pattern.

PART II
ENVIRONMENT PROTECTION

Introduction

To live a healthy and productive life, a clean environment is an imperative. Polluted air, water and degraded land not only cause diseases, but also adversely affect the production. The quantity of production depends on the quality of natural resources, i.e., environment. Till 17th century, environment did not lose its virginity, the progress achieved by man in science and technology led to the industrial revolution, which again paved the way to urbanization and exploitation of natural resources. Rapid growth of industries, urbanization, population and over consumption resulted in the depletion of natural resources, pollution, soil erosion, acid rains, depletion of ozone layer, extinction of species, green house effect and other health hazards to men and cattle. They have become a threat to the very survival of life on earth. Then realization came that the protection of environment is inevitable for a healthy and productive life. The UN Conference held on June 14, 1972 at Stockholm alerted the nations about environmental problems. There has grown up a serious concern all over the world about the rivers turning murky, fish rotting on seashores, tree withering, cities choking with foul air, toxic chemicals being cycled into food stuffs and disease epidemics appearing so frequently. If environment is not protected, the present generation cannot live a healthy life and the needs and aspiration of future generations will not be fulfilled, which are important aspects of sustainable development.

Therefore, protection of environment is inevitable for a healthy and productive life of present generation and for meeting the needs and aspirations of future generations.

State's Intervention in Protecting Environment

Government's intervention in protecting environment is not new. As long back as in 1237, King Edward I of England promoted the passage of a law, outlawing the use of certain types of coal. Charles II, in 1961, commissioned John Evelyn to make a report on London's air pollution. Napoleon ordered in 1810 that measures be taken by all factories to prevent damage or any kind of trouble to neighbours, crops, buildings, etc. Smoke ordinance was passed in the US by the City Council of Chicago in 1874. Similar regulations were soon imposed in all industrial countries (Sethi, Indrajeet, *et al.,* 1991). Stockholm Conference on Human Environment in 1972 alerted the governments to take measures to protect the environment and to formulate environmental policies. Nevertheless, it was only during the past thirty years that our world has really become 'Environment Conscious'.

Indian Government's Environment Protection Policy

As in many other countries, environmental planning took formal shape in India as a consequence of the Stockholm Conference held in 1972. India, through Mrs. Indira Gandhi, participated in this Conference very meaningfully and it was a historic event of planet wide importance in the protection of the environment. Indian government initiated the steps to protect the environment through legislation by setting up of the Ministry of Environment and Forests, Pollution Control Boards, National Parks and Sanctuaries, special projects, etc.

The Department of Environment was set up in 1980 to serve as the focal point in the administrative structure of the government for planning, promotion and co-ordination of environmental programmes. The present Integrated Department of Environment, Forests and Wild Life in the Ministry of Environment and Forests was created in September 1985. The Ministry's main activities are the survey and conservation of flora, fauna, forests and wild life, prevention and control of pollution, afforestation and regeneration of the degraded areas of the environment. These are to be achieved through impact assessment support to organizations implementing the programmes, environmental and forestry research, extension education and training to augment the requisite manpower, collection, collation and dissemination of environmental information and creation of environmental awareness (Sharma, 1994).

Environmental Legislation in Pre-Independent India

Though environmental awareness has grown in the recent decades only, even before independence, government tried to conserve the environment through the following acts :

- The Shore Nuisance (Bombay and Kolaba) Act, 1853.
- The Orient Gas Company Act, 1857.
- The Series Act, 1867.
- The Northern Indian Canal and Drainage Act, 1873.
- The Obstruction in Fairways Act, 1881.
- Indian Easement Act, 1882.
- The Indian Fishers Act, 1897.
- Bengal Smoke Nuisance Act, 1905.
- The Indian Ports Act, 1908.
- The Inland Stream Vessels Act, 1917.
- Motor Vehicle Act, 1939.
- The Factories Act, 1948.

Besides these Acts, in the Indian Penal Code, 1860, there are some sections dealing with control of pollution. They are:

Section 277: According to this section, whoever voluntarily corrupts or fouls the water of any public spring or reservoir, so as to render it less fit for the purposes for which it is ordinarily used, shall be punished with imprisonment of either description for a term which may extend to three months, or with fine, which may extend to five hundred rupees or with both.

Section 284 : According to this section, whoever does, with any poisonous substance, any act in a manner so rash or negligent as to endanger human life, or to be likely to cause hurt or injury to any person, or knowingly or negligently omits to take such order with any poisonous substance in his possession as is sufficient to guard against any probable danger to human life from such poisonous substance, shall be punished with imprisonment of either description for a term, which may extend to six months or with fine, which may extend to one thousand rupees or with both.

Environmental Legislation in Post-Independent India

In the post-Independent India, the following Acts have been enacted to control the environmental degradation:

River Boards Act, 1956

Certain states passed special laws to combat the problem of pollution of their water resources. Firstly, the state of Orissa passed the Orissa River Pollution Prevention Act, 1953. Then Maharashtra, one of India's most industrialized and one of densely populated states, passed the Maharashtra Prevention of Water Pollution Act, 1969. Then the Central Government ultimately passed Rivers Boards Act, 1956 for the prevention of pollution of the water of the inter-state rivers (Chakraborty, 1994).

The Atomic Energy Act, 1962

To control radioactive pollution in India, the Atomic Energy Act, 1962, was passed. The regulation of nuclear energy and radioactive substances in India is now governed under this Act. Thus, statutory obligation is imposed upon the central government to prevent radiation hazards, guarantee public safety and the safety of workers handling radioactive substances and the safe disposal of radioactive wastes.

The Insecticides Act, 1986

The Insecticides Act was passed by the parliament to implement the recommendation of the Kerala and Madras Food Poisoning Cases Inquiry Commission. The Act provided establishment of a Central Insecticides Board to advise the centre and the state on technical aspects of the Act. The manufacture and distribution of insecticides are now regulated through licensing under this Act and violation of which leads to the prosecution and penalties.

The Wildlife Protection Act, 1972

Parliament enacted the Wild Life Protection Act, 1972, pursuant to the enabling resolutions of 11 states under Article 252 (1) of the Constitution. The Act provides for establishment of State Wild Life

Advisory Board, regulation on for hunting wild animals and birds, developing sanctuaries and national parks and regulations in the trade of wild animals and animals products.

The Water (Prevention and Control) of Pollution Act, 1974

In 1974, the parliament came out for the first time with a comprehensive legislation for controlling water pollution by enacting the Water (Prevention and Control of Pollution) Act. The Act was passed with the object of prevention and control of water pollution and of restoring the wholesomeness of water quality. The Act provides for the constitution of a Central Board for the prevention and control of water pollution. The Act also provides for the constitution of state boards for the prevention and control of water pollution in states.

The Board's functions include advising central government concerning the prevention and control of water pollution through coordination of efforts by State Boards, giving of technical assistance and guidance to states, sponsoring of research and training of persons engaged in the field of water pollution. The Act was amended in 1988 to strengthen the Act's implementation provisions. Now, a board is competent to close a defaulting industrial plant or withdraw its supply of power or water by an administrative order and a citizen's suit provision bolsters the enforcement machinery (Chakraborty, 1994).

The Water (Prevention and Control of Pollution) Cess Act, 1977

The Water Cess Act was passed to augment the resources of the Central and State Water Boards. The Act envisaged incentives for adopting pollution control and authorized government to impose cess for water consumption.

The Forest (Conservation) Act, 1980

To stop the growing deforestation and the resulting environmental degradation, the parliament enacted the Forest (Conservation) Act in 1980. The Act was again amended in 1988. Now, under the Forest Act as amended in 1988, a prior approval is essential for any state to "dereserve" a reserved forest, use forest land for non-forest purposes, assigns forests land to a private person or corporation or clears forest land for the purpose of reforestation. There is an advisory committee constituted under the Act to advise the centre for these approvals.

The Air (Prevention and Control of Pollution) Act, 1981

To oblige the UN Conference on the Human Environment held at Stockholm in June 1972, the parliament enacted the Air (Prevention and Control of Pollution) Act, 1981. The framework of the Act is almost in the line of Water Act, 1974. Under the Air Act, all industries operating within designated air pollution control areas shall have to obtain a permit or consent from the respective state board. The states are required to prescribe emission standards for industry and automobiles in consultation with the Central Board.

The Air Act was amended in 1987 to strengthen the enforcement machinery and prescribing stiffer penalties. Under the 1987 Amendment Act, the State Boards may close down a defaulting industrial plant or may stop its supply of electricity or water and also may move to a competent court to restrain emissions that exceed the prescribed standard.

Environment (Protection) Act, 1986

The Bhopal Gas mass disaster on 3rd December, 1984 led the Government of India to enact the Environment (Protection) Act, 1986 under Article 253 of the Constitution. This is a broad-based environmental legislation. Under section 2(a) of this Act, environment means and includes water, air, land and the inter-relationships among water, air, land and human beings and other living creatures, plants, micro-organisms and property. Section 3(1) of the Act empowers the centre "to take all such measures as it deems necessary or expedient for the purpose of protecting and improving the quality of the environment and preventing controlling and abating environmental pollution" (Chakraborty, 1994). Thus, under this Act, the Central Government is authorized to develop new national standards for the quality of the environment to regulate cities of big industries to prescribe procedure for manufacturing hazards for preventing accidents and to collect and disseminate information regarding environmental pollution.

Motor Vehicles Act, 1988

This Act came into force from 1st July, 1989. It provided that regarding construction, equipment and maintenance of motor vehicles from October 1, 1989, every motor vehicle should comply with certain emission standards.

To help the owners of cars and scooters maintain the prescribed level of exhaust emissions, the Directorate of Transport in Delhi has established Free Pollution Checking centres at each of its offices in Delhi. Besides this, mobile teams are also covering different parts of the city. Delhi Administration has also been providing free facilities at different petrol stations all over the city for checking exhaust carbon monoxide levels from cars and scooters.

Setting up of Pollution Control Boards

Following the Water (Prevention and Control of Pollution) Act, 1974, which became effective from 23rd March, 1974, the Central Board for Prevention and Control of Water Pollution was constituted in September 1974. The matters related to Air Pollution were also looked after by CBPCWP. To advise the respective state governments on matters related to water and air pollution, State Boards were also set up. The CBPCWP coordinated the activities of the State Pollution Control Boards. While amending the Water (Prevention and Control of Pollution) Act, 1974 in 1988, the Central/State Boards for the Prevention and Control of Water Pollution were renamed as Central/State Pollution Control Boards, as these Boards also deal with air pollution (Sharma, 1994). Consequently, now there is a Central Pollution Control Board (CPCB) that makes recommendations and advises the central government on pollution matters. The Board advises the Pollution Control Division of the Ministry of Environments and Forests, New Delhi. There are also State Pollution Control Boards (SPCB) to advise respective state governments. Except the state of Manipur, Mizoram, Nagaland, Arunachal Pradesh and Sikkim, all other states have their SPCBs. After the amendment to the Water (Prevention and Control of Pollution) Act, 1974 in 1988, the Boards have been given powers to close or stop supply of Water and electricity of offending establishments. The citizens may file criminal complaints against offenders after 60 days notice to Boards. Even at the time of establishment of industry, the persons have to take consent of the Boards.

Nehru Foundation for Development

Since 1965, Nehru Foundation for Development (NFD) has been promoting educational efforts in the areas of science, nature study, health, development and environment through its associate institutions — Vikram A. Sarabhai Community Science Centre, Sundarvan, CHETNA and VIKSAT.

Environmental Education

Centre for Environment Education (CEE) was established in August 1984 to play a pivotal role in the nationwide effort to increase environmental awareness. The centre is supported by the Ministry of Environment and Forests, Government of India and affiliated to the Nehru Foundation for Development, Ahmedabad.

The main objective of CEE is to create environmental awareness among children, youth, decision-makers and the general community. To achieve this, CEE develops innovative programmes and educational materials, and field tests them for their validity and effectiveness. The purpose is to provide models that could be replicated elsewhere with modifications to suit local conditions.

CEE is setting up Regional Cells in different zones of the country in order to facilitate effective co-ordination, monitoring and follow up environmental education programmes across the country in a decentralized manner. At present, two Regional Cells are functioning from Bangalore (CEE South) and Guwahati (CEE North-East):

- Environmental Education in School
- Interpretation
- Training
- Eco-development
- Experiencing nature
- Media
- Networking
- Urban programmes
- Industry initiatives (Centre for Environmental Education's Annual Report, 1993-94, p. 2).

Department of Non-Conventional Energy Sources

Due to rapidly depleting conventional energy sources, countries all over the world have been forced to concentrate on tapping the vast potential of non-conventional energy sources like solar, wind and tidal energy. While the responsibility for harnessing the potential for energy by conventional technology lies with the Department of Power/Central Electricity Authority and the State Governments, the Department of Non-Conventional Energy Sources (DNES) is actively involved in Research and Development activity for developing non-conventional know-how technology.

National Wastelands Development Board (NWDB)

With the objectives of increasing tree and other green cover on wastelands, preventing good land from becoming wasteland and to formulate within the overall Nodal Policy, perspective plans and programmes for the management and development of the wastelands in the country, National Wastelands Development Board was set up in 1985.

In addition to above organizations, Industrial Technology Research Centre (ITRC), National Environmental Engineering Research Institute (NEERI), Tata Energy Research Institute (TERI) are some notable organizations involved in environmental promotion. Design, purpose and effectiveness of management together form a solid basis of conservation of biological diversity (Sharma, 1994). Due to the steps taken by the Indian Government to conserve the biological diversity, India was recognized as one of the 14 countries, which assumed prominence in terms of the conservation of biological diversity and got seventh place in this regard at Earth Summit in 1992 (Ramakrishna, 2000).

National Parks and Sanctuaries

At the 15th meeting of IBWL held on 1st October, 1982, the then Prime Minister, Late Indira Gandhi, gave a 12-point strategy for an Action Plan for the conservation of wildlife in India. This included the establishment of a network of scientifically managed protected areas, including National Parks, Sanctuaries, Biosphere Researches and other areas. At present, there are 84 National Parks and 477 Sanctuaries in India.

Special Projects for Endangered Species

Some special projects were started by the government to protect selected wildlife such as Project Tiger, Gir Lion Project, Crocodile Breeding Project, etc. These projects aim at combating and increasing the deteriorating population of certain endangered species. For example, when Project Tiger was started in April 1973, there were 25 tiger reserves in 14 states. At that time, the population of tigers was only 1800 in these reserves. Now, population of tigers in these reserves has increased to 3,435 (Ramakrishna, 2000).

Conservation of Wildlife

For the conservation of wildlife, the Government of India has taken up various steps by setting up different organizations, through legislation and by initiating other conservation programmes as follows:

Indian Board for Wildlife (IBWL)

This is the main advisory body to Government of India. It was first constituted in 1952 as an advisory body under the name 'Central Board for Wildlife'. Later, it was renamed as IBWL. At its first meeting, the Board made recommendation for a unified legislation for wildlife conservation in India. Accordingly, the Wildlife (Protection) Act was enacted in 1972, which has been adopted by all states.

Wildlife Preservation

There is a central body, 'Wildlife Preservation' headed by the Director, Wildlife Preservation, Government of India. To assist the Director in implementing the Wildlife (Protection) Act, 1972, there are four Regional Deputy Directors—one each at New Delhi, Mumbai, Calcutta and Chennai. They are responsible for implementation of the Convention of International Trade in Endangered Species (CITES) and also assist the local officers in wildlife protection and enforcement of regulations in trade and commerce in wildlife, including their import and export.

Protected Areas Network (Conservation of Biological Diversity)

In situ conservation of wildlife includes a comprehensive system of protected areas. There are different categories of protected areas, which are managed with different objectives for bringing benefit to society. These include : (i) National Parks, (ii) Sanctuaries, (iii) Biosphere Reserves, (iv) Nature Reserves, (v) Natural Monuments, (vi) Cultural Landscapes, etc. These areas may vary considerably in size.

National Policy on Environment

A National Environmental Policy statement was announced in February 1992 (*The Hindu*). Some of the important aspects of the policy statement are:

1. The government made it compulsory for all manufacturing industries to annually make a public statement on pollution caused by them, by way of emissions and effluents discharged by (Environmental Audit);
2. The medium and large-scale industries are to be made fully responsible and accountable for the waste they produce;
3. New units are to be encouraged to go in for clean technologies;
4. Effluent Treatment Plants (ETP) are to be set up for clusters of small industrial units wherever possible;
5. Encourage recycling of all waste products; and
6. Exercise and customs rebate for pollution control equipment is to be reviewed (*The Hindu*, 1992).

Besides preventing pollution at source; encouraging, developing and applying the best available practicable technical solutions; ensuring that polluter pays for the pollution and control arrangements; focusing protection on the polluted areas and river stretches and involving the public in decision-making with the objective of integrating environmental considerations into decision-making at all levels constitute other aspects of the environment policy (Chakravarthi, 1994). Thus, through a number of measures, government is seeking to protect the environment.

Importance of Communication in Various Programmes

Communication was recognized as an important element in the successful implementation of various development programmes.

Especially for environmental protection and successful implementation of family planning, communication and education were expected to play a vital role by creating awareness among the people.

Conclusion

Though the concept of sustainable development is relatively new one, certain policies and programmes towards fulfilling the various objectives of sustainable development were initiated by the government long ago. In order to eradicate poverty, Indian Government introduced a myriad of programmes, which include community development programme, Small Farmers Development Agency (SFDA), Integrated Rural Development Programme (IRDP), Swarna Jayanti Gram Swarozgar Yojana (SGSY), etc. Similarly, though government started showing more interest on environmental protection from 1972 (Stockholm Conference) onwards, even before that, government evinced some interest in protecting the environment through legislation, and by setting up some organizations. Population control has remained one of the overriding objectives of the Government of India. The nature of all these programmes demand a good communication system between the planner and the beneficiary. The planner needs to understand the needs, aspirations, capabilities and limitations of the target beneficiaries; while the beneficiary too needs to know thoroughly about the various programmes and schemes meant for him or her. Besides, the environmental protection and family planning programmes also call for awareness and participation on the part of the people. Therefore, communication has been considered to be one of the key elements in the success or failure of the various programmes, which constitute different dimensions of sustainable development.

REFERENCES

Balakrishna, P. (1995), "To Change the Plight of Poor, the Direction of Reforms Should Change," *Yojana*, (Telugu) May 95, *Sumputi*: 22, *Sanchika*: 12, Publications Division, Hyderabad, p. 34.

Bose, E., M.T. Vu, A. Jevin, R. Bulatao (1992), World Population Projection, 1992-93. Edition (John Hopkins) University Press, Baltimore, MD, published for the World Bank.

Chakrabarty, N.K. (1994), *Environmental Protection and the Law*, Ashish Publishing House, New Delhi, pp. 53-68.

Chakravarthy, T.K. (1980), *Development of Small and Marginal Farmers and Agricultural Labourers: An Overview of Policies and Programmes*, NIRD, Hyderabad, 1980, p. 24.

Compendium of Instruction on SFDA/MFAL, Government of India, Ministry of Agriculture and Irrigation, Department of Rural Development, September 1975, p.1.

Centre for Environmental Education (1993-94), Annual Report, Nehru Foundation for Development, Ahmedabad, p. 2.

Dandekar, V.M. and Nilakanth Rath (1971), *Poverty in India*, Sangam Press, Pune, 1971, pp. 15-35.

Dilli, K.T. (1996), *Poverty the Worst Form of Pollution*, Third Concept, New Delhi, January, pp. 25-29.

Eighth Five Year Plan 1992-97 (1992), Planning Commission, Government of India, New Delhi.

First Five Year Plan, (1951), Planning Commission, Government of India, New Delhi.

Fourth Five Year Plan 1969-74, Planning Commission, Government of India, New Delhi.

Giriappa, S. (1992), "IRDP and Poverty Alleviation", *Journal of Rural Development,* NIRD, Hyderabad, 1992, p. 486.

Green, C. (1992), *The Environment and Population Growth Decade for Action*, Population Reports, Series, M. No. 10, p. 11.

Gupta, S.P. (1995), "Economic Reform and Its Impact on Poor", *Economic and Political Weekly,* June 3, New Delhi.

Gupta, V.S. (1989), Environmental Reporting Some Issues, *Vidura*, May-June 1989, p. 3.

John Bongarts (1994), *Population Policy Options in the Developing World*, Science, Indian Penal Code, 1860, Vol. 263, 11 February.

Jos Chathukulam and Kurien, V.K. (1995), "Jawahar Rozgar Yojana : An Assessment ?" *Economic and Political Weekly*, February 11, pp. 393-344.

Labour Enquiry, Summary Report (1974-75), Labour Bureau, Chandigarh, Ministry of Labour, p. 15.

Laskar, S.I. (1988), *Directive Principles of State Policy in Indian Constitution*, Deep and Deep Publications, New Delhi, pp. 26-29.

Madhavi, C. (1993), *Impact of Industrial Pollution on Social Relations: A Case Study of Sultanpur*, M. Phil. Dissertation, Department of Sociology, University of Hyderabad, p. 41.

Maithani, B.P. and Haloi, K. (1988), "Implementation of IRDP: Nagaland Experience," *Journal of Rural Development,* NIRD, Hyderabad.

Manasa, N. (1995), "Global Fight Against the Hunger is Confined only to the Lip Service", *Eenadu*, A Telugu Daily, 13-03-1995, Ushodaya Publication, Hyderabad.

Morley Mohan Lal, G. (1988), *Poverty Alleviation: The Indian Experience*, Himalaya Publishing House, Bombay, pp. 53-60, 288-324.

Prasad Kamta (1985), *Planning for Poverty Alleviation*, Agricole Publishing Academy, New Delhi, 1985, pp. 31-153.

Prasad Gargi (1995), Cutting the Ground under Land Reforms. *The Hindu*, Sunday, November 12, p. 7.

Prasad, Mani Shankar (1996), *Need for Environmental Awareness, Third Concept*, January, New Delhi.

Ram Reddy, and and Haragopal, G. (1985), *Public Policy and the Rural Poor in India*, Centre for Economic and Social Studies, Hyderabad, pp. 11-92.

Ramakrishna, T. (2000), *Jeevaavarana Pariraksh anaku Vanyaprani Samrakshana Dehweyam* (The purpose of conserving wildlife is to conserve the life sustaining system), *Yojana* (Telugu), October 2000, Hyderabad, pp. 2 and 42-43.

Rao, M.S.R.K. (2000), *Grameena Bharata Punarnirmanam: Parivarthana Kosam Pathakalu* (Reconstruction of Rural India: Schemes for the Changes), *Yojana* (Telugu), October, Hyderabad, pp. 10-14.

Reddy, Sphurthi (2001), *Janam Janam Prabhanjanam* (Telugu) (People! People! Over number of people), *Vaartha* (Telugu), Sunday Magazine, 8th April, pp. 12-15.

Ray, C.N. (1992), *Journal of Rural Development*, NIRD, Hyderabad, pp. 97-98.

Savita Varmani (1989), *Land Reforms in India: Evaluative Study of Surplus Land Distribution Allottees in Haryana*, in Sharma, M.L. and Punia, R.K. (eds.), *Land Reforms in India*, Ajanta Publications.

Satish Sarangi and Gary Cohen (1995), "A Tale of Two Industrial Estates," *Economic and Political Weekly*, June 17, pp. 1419-1421.

Second Five Year Plan (1956), Planning Commission, Government of India, New Delhi, p. 554,

Sharma, P.D. (1994), *Ecology and Environment*, Rastogi Publications, New Delhi, pp. 485, 354-356.

Singh, D.V., Jagdish Chand and Tulsi Raman (1989), "Impact of Land Reforms on the Socio-economic Structure of Farming Families: A Case Study in Himachal Pradesh " in M.L. Sharma and R.K. Punia (eds.). *Land Reforms in India*, Ajanta Publication, New Delhi, pp. 17-18.

Swarnjayanti Gram Swarojgar Yojana (SGSY) Guidelines, Government of India, Ministry of Rural Development, New Delhi.

Sixth Five Year Plan 1980-85 (1980), Planning Commission, Government of India, pp. 374-375.

Seventh Five Year Plan 1985-90 (1985), Planning Commission, Government of India, pp. 282-287.

Sethi, Indrajit, M.S. and Iqbal, S.A. (1991), *Environmental Pollution: Causes, Effects and Control*, Commonwealth Publishers, New Delhi.

Tandon, P.K. (1995), *Impact of New Economic Policy on Peasantry*, Third Concept, February, New Delhi.

The Hindu (1992), The New Environmental Policy Announced Article: *The Hindu*, February 22, quoted by Madhavi, C. (1993), *op. cit.* p. 41.

Third Five Year Plan (1961), Planning Commission, Government of India, New Delhi.

UNDP (1994), Human Development Report, Oxford University Press, New Delhi, p. 27.

Upadhyaya, Ramesh (1995), *Poverty Alleviation Tops Agenda: Mishra*, An Interview with Dr. Jagannath Mishra, *The Hindu*, Hyderabad, July 12, p. 15.

World Development Report, 1992, Oxford University Press, New York, p. 2.

World Commission on Environment and Development, (WCED) (1987), *Our Common Future*, Oxford University Press, New York Press, pp. 2-145.

5 A Profile of Medak District with Special Reference to Environment and Development

Introduction

As discussed in the previous chapter, Government has initiated various plans and programmes for the environmental protection, population control, poverty alleviation etc., which constitute various components of sustainable development. Examining the role of communication in these aspects of sustainable development being the aim of the present study, an empirical study has been conducted in Medak District of Andhra Pradesh. An attempt has been made in this chapter to identify and describe the condition of poverty, environment, population etc., as well as the Government plans and programmes to promote sustainable development in the district. This district has been selected for the following reasons:

(a) It is one of the backward districts in Andhra Pradesh,
(b) It consists of both industrial and agricultural area,
(c) The district has both urban and rural population,
(d) This district experienced the worst form of industrial pollution, and
(e) Various NGOs are functioning in the district, aiming at sustainable development.

Thus for all these reasons, Medak District has been chosen for the empirical study. In the following chapters, analysis on specific poverty alleviation programmes and environmental awareness, has been presented.

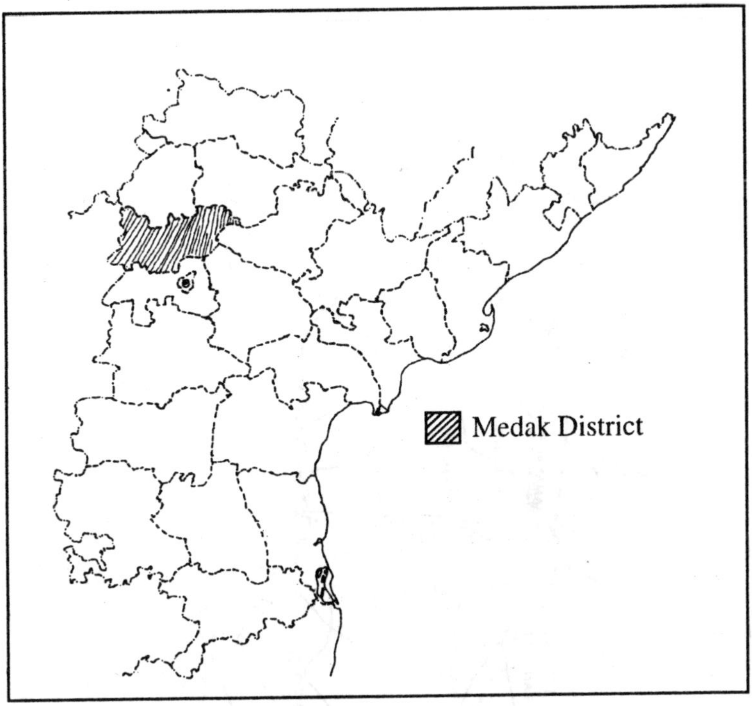

Map 5.1 : Map of Andhra Pradesh

General Introduction about Medak District

Geographical Area

Medak District is located in the Telangana region of Andhra Pradesh. The district lies between 17°, 27′ and 18° 19′ of Northern Latitude and 77° 28′ and 79° 10′ of Eastern Longitude. It is bounded on the north by Nizamabad and Karim Nagar Districts, on the east by Warangal and Nalgonda Districts, on the south by Rangareddy District and on the west by Bidar District of Karnataka State. The district Headquarters is located at Sangareddy. Total area of the district is 9699 sq. kms.

Historical Background of the District

The district derived its name from Medak, the then Headquarters town

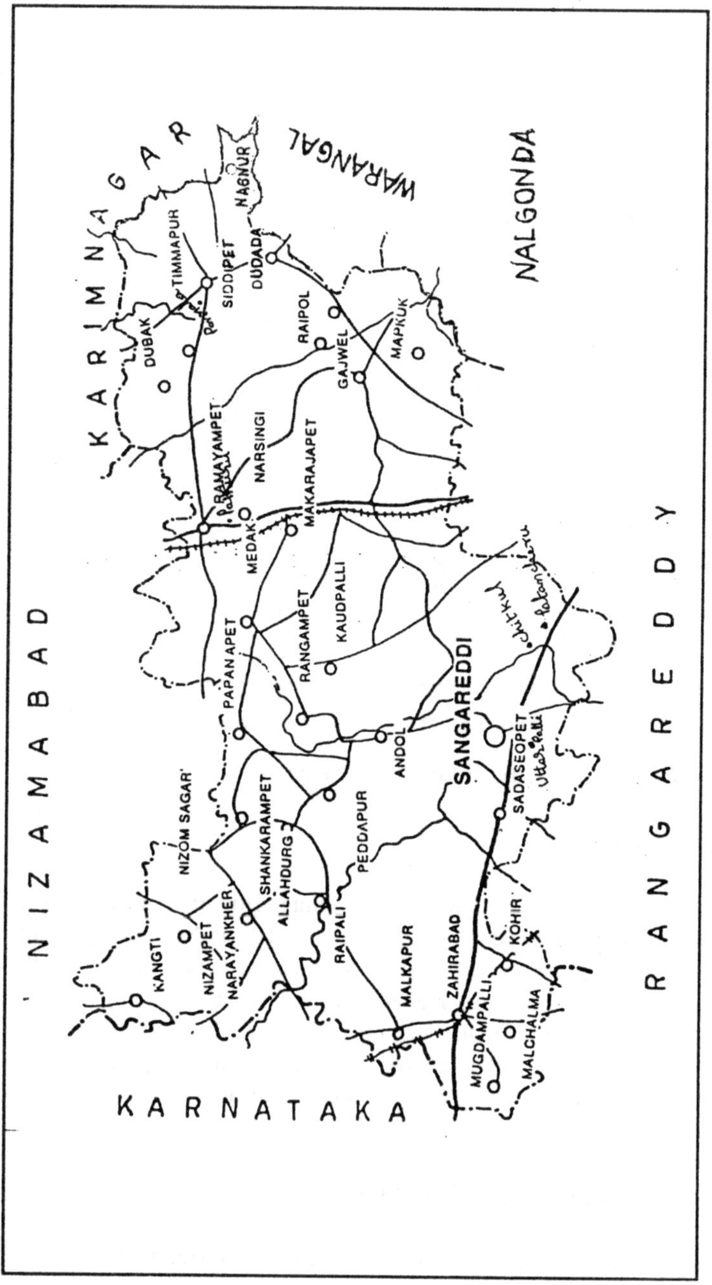

Map 5.2 : Map of Medak District

of the Taluk of the same name. Medak was orginally known as Methukudurgam, which subsequently changed to Methuku due to the growth of fine and coarse rice in this area (Bhatt, 1998) while the Sultans of Golkonda called it as Gulshanabad, Nizam named it as Medak (Lavanya, 1998)

Its political history commenced with the advent of the Mauryas who extended their sway to the South during the reign of Ashoka. Medak District became part of the Kakatiya Kingdom, the Bahmani Kingdom and later the Golkonda Kingdom. Finally, on the fall of the Qutubshahi Dynasty, it was annexed to the Mughal Empire. During the formation of Hyderabad State by Asaf Jahi, this district was detached and included in the Nizam's Dominions. It finally became a part of Andhra Pradesh with effect from 1st November, 1956 under the Scheme of Re-organization of States.

This is the only district in Andhra Pradesh to have a name of one town and district headquarter is another town. The district has two Parliamentary Constituencies—Medak and Siddipet. The district is divided into three Revenue Divisions, namely Medak, Sangareddy and Siddipet. The district has 10 Assembly Segments, viz. Gazwal, Andole, Siddipet, Dommat, Narsapur, Zahirabad, Narayan Khed, Ramayam Pet, Sangareddy and Medak.

Medak District is divided into 45 mandals as follows : Medak, Manoor, Kangti, Kalher, Narayankhed, Regode, Shankarampet (A), Alladurg, Takmal, Papannapet, Kulchram, Shankarampet (R), Ramayampet, Dubbak, Mirdoddi, Jagadevpur, Gajwel, Doultabad, Chegunta, Yeldurthy, Kowdipally, Andole, Raykode, Nyalkal, Jarasangam, Zahirabad, Kohir, Munipally, Pulkal, Sadasivpet, Kondapur, Sangareddy, Patancheru, Ramchandrapuram, Jinnaram, Hathnura, Narsapoor, Shivampet, Toopran, Siddipet, Nangunur, Kondapak, Wergal, Mulugu and Chinnakodur.

The district has a total 1265 villages, 809 Grama Panchayats and 11 Panchayat Samithis. The district was represented by some eminent political leaders in both Lok Sabha as well as State Legislature. Prominent among them are the former Prime Minister Mrs. Indira Gandhi who was elected to Lok Sabha from Medak (1977) and T. Anjaiah, Former Chief Minister of Andhra Pradesh.

Demographic Profile of the District

Total population of the district is 22,69,800 persons as per 1991 census.

This population consists of 11,52,079 (50.7 per cent) males and 11,17,721 (49.24 per cent) females. Rural population of the district is 19,41,313 persons (85.52 per cent) out of whom 9,83,272 (50.6 per cent) males and 9,58,041 (47.35) females and Urban population is 3,28,487 (14.47 percentage) 1,68,807 (51.38 percentage) males and 1,59,680 females (48.61 per cent) the Scheduled Casts and Scheduled Tribes population of the district (as per 1991 Census) is 4,05,722 (17.87 per cent) persons and 95,042 (4.18 percentage) persons respectively. The Rural-Urban breakup of these people is as shown below:

Rural (i) Scheduled Castes : 3,72,249 (19.17%)
(ii) Scheduled Tribes : 92,098 (4.74%)
Urban (i) Scheduled Castes : 33,473 (10.19 %)
(ii) Scheduled Tribes : 2,944 (0.89%)

Main languages spoken in the district are Telugu, Urdu and Hindi. Majority of the people in the district are Hindus, followed by Muslims, Christians, Sikhs, Buddhists and Jains respectively. The biggest church of South Asia is situated in Medak.

Economy of the District

Medak District is known as one of the most backward districts in Andhra Pradesh (Suresh Kumar, 2000). It is prone to recurring drought (Raj Sekhar, 1995). Out of 45 mandals in the district 41 (91%) are drought effected (Rao, 1997). Agriculture and allied occupations are the main source of living for majority of the people in the district. Though it's was industrially backward prior to 1970-71, due to government policy of concessions to the entrepreneurs, industries were also set up in the district between 1971-80.

Agriculture and Irrigation

The principal crop of the district is paddy. The paddy cultivated during Kharif Season is known as *Abi* crop and those of *Tabi* Season is Rabi crop. The other important crops of the district are Jawar, Ragi, Groundnut, Castor and Pulses. The district is not watered by any big river. The only river of some consequence, is the Manjira, which is a tributary of the Godavari. This river rises in Bidar District and enters Medak District in the south-eastern direction. It flows for about

96 kms in the western and north-western Taluks of Narayan Khed, Zahirabad, Sangareddy, Narsapur and Medak in this district. The other important streams are the Haldi or Pasupu yeru and the Kudlair. Pasupu yeru is a tributary of the Manjira and enters the district from the north and flows through Medak town. Kudlair is in Siddipet Taluk. Another stream Nakkavagu is the source of water for about 15 to 20 villages, which serves drinking water and irrigation purposes. Starting from Gangaram it touches Ramachandrapuram, Usikaybavi, Pocharam, Bachugudem, Lakdaram, Byalthole, Pedda Kanjerla, Chidruppa etc. Since there are no big rivers in the district, tanks are the main sources of water. Among these tanks, the tank of Malkapuram is a prominent one. Total land with the irrigation facility in the district is 1,21,000 hectares, out of which 79,000 hectares under tanks, 31,000 hectares under wells, 8,000 hectares under canals and 3,000 hectares under other sources is cultivated (Lavanya, 1998).

Industrialization

Medak is one of the industrialized districts in Andhra Pradesh. Patancheru is one of the industrial areas located in the district. The foundation for the industrialization was laid down in 1962 when the Industries Department of Andhra Pradesh had earmarked an area of 56.26 acres near Patancheru for industrial development. Later on, Andhra Pradesh Industrial Infrastructure Corporation which was formed in 1973 further developed the area in five phases. In all the five phases, 276 indsutries and an additional 31 industries were set up in and around Patancheru (Reddy, D.N., 1992).

Products of this industrial area range from Chemical, Pharamaceutical, Agrochemical, Paper, Paints, Cellulose, Steel to refineries, apart from a number of a machine works. Employment generated by these industries is for about 25,000 persons (Rao, *et al.*, 1990).

Another notable industrial area is located near a village Bollaram in Jinnaram Mandal of Medak District. Certain area near Bollaram village was earmarked by the Andhra Pradesh State Non-Resident Indian Investment Corporation (ANRICH) to set up Industries, under the NRI category, have also come up in this area. Industries here are predominantly Pharmaceutical Units, and their products, include bulk drugs like Sulpha Melthoxazole, Ebuprofen, Trimethoprim and Paracetamol. Totally there are 53 industries.

Both the industrial areas lack proper infrastructural facilities like water supply, roads and sewer lines, which have not been developed properly. Much of the process water needs are met by individual bore wells. Sewer lines are almost absent. Many units also depend on the tanker supply of water. Roads are improperly developed (Reddy, 1992).

Poverty in the District

As mentioned earlier, Medak District is one of the most backward districts in Andhra Pradesh. 85 per cent of people are living in rural areas. Agriculture and allied occupations are main source of income for majority of people in the district. The district is not covered by any major river. It is prone to recurring droughts. Out of 3,54,514 rural families, 1,56,090, i.e. 44 per cent of the families are living below poverty line. The percentage of literates is much lower than the state's average in the district. It is 32.41, whereas State's average is 42.5.

Amenities

Villages having one or more amenities in Medak district as per 1991.

Table 5.1 : Amenities in Medak District

Sl.No.	*Amenities*	*Number of Inhabited Villages*	*Percentage*
1.	Education	1201	98.36
2.	Medical	403	34.26
3.	Drinking Water	1200	98.12
4.	Post and Telegraph	21	50.78
5.	Market/Hat	0	00.00
6.	Communications	677	55.36
7.	Approach by Pucca Road	593	48.49
8.	Power Supply	1205	98.53

Source: S.C. Bhatt, 1998.

Table 5.1 shows that though most of the villages have some basic amenities, viz., education, drinking water and power supply, nearly half of the villages do not have water and power supply, and nearly half of the villages do not have other basic amenities viz., Medical, Post and Telegraph, Market, Communications and approach *pucca* roads.

Population Growth : The decennial growth rate of population of the district as a whole in relation to the state between the period between 1981-91 is higher than the state's average as shown below:

Table 5.2 : State and Medak : Decennial Growth Rate of Population 1981-91 (Per cent)

State and District	*Total*	*Rural*	*Urban.*
A.P.	23.91	18.21	42.64
Medak	25.13	21.55	51.49

Source : DRDA Office, Sangareddy.

Non-Governmental Organisations Operating in the District

In Andhra Pradesh there are a number of voluntary organisations involved in Rural Development, in organising the rural poor and in the implementation of Welfare Oriented Programmes. Madhavan's Survey in 1987 could identify 717 organisations in A.P. out of which Andhra region accounts for 287 (40%), Rayala Seema 158 (21.9 %) and Telangana 272 (38 %) respectively (Madhavan and Rao, 1988).

There are 27 Non- Governmental Organisations operating in Medak District aiming at poverty alleviation, promotion of State and District savings, environmental protection, health awareness, family planning etc. Among these organizations, Deccan Development Society (DDS) and HELP are functioning in Zahirabad Mandal. Andhra Pradesh Mahila Samatha Society, St. John Ambulance Association and Action Co-Op are operating in Sangareddy Mandal. AWARE and ROADS are functioning in Narsapur area. While Toopran is concentrating its activities in Toopran Pragati and Cheyuchata are working in Chegunta, Sahayata and Hard, Shanti Rural Development Society, PEACE are operating in Ramayampet, Dubbak and Jayadevpur Mandals respectively. Besides, Deen Dayal Development Society, SAIDS and Tribal Development Society are operating in Gazwel, Doulthabad and Medak Districts respectively.

Environmental Problems in the District

Medak being a district having a good number of industries, forest area and an abattoir called Alkabir, has drawn the attention of environmentalists, social scientists and activists. With Industrial development came environmental degradation so much that Medak today finds prominent mention among environmental disaster areas of the World (Madhavi, 1993).

Industrial Pollution

Effluents of Bollaram and Patancheru industries are released into the open places which accumulate in roadside drains and pits. As a result, ground water within the industrial area is polluted and is unfit for process water. One Ice-Producing factory, G.P. Ices, had to be closed down several times due to non availability of unpolluted water. All effluents of Patancheru Industries ultimately join Nakka Vagu after allowing for seepage at various pits and drains. Discharges at Bollaram are also let out and join an irrigation tank, Asanikunta, after taking the gravitational course.

Consequently, ground water all along the Nakkavagu is polluted and at the surface level, the water flow constitutes nothing but effluents. It gets diluted only during rainy season. An independent estimation puts the waste water flow in Patancheru at 5 million litres per day (Reddy, 1992) over a period of time crops and lands were degraded in villages, such as, Pocharam, Ganapathigudem, Inole, Lakdaram, Bachugudem, Pedda Kanjerla, Chitkul and Ismail Khan Pet. With the contamination of ground water, availability of pure drinking water for villages became a distant dream.

After effluents from Bollaram industries started exceeding the capacity of Asanikunta, its bund was deliberately breached by the industries in 1986. It resulted in the inundation of down stream agricultural fields and pollution of wells by the stream side and contamination of Posamundram, a tank serving the needs of Kishtareddipet Village.

Considering the gravity of problem and following the intense public pressure, the Revenue Divisional Officer, Sangareddy issued a notification dated September 4, 1986 in proceedings 1004/86 which declared that Nakkavagu waters are unfit for drinking and for any human needs due to industrial pollution. Again on 19th April, 1989, Joint Director (Agriculture) Sangareddy declared Nakkavagu waters unfit for irrigation purposes. Even though in the case of Bollaram no declaration has been made. "The Revenue Divisional Officer Sanagareddy has reported that the untreated effluents discharged by various industries of Bollaram industrial area in general and by

M/s. Andhra Pradesh Met. Engineering in particular joining the Asanikunta, an irrigation source had overflown and the polluted water joined the feeding canal of the Ayacut of Sultanpur village and damaged crops."

According to Government's Assessment, from 1984-89, total land affected, due to industrial effluents of Patancheru and Bollaram is 1382.28 acres. Another estimate by the National Environmental Engineering Research Institute (NEERI), Nagpur in 1991, calculates the damaged land as 1,717 acres belonging to 581 farmers. Despite extensive cattle loss, no precise figure is available. Quoting farmers, the NEERI report puts the figure as 1,323 animals.

Villagers are suffering from alien diseases like epilepsy, skin and throat problems, respiratory diseases, conjunctivitis, glaucoma, cancer, leukemia and paraplegia. NEERI Report cites farmers as saying that pregnant women are delivering still born babies. It indicates that even future generations are affected. Girls are not attaining puberty at proper age, 27 per cent of the girls have been affected like this (Srinivas, 1994). Menses in women also, instead of at 28 days interval is taking place after three months gap. Married women are not conceiving. In Sultanpur village alone in 1989, there have been nearly 6 deaths due to cancer (Reddy,1992).

250 Industries in Patancheru industrial area, directly or indirectly provided employment to nearly 25,000 people. But due to the pollution of Nakkavagu, lives of 30,000 people in 15 villages become miserable (Reddy, 1994).

Besides, contrary to the belief that industrial development strengthens agricultural economy, pollution has displaced several, traditional professions through dislocation of agriculture operations. Local fishermen were also forced to abandon their profession since there are no fish resources in polluted tanks and streams. Even the washerman community is caught in this survival crisis, as there is no fresh water available to wash clothes.

Once prosperous farmers become marginalized because of the declining of their lands fertility due to polluted water. *The Week* dated 24th March, 1991 reported that "By July 1986, thousand acres had been ravaged by pollution and by March 1991 another 4,000 acres of farm land in the villages around Patancheru and Bollaram, rendered barren. Thus the rate of land degradation is reported to be growing at the rate of 1000 acres a year (Madhavi, 1993).

The Patancheru Anti-Pollution Committee (PAPC) in a

memorandum submitted to the Union Minister of State for Planning Mr. Bhage Govardhan on 29th July, 1990. Stated that 1250 acres of farm land has been destroyed by polluted water of Nakkavagu displacing 500 families (Madhavi, 1993). Thus industrial pollution affected the health, wealth and lives of the local people.

In the middle of the 1980s a strong environmental movement was started against the Patancheru industrial pollution. It was spear headed by Citizens Against Pollution (CAP) and Patancheru Anti-Pollution Committee (PAPC). The movement yielded some good results as discussed in Chapter 7.

Poverty Alleviation Programmes Implemented in the District

The poverty alleviation programmes which have been implemented in the state of Andhra Pradesh, also have been implemented in Medak district. Integrated Rural Development Programme (IRDP), Development of Women and Children in Rural Areas (DWCRA), Training for Rural Youth and Self Employment (TRYSEM), Supply of Improved Toolkits to Rural Artisans (SITRA), National Old Age Pension Scheme (NOPS), National Maternity Benefit Scheme (NMBS) etc., are the poverty alleviation programmes implemented in the district. In 1999 Swarna Jayanti Gram Swarojgar Yojana (SGSY) was introduced.

Communication Flow about the Poverty Alleviation Programmes

The communication flow about the poverty alleviation programmes is of vertical nature. In DRDA office a plan is prepared about the poverty alleviation programmes to be implemented. Generally every year some villages are covered banks-wise (within the jurisdiction of certain banks) and thus care is taken to cover all the villages district. Then information along with this yearly plan is sent to Mandal Revenue Officer for preparing the action plan. Mandal Revenue Officer is asked to identify the assets that are to be given to the target beneficiaries in these villages. Taking into consideration, the needs, aspirations and potentialities of the target beneficiaries in these villages. Village Development Officer, Field Officer, M.D.O., & E.O.R.D (Extension Officer Rural Development) discussed and decided about the assets to be given. They decide the dates to hold the *Gram Sabha* meeting. Then people are informed through *Dandora* (traditional public announcement systems of attracting attention through drumbeat). On the day of *Gram Sabha* government officers such as, Mandal Development Officer, Village Development Officer, Bank Manager, Field Officer etc, attend the *Gram Sahba* (Village Assembly) meeting, which is also attended by the people of the village where people are informed about the schemes.

Generally whoever feel that they should get some help attend this meeting. Therefore, in *Gram Sabha* meeting itself, they register their names and proposals. Then these forms are sent to DRDA office where these are sanctioned and sent back to mandals and bankers. Asset is generally the choice of people. If such a scheme is not available, beneficiaries are suggested to take other schemes.

Often the priorities of the VDO and Bank Officers vary regarding the selection of the beneficiaries. While the VDOs prefer the poor people, Bank Officers prefer the persons whose financial condition is better, so that they would clear the loan. As the bank officers have the deciding power, ultimately they select the beneficiaries who have certain level of affluence. Thus some times even the purpose of the programme is defeated.

The programmes, which have been initiated and implemented in Andhra Pradesh in order to promote sustainable development, also have been implemented in all districts including Medak district. The former Chief Minister of Andhra Pradesh, Mr. N. Chandrababu Naidu is not only considered as a High-tech Chief Minister, but also as a green Chief Minister. *Down to Earth,* a leading science and environment fortnightly collected information from its readers and environmentalists to measure the effectiveness of the Chief Ministers (CMs) in promoting sustainable development. According to this information, while a few CMs—Pawan Kumar Chamling of Sikkim and Digviyay Singh of Madhya Pradesh have been given high marks by environmentalists of their respective states, *Down to Earth* readers in Andhra Pradesh have rated Chandrababu highly (Agarwal, Anil,1999). After coming to power, the Chief Minister of Andhra Pradesh Mr. Chandrababu Naidu introduced several developmental programmes, including the *Janma Bhoomi* programme and other projects such as the Joint Forest Management and Watershed Development.

He launched the Janmabhoomi, Watershed Management and Joint Forest Management (JFM) programmes to bring about sustainable development in the State (*Down to Earth*, February, 1999). He has also initiated several self help groups such as the Water Users Association to involve farmers in the management of irrigation systems, Development of Women and Children in Rural Areas (DWCRA) groups, and village education and health committees. The Janmabhoomi, JFM and DWCRA programmes have been successful (*Down to Earth*, 1999).

Janmabhoomi

The *Janmabhoomi* programme was launched in May 1997. In this, people identify their problems in *Gram Sabhas*, village meetings which are conducted by the nodal officers of the particular region, and send project proposals to the government. *Gram Sabhas* are conducted in areas with a population of more than 200 people. The five core areas of *Janmabhoomi* are community work, primary education, primary health, family welfare and environmental protection. The works are taken up under two categories—earth work and non-earth work. The former includes building of roads, canals and drains. The government and public contribute equally for every project. Non-earth work includes plantation of trees, meeting educational, health, fodder and drinking water needs. Here, the public pays 30 per cent of the cost of the project in the form of shramdhan (voluntary labour) and government pays the rest. All the projects are executed within stipulated time period. In Medak District 6641 works worth Rs. 108.71 crores were completed by February 2001, presently 954 works worth Rs. 17.06 crores, are going on in the district.

Clean and Green

Clean and Green programme was initiated as part of *Janmabhoomi* on 10th September 1998. Tree plantation, cleaning the environment, surroundings, providing proper drainage system, promoting the construction of toilets etc. are the important activities of this programme. Under this programme, silt of 10,525,462 kms has been removed, and the garbage of 1,10,462 tonnes was removed in 9 rounds. Similarly 3,353 market places, 6,039 abattoirs, 2,337 municipal parks and the premises of 3.57 lakhs organizations have been cleaned. Besides 1,137 lakh saplings have been planted. In the state (Clean and Green folder N.D). For this purpose, every 3rd Saturday has been observed as Clean and Green day. As part of clean and green programme 40,567 individual sanitary latrines were sanctioned and 18,486 latrines worth Rs. 310.32 lakhs have been completed in Medak District. During the year 2000-2001 alone 1,29,256 saplings were planted in the district. Besides, water was chlorinated, garbage was removed, market places, slaughter houses and municipal parks were cleaned in the district. On 5th July, 2000 itself, 157 sources of drinking water were chlorinated, 38 tonnes of garbage was removed and five market places, slaughter houses, and 9079 metres of drainage systems, were cleaned in the district as part of this programme.

Watershed development is another focus area of the government. The State Government has made a four year (1995-96 to 1998-99) watershed development plan. It has already invested more than Rs. 3,000 crore on 4239 watershed projects covering 2.1 million hectares (Hg) of land. The Chief Minister of A.P sought help from Anna Hazare, the person behind *ralegani siddhi's* success. According to Rajamani (1999) "Some of the watershed projects based on Anna's methods have helped farmers cultivate two crops a year."

In Medak District, 238 watershed programmes worth Rs. 2,431 lakhs are going on. Besides construction of check dams, social forests are also grown as part of this programme. In Medak District in 600 hectares of land 12.5 lakhs plants, consisting of different varieties were planted. This programme is also helping the people in the form of employment. The District Collector of Medak District (Shanti Kumari, 2001) stated that through micro watershed project water harvesting programmes are going to be organized a large scale. By implementing this project, over 10,000 acres of the land will be brought under cultivation.

Conservation of Forests and Wildlife

Out of the 9662 kms of the district 962.79 kms, which form 9.9 per cent of total geographical area is occupied by forests. The forests of Medak District are distributed in 239 forest blocks. The forest is prone to injuries. The main agencies causing damage in order of importance are man, cattle, goats, and forest fires (Hazari, 1996). The result of the injuries cause deterioration in quality condition and mixture of the forest crop. Therefore, the forests are sought to be protected through the joint forest management programme.

Joint Forest Management

The Joint Forest Management Programme was launched in Andhra Pradesh nearly seven years ago. In 1995 there were merely 200 Vana Samrakshana Samithis (VSS) by February 1999 the number increased to 6,271 with a total of 1.4 million hectares of forest land under the programme. Under this programme, government has entrusted the villagers with the task of regenerating and protecting the forest. The entire timber and bamboo produce is given to VSS members (*Down to Earth*. February, 1999). In the forest areas of Medak District, Vana Samrakshana Samithis were established to protect the forest.

In order to protect the wildlife, 23 wild life sanctuaries have been set up in Andhra Pradesh. Out of these 23 sanctuaries, 2 are located in Medak District at Pochampalli and Manjira respectively (Sujata: 1998). The Pochampalli wildlife sanctuary with an area of 130 kms is spread over the districts of Medak and Nizambad. The bio-diversity component of the sanctuary aims at:

(a) Improved management in protected area.
(b) Implementation of Eco-Development activities in villages around the sanctuary.
(c) Support for research, training, and extension work in Bio-diversity conservation.
(d) Formation of Eco-development committees.
(e) Development of water sources in the forest, like, construction of check dams and percolation tanks.
(f) Providing alternate energy sources like bio-gas plant and fuel efficient chullahs.
(g) Alternate income generation schemes.

Nestling between the Manjira and Singoor barrages lies the Manjira wildlife sanctuary, spreading over an area of 20 sq. kms. It is situated at 5 kms distance from Sangareddy, the Headquarters of Medak District. The sanctuary follows the course of river Manjira over a length of 36 kms with an average width of 500 to 800 metres. The Sanctuary is the abode for a number of resident and migratory birds in addition to being the home for the marsh crocodile, which is known as "Muggor".

Environmental Education Centre

Manjira wildlife sanctuary has got an environmental education centre. With a museum, library and auditorium, this centre helps to educate the visitors about nature conservation and maintenance of ecological balance. Stress is laid on conservation of the most precious resource to man-water. The centre also shows films on nature and wildlife everyday on 16 mm projector. Besides, video films are also screened.

Information and Communication

There is a Public Relations department functioning with an objective of giving relevant information to the target group through suitable media (Johnson,1993). Since issues may vary from district to district, the public relations department conducts a study in the district and identify the important issue or programme to be propagated. Similarly for such information dissemination purpose Mandals and Villages are also identified.

In the information dissemination process, multimedia, which include exhibitions, postures, banners, pamphlets, traditional folk media, video films, 16 mm films, audio cassettes, public meetings, rallies etc. are used in every district. Officials and staff concerning the programme about which, information is disseminated, also work along with staff of information/public relations department. At village level, *Gram panchayats*, voluntary organizations also participate in the information disseminations movement. District Public Relations officers act as conveners of these committees.

Conclusion

Medak District is one of the backward and environmentally affected districts in Andhra Pradesh. The main occupation in the district is agriculture. Yet only 43.98 percentage of its total area consists of cultivable land. There is no major river flowing in the district. Tanks are the main sources of water for cultivation. Canals, bores and wells being the other sources. The district is prone to recurring droughts. The families living below the poverty line are 44 per cent, much higher than the state and country's overage, while the literacy rate is 32.41 per cent much lower than the average of the state and the country.

Another dimension of the district is, it is one of the industrialized districts in Andhra Pradesh. The industrialization in the district, resulted in the concomitant negative effects—air pollution, water pollution, soil degradation, causing misery to around 50,000 people. Industrial pollution in the areas, such as, Patancheru being the worst form of pollution, people in the district have suffered more from the industrialization than the number of people who have been benefited by the industrialization in the district. The situation led to the organization of a strong environmental movement against industrial pollution and the movement has yielded some good results.

The district is also endowed with thick forests as well as the rich flora and fauna. Due to the various human activities the condition of the forests started to get deteriorated. The forests in the district are sought to be protected through joint forest management. For this purpose the *Vana Sanrakshana Samithis* (VSS) have been set up in the villages near by the forests. Thus the forests are sought to be protected through people's participation. For conserving the wildlife, two wild life sanctuaries has been set up in the district. The Manjira wildlife sanctionary also have an environmental education centre, which aims at imparting environmental education to the visitors.

Prevalence of poverty being a major problem in the district, various poverty alleviation programmes were implemented. These programmes include IRDP, DWCRA, SITRA, TRYSEM, old age pension scheme, maternity benefit scheme etc. The state government's programmes *Janmabhoomi* watershed management and Clean and Green are aiming at promoting the environment in the district. Over a 25 Non-Governmental Organizations (NGOs) are operating in the district, working for the fulfillment of the different goals of sustainable development in the district. Thus in Medak District, various programmers are going on towards the sustainable development. For the success of these developmental and environmental protection programmes, communication has a key role to play. Therefore, this has been examined and presented in the following chapters.

REFERENCES

Agarwal, Anil (1999), "Getting Greener". *Down to Earth*, New Delhi, Feb. p. 22.

Bhatt, S.C. (1998) *The Encyclopaedic District Gazetters of India*, Gyan Publishing House, New Delhi, Vol. pp. 241-256.

Clean & Green Folder (N.D) "Pudamithalliki Pachathoranam Prajalandariki

Arougyam Abharanam" "The Green garland to mother earth is health to all" Department of Public Relations, Government of Andhra Pradesh, Hyderabad.

Down to Earth (February 1999) Chandrababu of Hyderabad (Analysis). Down to Earth February15, pp. 40-44.

Hazari M.A.M. (1996), Working Plans for the forests of Medak District, Forest Department, Government of Andhra Pradesh, Hyderabad, pp. 46-47.

Johnson, Ch (1998) "Samachara Saakha Nuthana Prachara Prakriya - Keelaka Rangalapai Dhristi" (New information dissemination process of information Department—Focus on Key areas) *Andhra Pradesh* (Telugu), August, Hyderabad, pp. 39-40.

Lavanya, Bandla (1999), Medak Zilla (Mana Zillaalu Series), *Andhra Pradesh,* March, Department of Information and Public Relations, Hyderabad, pp. 63-65.

Madhavan P.K.S. and Rao G.S. (1988), "A.P. An Appraisal (Mimeo) Aware, Hyderabad, p. 70 cited by Prasad SDJM in Role of Voluntary Organisations in Rural Development, M. Phil Dissertation. Department of Economics, University of Hyderabad, 1992.

Madhavi, C. (1993), Impact of Industrial Pollution on Social Relations: A case Study of Sultanapur, M. Phil Dissertation. University of Hyderabd, Hyderabad pp. 31-49.

Rajamani, R. (1999) quoted *in Down to Earth* February15, *op. cit.* p. 42.

Raj Sekhar, N. (1995), Role of Voluntary Organizations in Rural Development : A Case Study of Deccan Development Society. M.Phil. Dissertation, University of Hyderabad, p. 54.

Rao, B.V. S. *et al.* (1990), *Andhra Pradesh Paryavoramna Paristhithi,* (The Status of A.P. Environment) Praja Nevedika Academcy of Gandhian Studies, Hyderabad, p. 138.

Rao, P.L.V. (1997), "Drought in Telangana" in S. Simhadri and P.L. Vishweshwara Rao, (eds.) *Telangana Dimensions of Under Development*, Centre for Telangana Studies, Hyderabad, March-June, p. 105

Reddy, D.N. (1992) Public Policy for Environmental Protection : A study of its implementation in an Industrial area. M.Phil. Dissertation, Department of Political Science, University of Hyderabad, Hyderabad, pp. 70-80.

Reddy, D.N. (1994), "Patancheru–Parisramika Kalushyam (Patancheru Industrial Pollution. *Paryavarana Bharathi,* Hyderabad, March-June, pp. 8-4.

Shanti Kumari (2001) " Atu Jala Samrakshana—Itu Ceiling Bhoomula Abhivruddi" (on one hand the water harvesting and on the other hand the development of ceiling lands). District Collector of Medak, Shanti Kumari's interivew with news today, *Eenadu* (Telugu) March 15, Medak Dist. edition, Sangareddy.

Srinivas, Satya G. (1994), *Paryavaranam* - Sthree (Environment and Woman) *Paryavarana Bharathi,* March-June, Hyderabad, pp. 12-15.

Sujatha, Gottipati (1998), "Paryavarana Samatulyataku Vanya Pranule Pranam" (wildlife is lifeline to maintain environmental equilibrium") *Andhra Pradesh* (Telugu) Hyderabad, October issue, pp. 31-33.

Suresh Kumar, Garlapati (2000) "Methuku Seemalo Prapatu Dhorani" *Suprabhatham* (Telugu) Nov. 4, p. 15.

Udayam (1991), Hyderabad, 20 April, 1991, pp. 1-2.

6 Role of Communication in the Success or Failure of the Poverty Alleviation Programmes

(With Special Reference to DWCRA and IRDP Asset-giving Schemes)

Introduction

Generally, it is believed that those who are aware of the schemes or benefits meant for them can avail and utilize those schemes or benefits in a better way. Sometimes, due to lack of awareness, even educated people fail to avail themselves of some provisions or benefits meant for them. As such, what about the uneducated and poor people in rural areas in terms of utilizing the poverty alleviation programmes meant for them? To what extent do they have awareness about these programmes? What are the channels of communication or sources of information creating such awareness? To what extent is the awareness responsible for utilization of these schemes and what is the overall impact of the poverty alleviation schemes on the beneficiaries? These are the questions to be addressed from communication point of view, while analyzing the role of communication in the success or failure of the poverty alleviation programmes.

In order to find out answers to these questions, a survey has been conducted in two villages, Uttarpally and Pathuru, located in two different revenue divisions—Sangareddy and Medak—respectively in Medak District. This survey has been conducted among the target beneficiaries of IRDP and DWCRA—both those who have availed of these schemes and those who have not availed them. An attempt also has been made to evaluate the improvement in the quality of life of those who have been profitted by these schemes. Findings of the survey have been presented in this chapter. This chapter has been divided into two parts – Part I and Part II. Part I deals the profile of the villages selected for the present study and the role of communication in relation to DWCRA. Part II, focuses on the role of communication in relation to the utilization of IRDP has been dealt with.

Before presenting the findings, it would be pertinent to provide the profile of the villages taken for this study, poverty alleviation programmes implemented in these villages, profile of the beneficiaries, etc. These details are as follows:

PART I

Section A

A Profile of the Villages Selected for the Study

Uttarpalli

Uttarpalli is located in Sangareddy Mandal of Medak District. It is situated at 8 kms. away from the district headquarters, Sangareddy. The population of the village is 1267, out of which 660 (52.09%) are males and 607 (47.98%) are females. One remarkable feature of the village is, except infants, almost all the villagers are literates. Under **Akshara Prabha* and *Akshara Sankranti*, an attempt is being made to achieve total literacy in the village.

The total area of the village is 1700 acres. The main source of the livelihood for the people of this village is agriculture. This village has 1400 acres of cultivable and 150 acres of uncultivable land. Out of the 1400 acres of cultivable land, wetland comprises of 200 acres and the remaining 1200 acres are dryland. Fallow land is nearly 100 acres. The crops raised in the village are paddy, sugarcane, turmeric, onion, jowar, wheat, blackgram, greengram, redgram and groundnut. Besides, vegetables like tomatoes, brinjal, green chilli and *bhindi* (ladies-finger) are produced in the village.

Sources of irrigation in the village are wells and borewells. There are six wells and 50 to 60 borewells. 90 per cent of the families in this village own at least some minimum area of agricultural land. Though agriculture is the main occupation of the villagers, simultaneously, many of the villagers work as casual agricultural labourers. Besides,

* *Akshara Prabha* and *Akshara Sankranti* are the literacy progammes, which aim at achieving total literacy.

those who have traditional occupations are engaged in such traditional occupations, as sheep rearing, washing clothes, etc.

Infrastructural Facilities

There is a government primary school in the village. For high school studies, the students of this village go to Mallepalli, which is 4 kms. away from Uttarpalli. There are a good number of students (around 250-300) studying this village. Everyday, twice a day, *i.e.* morning and evening, there is bus service between Sangareddy and Uttarpalli. This village was electrified nearly 25 years ago by Andhra Pradesh State Electricity Board (APSEB).

There is no primary health centre in the village. Every month or every fortnight, a doctor and nurses visit the village. Generally, people of this village go to Sangareddy for medical treatment. Similarly, there is no veterinary care centre in the village. The livestock are to be taken to Sangareddy for treatment. But, after the introduction of *Janmabhoomi* programme, a veterinary doctor started visiting this village.

In the year 1991, an overhead tank was constructed by the panchayat to provide drinking water under the *Rakshita Manchineeti Pathakam* (Protected Water Supply Scheme). The water is drawn from the bore into the overhead tank and supplied to the entire village through six taps located at six different corners of the village. Besides, there are three boring pumps. But these are not working properly. Presently, the villagers are facing an acute water problem.

Religion-wise, out of 335 families of the village, there are 320 Hindu, 10 Muslim and 5 Christian families. Nearly, half of the households in the village belong to Kuruma Caste (Backward Class) followed by Scheduled Castes and other Castes. There is no Scheduled Tribe family in the village. Occasionally, for example, on the occasion of festivals, folk forms are performed in the village. In addition to that, to propagate about the development programmes also, these performances are given in the village. There are nearly 30 television sets and 120 radio sets in the village.

Poverty Alleviation Programmes in the Village

According to an estimation, 70 per cent of the people in this village are living below the poverty line. Therefore, in order to eradicate poverty, government has introduced various poverty alleviation programmes, which include Integrated Rural Development Programme (IRDP), Chief Minister's Empowerment of Youth (CMEY) and Development of Women and Children in Rural Areas (DWCRA). The present study aims at analyzing the role of communication in the success or failure of these poverty alleviation programmes — IRDP asset-giving programme and DWCRA. As part of IRDP asset-giving programme, assets, such as surface bore, submersible bore, and sheep units were given to 13 beneficiaries in 1997-98.

DWCRA Groups

Under the DWCRA programme, 12 groups have been formed in this village. Each group, consisting of 15 members, a total of 180 women are covered under this programme. All the groups are functioning well without any discrepancies. But the key activities have not yet started. Women belonging to all communities in the village, viz. Scheduled Castes, Backward Classes, and other castes are included in these groups.

Pathuru

The village, Pathuru, is located in Medak Mandal of Medak District. It is situated 8 kms. away from Medak town and 60 kms. away from Sangareddy, the district headquarters. The total population of the village is 2,332, out of which 1,113 are males and 1,219 are females. 20 per cent of people in the village are literates, of whom 90 per cent are men and 10 per cent are women.

The total area of the village is 2,991 acres. The total cultivable land in the village is 1,372, of which 1,025 acres is dryland and 347 acres is wetland. An area of 1,500 acres of this village is occupied by forests. The cultivable land of Pathuru is irrigated by eight small tanks. In addition to these tanks, the land is also irrigated by a canal, Pushpalavaagu, which reaches Pathuru from distance 5 kms. The main crops raised in the village are maize, paddy and sugarcane. About 90 per cent of people in this village depend on agriculture for their livelihood.

The population of those belonging to Scheduled Caste in this village is 301; Scheduled Tribe population is 381 and the remaining population consists of Backward Classes and Forward Castes. Except five or six families, every family has some minimum area of cultivable land. Around 20 per cent of people in this village are living below the poverty line.

There is an overhead water tank. This tank is filled by bore water, which is supplied to the villagers through 35 water taps, which are located in different corners of the village. Besides, there are 14 boring pumps and 8 wells. There is one upper primary school in the village. In addition to this, there are two *Anganwadi* centres. There is no Primary Health Centre (PHC) in the village. But on every alternative day, health workers (nurses) and occasionally, a doctor visit this village. Besides, there are two Registered Medical Practitioners (RMP). Though there is one veterinary hospital, there is no doctor. For medical treatment, livestock are taken either to Medak or Haveli Ganapur, which is 5 kms. away from the village.

Communication

Since Pathuru is situated on the roadway between Medak and Siddipet, people of this village have easy access to buses and auto-rikshaws, thus there is good surface communication between Pathuru and Medak. People also have access to newspapers, radio and television. Eight copies of *Vaartha* are circulated everyday in the village. There are 30 TV sets, nearly all the sets have cable connection. The village has a post office and telephone facility. Occasionally, traditional folk media performances are given, e.g. on the occasion of *Dasara* and *Ugadi*. If government wants to convey any message to the people, the people are informed through *Dandora* (drumbeat), which is followed by *Gram Sabha* Village Meeting. Now, womenfolk of the village are well-organized in the form of DWCRA groups. Therefore, it has become easier to meet or inform womenfolk through DWCRA groups.

Poverty Alleviation Programmes in the Village

Poverty alleviation programmes introduced in the village are: IRDP, DWCRA, CMEY, Old Age Pensions, Widow Pensions, *Annapurna* and *Antyodaya* schemes. As the present study focuses on IRDP asset-giving programme and DWCRA, details about the implementation of these programmes in Pathuru are as follows:

Under the IRDP asset-giving programme, in the years 1995-96 and 1998-99 assets were given to the beneficiaries. These assets include submersible pumpset, pipeline and surface bore motor.

Section B

DWCRA Groups

Compared to Uttarpalli, DWCRA groups were started much earlier in Pathuru. Here, from January 1995 onwards, DWCRA groups were formed. Now, there are 18 DWCRA groups in the village. It was said that out of these 18 groups, four groups are not functioning properly. The key activities have not yet started. Recently, gas stoves have been distributed to four groups. Each group consists of 15 members, and a few groups, over 15 members; over 270 women of this village have been covered under this programme. Women belonging to all communities, viz. Scheduled Castes, Scheduled Tribes, Backward Classes and other castes are included in the groups.

Data Analysis

In order to analyze the role of communication in the success or failure of these programmes and to evaluate the overall impact of these schemes, a survey has been conducted among the beneficiaries of IRDP asset-giving scheme and the DWCRA. A survey has also been conducted among the target beneficiaries of IRDP and DWCRA, who could not avail of the scheme to find out why they could not avail of the scheme and to what extent the lack of communication or awareness is responsible for not utilising the schemes.

Awareness about DWCRA among the Beneficiaries

From the survey, it has been found that all the beneficiaries of DWCRA scheme are aware of this programme. But interestingly, some members of this scheme in Uttarpalli know and pronounce DWCRA groups as 'doctor' groups. Similarly, in Pathuru, 25 per cent of respondents do not know about DWCRA. For them, DWCRA is *isthirakula* loan (loan for making leaf plates). This is due to the fact that DWCRA in Pathuru has been equated with and termed as *isthirakula* loan.

Sources of Information about the Scheme

Beneficiaries of DWCRA came to know about the scheme through friends, family members, sarpanch, group leaders and government officials/personnel.

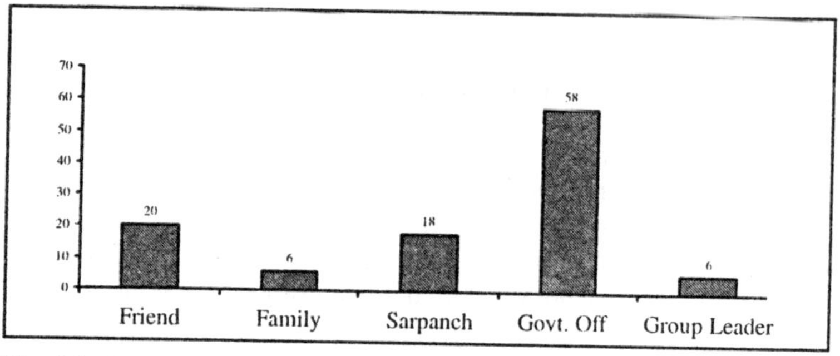

Fig. 6.1 : Sources of information about DWCRA to the beneficiaries

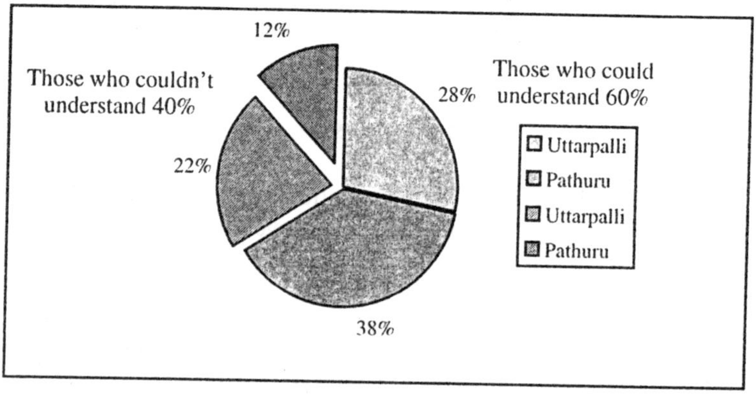

Fig. 6.2 : Understanding about the scheme among the DWCRA beneficiaries

As shown in Figure 6.1, for majority of the respondents (58 per cent), government personnel have been the source of information about DWCRA, followed by friends (20 per cent), *Sarpanch* (18 per cent), family members (6 per cent) and group leader (6 per cent) of respondents respectively. In Uttarpalli, respondents, who came to know through governmental personnel, said that they were told about DWCRA by Annasujamma, a motivator-*cum*-social worker, who came to Uttarpalli from Alluru. In Pathuru, the *Sarpanch* is found to be a source of information to a considerable number of people (18 per cent). Interestingly, most of the respondents, who said that they came to know through *Sarpanch*, belong to BC community to which *Sarpanch* too belongs. With regard to information about DWCRA, government officials being the main source of information next to close or intimate people, are playing an important role.

Understanding about the Scheme

For the success of any scheme, the target groups need to have proper understanding about various aspects of the scheme that they are availing of and about the benefits they can derive from the scheme that they are using. With regard to DWCRA though majority of the people (60 per cent) said that they could understand about DWCRA, a good number of people (40 per cent) said that they could not yet understand about DWCRA, as shown in Figure 6.2.

Understanding about DWCRA is more in Pathuru compared to Uttarpalli. It could be due to the reason that this scheme was introduced in Pathuru in 1995, much earlier, whereas in Uttarpalli, it was introduced in 1999.

Reasons for not Understanding the Scheme

In both the villages, out of 50 respondents, 30 claimed that they understood the programme. Out of 20 respondents, who said that they could not yet understand about the scheme, 14 respondents (70 per cent) said that no one told them about the scheme properly. Four respondents (20 per cent) said that adequate information was not provided. While one respondent (5 per cent) said that she heard about it while it was being explained, but failed to understand properly; another respondent (5 per cent) said that since she had not received anything from the scheme, she could not understand about the scheme.

Perceptions of those who have Understood the Scheme

Among those who said that they understood the scheme, 20 respondents (66.6 per cent) told that this scheme was about saving money, while six respondents (20 per cent) said that this was a scheme to provide loans to those who saved some amount of money. While three respondents (10 per cent) said that this was about *isthirakula* loan, one respondent admitted that she did not know about the scheme. It is interesting to note that while some beneficiaries perceived DWCRA as a scheme that promotes savings, others perceived it as a scheme that provides loans.

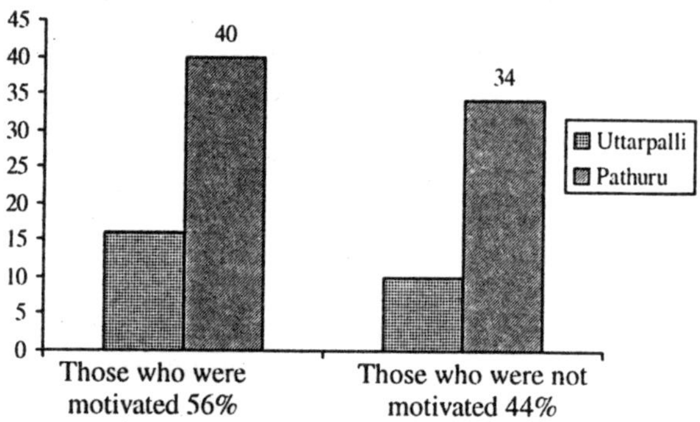

Fig. 6.3 : Motivation to the DWCRA Beneficiaries

Motivation about the Scheme

Motivation is inspiring a person to act in a particular manner. It is stimulating the interest of a person in an activity. As such, motivation is of a crucial importance with regard to poverty alleviation programmes. Among 50 DWCRA beneficiaries in Uttarpalli and Pathuru, 28 respondents (56 per cent) said that they were motivated to join DWCRA groups by various sources, such as friends, sarpanch and government personnel. While 22 respondents (44 per cent) said that they were not motivated by any one, but they joined on their own, as shown in Figure 6.3.

Motivation to the DWCRA Beneficiaries

Those who joined on their own said that they all belonged to the same community, i.e. *cooli* or agricultural labour community. Therefore, they said that they all talked to each other, discussed and formed the groups. Here, horizontal flow of communication in the social system has functioned as a propelling and motivating factor.

Sources of Motivation

The DWCRA beneficiaries of Uttarpalli and Pathuru were motivated by different sources. A total of 28 respondents (56 per cent) said that they were motivated by different sources. Out of them, for 11

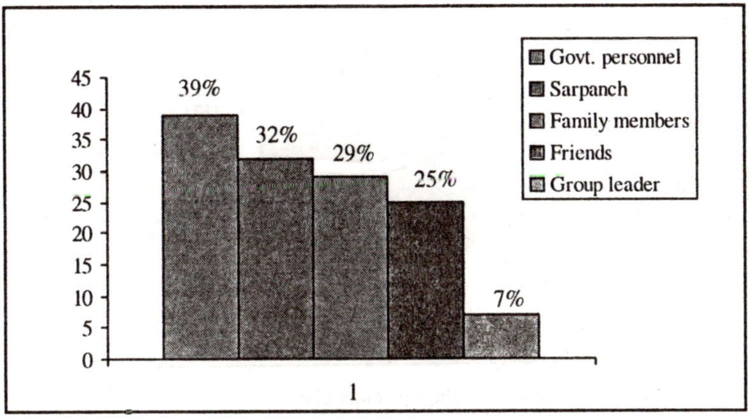

Fig. 6.4 : Sources of motivation to DWCRA beneficiaries

respondents (39.28) government personnel have been the source of motivation followed by sarpanch to 9 (32.1 per cent) respondents, family members to 8 (28.5 per cent) respondents, friends to 7 (25 per cent) respondents and group leader to 2 (7.1 per cent) respondents, as shown in Figure 6.4.

Sources of Motivation to DWCRA Beneficiaries

Government personnel being source of motivation to more number of people. Among the government personnel, Annasujamma of Alluru has been mentioned by the respondents in Uttarpalli, as their source of information and motivation. It seems that homophilous relationship between Annasujamma and villagers helped her to establish contact with women of Uttarpalli and to motivate them.

Improvement in the Financial Condition after Availing DWCRA

A total of 27 respondents said that there was some improvement in their financial condition after availing the scheme; out of them 23 respondents (85%) told that they were saving every month some little amount of money and thus there was some improvement in their financial condition. Two respondents (7.4%) said that there was improvement, as they had received gas stoves, while another two respondents (7.4%) expressed that they had got loan facility and a feeling of security. As shown in Figure 6.5, majority of the respondents

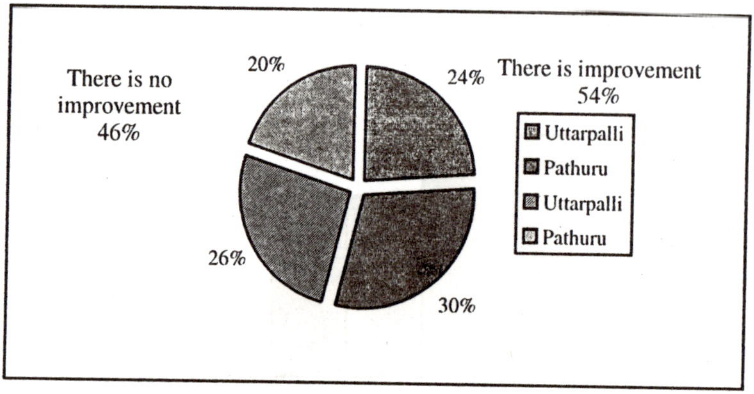

Fig. 6.5 : Improvement in the Financial Condition after availing DWCRA

(54 per cent) said that there was some improvement in their financial condition after joining the DWCRA.

Understanding about the Scheme before Joining

With regard to prior understanding about the scheme before joining it, out of 50, 31 respondents (62 per cent) said that they could not understand about the programme thoroughly before joining it. However, 38 per cent of the respondents said that after thorough understanding only, they joined the scheme.

Section C

Impact of the Scheme

The DWCRA groups in Pathuru are six years old, and in Uttarpalli, two years old. Therefore, an attempt has been made to evaluate the impact of the scheme on the financial condition and the quality of life of the beneficiaries.

Table 6.1 : Improvement in Financial Condition among Different Communities

Sl. No.	*Community*	*Beneficiaries in Uttarpalli*	*Beneficiaries in Pathuru*	*N*	*Total*	*Percentage*
1.	SC	7	7	30	14	46.6
2.	ST	–	–	1	–	0.0
3.	BC	4	7	17	11	64.4
4.	OC	1	1	2	2	100.0
Total		12	15	50	27	54.0

Among the respondents belonging to Backward Classes (BCs), out of 14 respondents, 11 respondents (78.5 per cent) said that there was improvement in their financial condition after joining the DWCRA groups, while among Scheduled Caste people, improvement in the financial condition has taken place in case of 14 respondents (46.6 per cent). It implies that those who are relatively better of are utilizing the scheme in a better manner.

Out of 23 respondents, who said that there was no improvement in their financial condition, 14 respondents (60.86 per cent) said that since they had not received anything from the government, there was no improvement in their financial condition. While seven respondents (30.43 per cent) said that they only their money was lent to them as loan and that too on interest; therefore, there was no improvement in their financial condition. Two respondents said that they were eating only if they worked and they were not receiving any financial benefit from DWCRA.

With regard to interest on DWCRA loan, there is a contrasting response in these two villages. While the respondents in Pathuru remained silent and to some extent happy with the interest, the respondents in Uttarpalli resented about it saying that they were forced to pay interest on the money, which they themselves saved, and felt that it was burdensome for them.

Improvement in the Quality of Life

About the improvement in the quality of life of people after availing

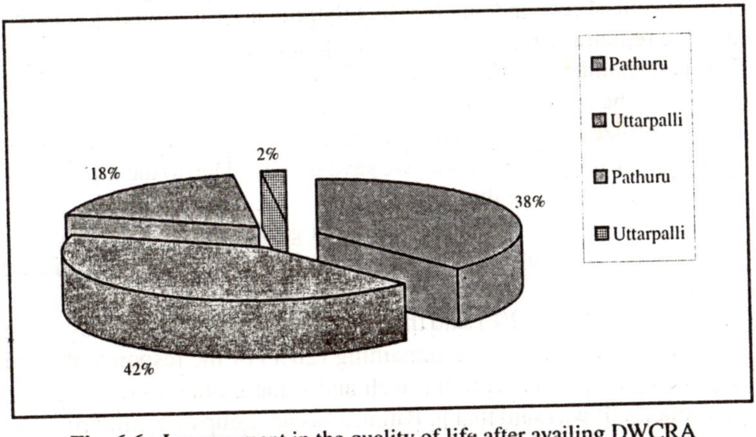

Fig. 6.6 : Improvement in the quality of life after availing DWCRA

DWCRA scheme, 40 respondents (80 per cent) told that there was no improvement in their quality of life, i.e. in terms of the quality of food, shelter, clothes, etc., while 10 respondents (20 per cent) said that there was some improvement in their quality of life after availing the scheme, as shown in Figure 6.6.

Though 80 per cent of respondents said that there was no improvement in their quality of life in terms of food quality, clothes, shelter, etc., some of them expressed that there was a remarkable change in their outlook. They said that after joining DWCRA, those who were illiterate, were becoming literate and those who were earlier confined to their homes, were now coming out from their houses and interacting with other members in society and thus becoming socially sensitive and active individuals. This view was expressed mainly in Uttarpalli, where under *Akshara Prabha* and *Akshara Sankranti*, total literacy programme is going on.

Among those who said that there was some improvement in their quality of life, for seven respondents (70 per cent), there is improvement in their food consumption, followed by educating children (10 per cent), wearing better clothes (50 per cent), improvement in shelter (50 per cent), bank balance (40 per cent) and cooking stove (20 per cent).

General Impression about DWCRA

The general impression about DWCRA among the beneficiaries is that majority of the people (64%) feel that it is a useful scheme, while 18 per cent feel that it is useful to some extent. While another 12 per cent of respondents feel that there is no use from this scheme, and the remaining 6 per cent of the respondents said they didn't know. While responding to the question, whether it is a useful scheme, some (80%) of the respondents in Pathuru said, "it is a useful scheme if it can be utilized properly. But we are poor people, we are unable to come out of starving. How can we save money? Due to the difficulties, we are unable to save the money."

About the DWCRA scheme that is going on in their respective villages, 90 per cent of the respondents belonging to Uttarpalli said that it was going on well in their village. In Pathuru, though majority of the respondents (72%) said that the DWCRA programme was going on well in their village, the remaining (28%) of the respondents said that their groups were running well and some groups were not going on properly. It was said that in Pathuru, some groups were not running properly due to the inability of members to pay every month 30 rupees. However, some of such respondents admitted that their husbands still took liquor, as they feel it was inevitable to forget their hard work.

Section D

Awareness about DWCRA among Target Beneficiaries who have not Availed the Same

Often, we find people saying that they could not do certain things or could not utilize certain schemes, for they did not know about those schemes etc. or due to lack of information or knowledge about them. As such, this situation exists more likely in case of people in rural areas, as majority of them are illiterate or less-educated. Therefore, a survey also has been conducted among the target beneficiaries of DWCRA, who have not availed themselves of the scheme, with regard to their awareness about the scheme. Findings of the survey have been presented in this section.

A Profile of the Respondents

For the purpose of the present study, 25 respondents in each of the two villages, viz. Uttarpalli and Pathuru, a total of 50 respondents have been taken through purposive sampling. All the respondents belong to lower income groups, i.e. annual income between Rs. 3000-6000, 6000-11,000. Out of 50 respondents, 34 (68%) did not receive any formal education. Now, they are learning-reading and writing.

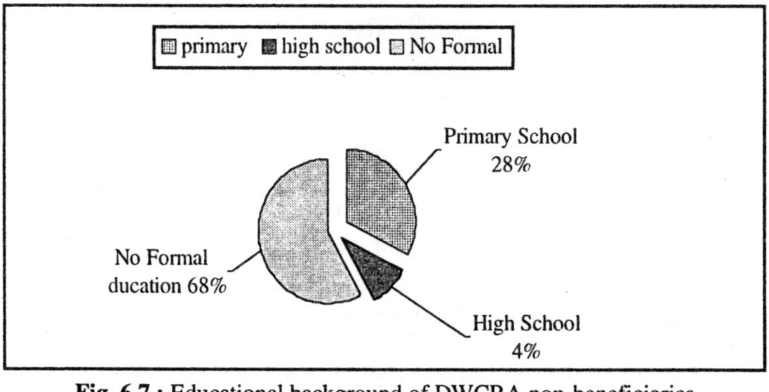

Fig. 6.7 : Educational background of DWCRA non-beneficiaries

14 respondents (28%) received primary school education and the remaining two respondents (4%) received high school education, as shown in Figure 6.7.

The respondents are in different age groups and they belong to Scheduled Castes, Scheduled Tribes and Backward Classes, as shown in Table 6.2.

Table 6.2 : A Profile of the DWCRA Non-Beneficiary Respondents by Age and Community

Age	*Uttarpalli*			*Pathuru*			*Total*
	SC	*ST*	*BC*	*SC*	*ST*	*BC*	
20 years and below	–	–	2	4	1	–	7
21 - 30	2	–	3	–	2	2	9
31 - 40	2	–	6	6	1	5	20
41 - 50	1	–	5	2	2	–	10
51 and above	1	–	3	–	–	–	4
Total	6	–	19	12	6	7	50

Awareness about DWCRA

Majority of the target beneficiaries, who have not availed of the DWCRA scheme (64%) are also aware of the DWCRA scheme, while 36 per cent of the respondents said that they had not heard about DWCRA, as shown in Figure 6.8.

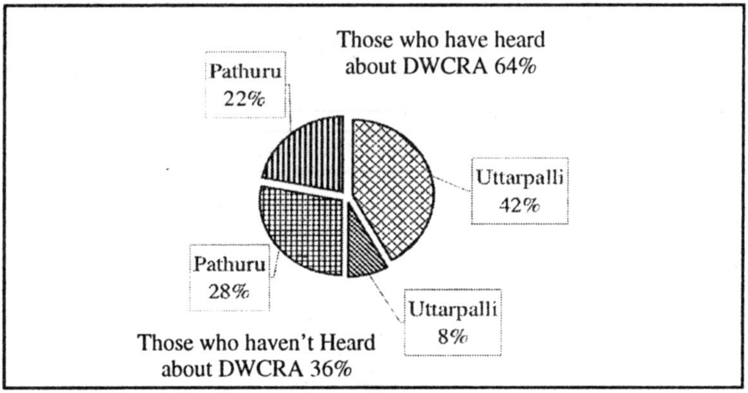

Fig. 6.8 : Awareness about DWCRA among the non-beneficiaries

Majority of the respondents, who know about DWCRA, are more in Uttarpalli compared to Pathuru.

Sources of Information to those who Know about DWCRA

A total of 32 respondents said that they knew about DWCRA. Out of them, some came to know about it through multiple sources, whereas others came to know through single sources. Among the sources of information about DWCRA, friends have been mentioned by 84 per cent of the respondents followed by *panchayat* members (46.8%), family members (18.75%), government officials (9.3%) and *sarpanch* (6.2%). It is shown in Figure 6.9.

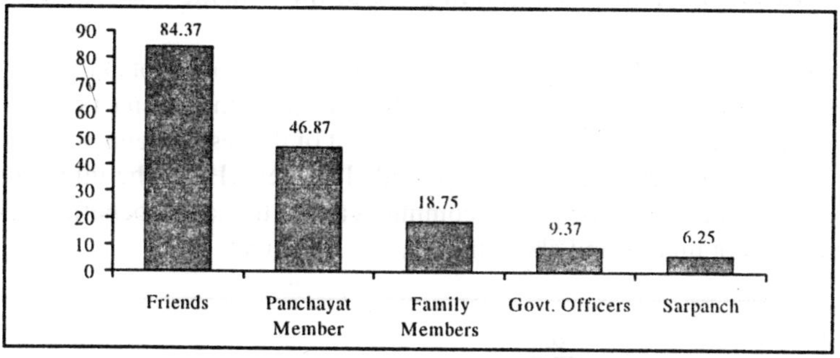

Fig. 6.9 : Sources of information to those who know about DWCRA

Friends have been mentioned as a source of information by 84 per cent of the respondents. From this, it is evident that interpersonal relations and interpersonal communication played an important role in spreading the information about the developmental programmes. None of the respondents, who availed the scheme, mentioned *panchayat* members as a source of information. But interestingly, 46.8 per cent of the respondents, who have not availed the scheme, have mentioned panchayat members as a source of information. The position of *sarpanch* and government officials also diminished as sources of information to the people, who have not availed the scheme. Here, informal sources seemed to be more influential than formal sources of information in spreading the information.

Understanding about the Scheme

When it came to the level of understanding about the scheme among the non-beneficiaries, only 14 (44%) out of 32 who said that they were aware of the scheme and could understood about the scheme. The remaining 18 respondents (56 %) said that they could not understand about the scheme. Among those who said that they had understood about the scheme, eight respondents (57.1%) told that the scheme was about saving money. Three respondents (21.4%) told that if they paid some amount of money every month, they would get money. And another three respondents (21.4%) said that through this scheme, loan was given. Here, interestingly, while one section of the respondents feel that it is a scheme to save money, others feel that it is a scheme, which provides loan.

Reasons for not Understanding about the Scheme

As many as 94.4 per cent of the respondents, who could not understand about the scheme, said that no one told them about the scheme properly. Another reason mentioned by 50 per cent of the respondents was that adequate information was not provided to them. Here, the inference is that due to lack of proper communication, the target beneficiaries could not understand about the scheme properly.

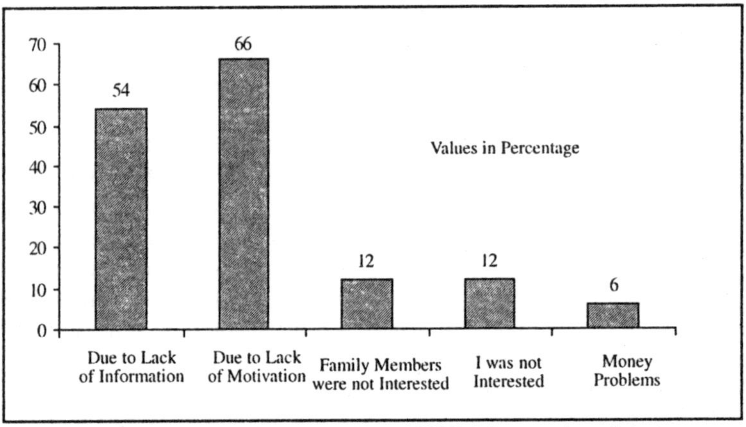

Fig. 6.10 : Reasons for not availing DWCRA by non-beneficiaries

Reasons for not Availing the Scheme

The target beneficiaries, under the present study, could not avail the scheme for multiple reasons.

Among the reasons for not availing the scheme, lack of motivation occupies the first position, followed by inadequacy in terms of information, resistance from family members, reluctance on the part of the individuals and money problems. Each of these reasons reveal the communication inadequacies and communication gap, as reason for the non-utilization of the schemes. Therefore, there is a need to bridge the gap between the planner and beneficiary to make these programmes successful.

Majority of the respondents expressed that had they joined the scheme, they would have been benefited. Their general impression about the scheme is that it is a useful scheme and going on well in their respective villages. Majority of the respondents (72%) are willing to become members of DWCRA groups if new groups are formed.

PART II

Section A

Awareness and Utilization of IRDP Asset-giving Scheme—Role of Communication

Integrated Rural Development Programme is a direct beneficiary-oriented scheme. It got widespread popularity due to its nature of providing benefits to the individuals in the form of loan with subsidy to purchase buffaloes, sheep unit, electric motors, etc. Communication, being assumed to be one of the important elements that play a crucial role in the success or failure of the scheme, a study has been conducted on the beneficiaries in two villages, viz. Uttarpalli and Pathuru, who have availed the scheme. A survey also has been conducted in these two villages among the target beneficiaries, who have not utilised the scheme. Findings of the empirical study have been presented in this part of the chapter.

A Profile of the Beneficiaries

In Uttarpalli and Pathuru together, 18 persons were covered under the IRDP asset-giving scheme. That means, as per the government records, assets were grounded in case of these beneficiaries. Initially, an attempt was made to cover all these beneficiaries, but since some of the beneficiaries were not available in these villages, 13 (78%) beneficiaries have been covered under the present study.

Interestingly, all the respondents belong to backward castes. Even out of the total 18 beneficiaries in two villages, there is only one beneficiary belonging to scheduled tribe, whereas there is no single

Table 6.3 : Educational Profile of the Respondents

Sl. No.	Educational Background	*Annual Income*						*Total*
		Uttarpalli			*Pathuru*			
		Below 6000	*6001- 11000*	*11001 and above*	*Below 6000*	*6001- 11000*	*11001 and above*	
1.	Illiterates	2	2	1	–	2	1	8
2.	5th and below	–	–	–	–	–	–	–
3.	5th – 10th	–	–	1	–	–	2	3
4.	10th – Graduation	–	1	–	–	–	1	2
	Total	2	3	2	–	2	4	13

beneficiary from scheduled castes. Although all the respondents under the present study belong to backward classes, there are some variations in terms of their education and income.

Table 6.3 shows that though in educational background, there are no remarkable variations between the respondents of Uttarpalli and Pathuru, there are glaring variations between the respondents in Uttarpalli and Pathuru in terms of income.

As shown in Table 6.3, in Pathuru, majority of the respondents belong to higher income groups, whereas in Uttarpalli, majority of the respondents belong to lower income groups.

Awareness about the Scheme

It is obvious, all the respondents, being the beneficiaries of the scheme, all of them are aware of IRDP asset-giving scheme. They acquired this awareness through different sources. Government officials have been mentioned as their source of information by 69.2 per cent of the respondents. In this regard, these respondents said that they came to know about the scheme through *Dandora* (announcing through drumbeat), which was followed by *Gramsabha* meeting, where government officials informed to the target beneficiaries about the scheme. Other respondents (15.3%) came to know through neighbours, while one each from both the villages, two respondents (15%) came to know through family members and sarpanch respectively.

Choice of the Asset

All the respondents said that the choice of the asset was purely theirs. They told that they had felt the respective assets they proposed and received would be useful to improve their financial condition, hence they applied for the same. It seems here government officials have given adequate freedom to the target beneficiaries to decide and apply for the assets, which can improve their lives.

Grounding of the Assets

Though government records show that all these 13 respondents, under the present study, have received the assets, three respondents (23%), two in Uttarpalli and one in Pathuru said that they had not yet received the assets. Therefore, there were only 10 (76.9%) respondents who received the assets. They received the assets between one and half years to two years back.

Present Status of the Assets

In Pathuru, all the respondents, who have received the assets, are using them and deriving some benefit. Contrary to this, in Uttarpalli, in case of three respondents (60%), out of the sheep they purchased, only few are existing. In case of two respondents (40%), assets were sold out and presently not existing. In case of one respondent, asset is existing but not working. The response in Uttarpalli shows us a grim picture about the utilization of IRDP scheme in this village.

Motivation about the Scheme

With regard to motivation in Uttarpalli, government officials were mentioned as source of motivation by four respondents (90%), while sarpanches and family members were mentioned as a source of motivation by two respondents (20%) respectively. One respondent said that he was not motivated by any one, but he joined on his own. In Pathuru, four respondents (90%) said that they were not motivated by anyone, but on their own they applied for the assets and got, while one respondent said that he was motivated by the government officers. The responses about the motivation in both the villages have been shown in figure 6.11.

Figure 6.11 shows that while 90 per cent of the respondents in Uttarpalli were motivated by the government officials, in Pathuru, 90 per cent of the respondents said that they themselves took the initiative, tried and got the assets. It is explicit here, beneficiaries in Pathuru

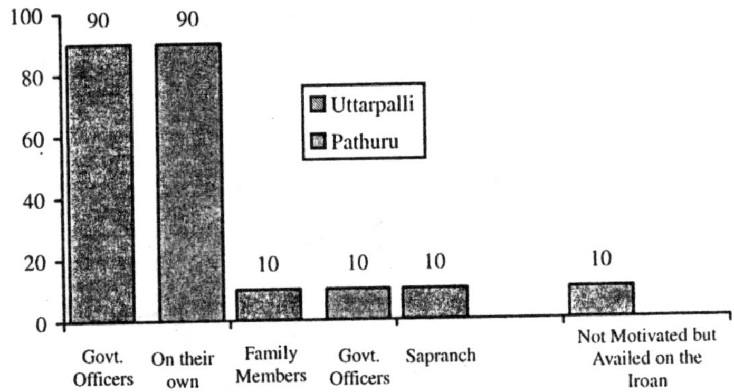

Fig. 6.11 : Sources of motivation to the IRDP beneficiaries

have more awareness about the programme than the beneficiaries in Uttarpalli, which led the beneficiaries into utilizing the scheme properly. Another factor being the certain level of the affluence of the beneficiaries in Pathuru.

Clearance of Loan

In terms of the clearance of the loan, there is a contrast between the respondents in Uttarpalli and Pathuru. In Pathuru, all the respondents cleared some Rs. 5,000 amount of loan in two instalments, whereas in Uttarpalli, only one respondent (20%) cleared an amount of Rs. 8000, while four others (80%) have not at all cleared the loan. The reasons mentioned for not clearing the loan were death of some sheep and not utilization of the asset due to the defect in the asset. Respondents in Pathuru said that since they could utilize the asset, they received some benefit from it and thus afforded to clear some amount of the loan.

Improvement in the Financial Condition after Availing the Scheme

In Uttarpalli, all the respondents said that there was no improvement in their financial condition after availing the scheme. As mentioned earlier, reasons for no improvement in the financial conditions are death of some sheep and non-utilization of the asset due to the defect in it. Contrary to this, in Pathuru, 90 per cent of the respondents said that there was some improvement in their financial condition after availing the scheme. They said that before getting the assets (bores and pump sets), they were dependents on the mercy of the rain for the cultivation, and they could not cultivate properly. But after getting the bores, they said that presently, they were cultivating well and thus there is some improvement in their financial condition after availing the scheme. Three respondents (60%) in Pathuru also said that there was little improvement in their quality of life after availing the scheme in terms of food, clothes, shelter, education of children, respect, etc. One respondent said that there was no improvement in his financial condition after availing the scheme, as he incurred loss at the time of installing the bore due to the failure of rigs and its subsequent shifting to another place.

General Impression about the Scheme

All the respondents in both the villages felt that it is a useful scheme. They suggested that this scheme should continue. Some of the respondents suggested that without giving much trouble to them, they should be given what they deserve to get from the government.

Section B

Awareness about the IRDP Among the Non-beneficiaries

Introduction

Though poverty alleviation programmes are meant for all the people living below the poverty line, only a few people are utilizing these schemes and the remaining people within the target group are left out. IRDP asset-giving scheme that was launched in Uttarpalli and Pathuru is a concrete example in this regard. Why is it happening so? Is it due to the communication gap or is there any limitation in the programme itself? If it is due to communication gap, how to overcome it? These are few questions to be addressed while analyzing the role of communication in relation to poverty alleviation programmes. Therefore, an attempt has been made to evaluate the awareness level about IRDP asset-giving scheme, sources of information, motivation, etc. For this purpose, a survey has been conducted among the target beneficiaries of IRDP asset-giving scheme in Uttarpalli and Pathuru.

The findings of the survey have been presented in this section, which are as follows:

Awareness about IRDP Asset-giving Scheme

Among the non-beneficiaries of IRDP asset-giving scheme, 75 per cent of the respondents are aware of the IRDP asset-giving scheme. In Pathuru, awareness about the scheme is more compared to the respondents in Uttarpalli, as shown in Figure 6.12.

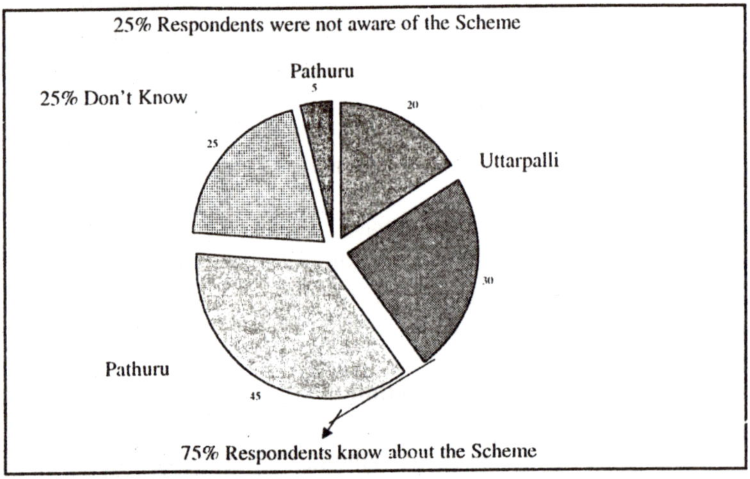

Fig. 6.12 : Awareness about IRDP among the non-beneficiaries

As shown in Figure 6.12, even among those who have not availed the IRDP asset-giving scheme in Pathuru, respondents have more awareness about the scheme than the respondents in Uttarpalli. It could be due to the proximity to Medak, good transportation facility (surface communication) between Medak and Pathuru, and the frequent visits of the VAO and other officials to the village.

Sources of Information about the Scheme

Respondents said that they came to know about the scheme through different sources. While some respondents came to know about it through single source, others came to know from multiple sources. Among the sources of information, as mentioned by the respondents, government officials occupy the first position (73.3%) followed by friends (20%), sarpanch (20%) and family members (13.3%), as shown in Figure 6.13.

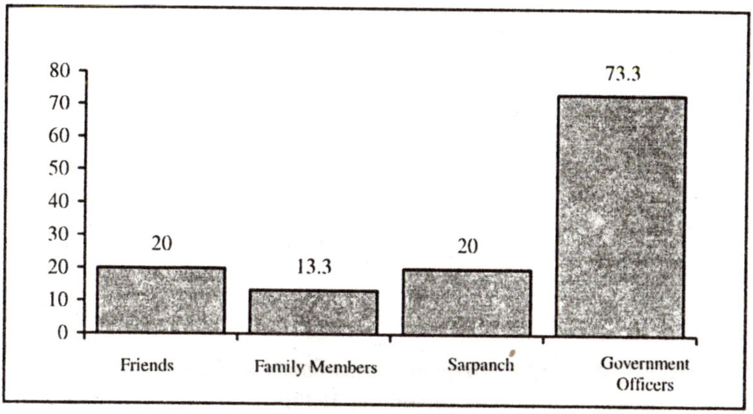

Fig. 6.13 : Sources of Information about IRDP to Non-Beneficiaries

Majority of the respondents in both the villages mentioned government officials as their source of information. They came to know through *'Dandora'*, which was followed by *Gram Sabha* meeting, where government officials informed people about the scheme. Few respondents also came to know through their respective mandal offices.

Reasons for not Availing the Scheme

As already mentioned, out of 20 respondents, 5 (25%) respondents said that they didn't know about the scheme. Therefore, obviously, in case of these respondents, lack of awareness is the reason for not availing the scheme. Even among those who know about IRDP asset-giving scheme, three respondents (15%) revealed that they could not avail the scheme due to lack of proper understanding. Another 11 respondents (55%) said that they tried but could not get any asset. Only one respondent (5%) said that he was not interested.

As shown in Figure 6.14, 73.3 per cent of the respondents tried for the assets, but they could not get due to limited opportunities. 46.6 per cent of the respondents said that they could not avail IRDP asset-giving scheme owing to the lack of information. In case of these

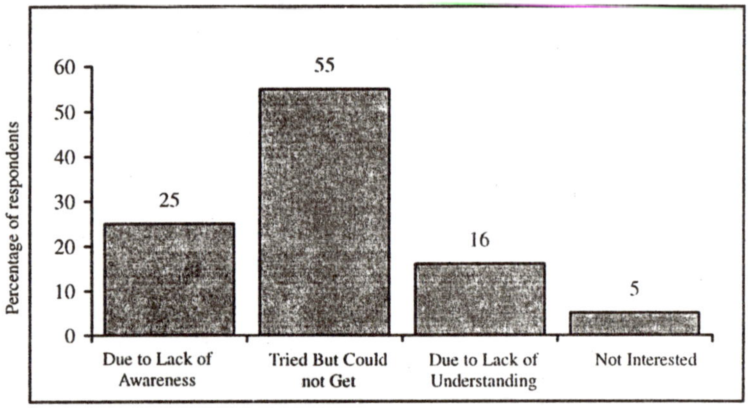

Fig. 6.14 : Reasons for not availing IRDP

respondents, dearth of adequate information and communication is reason for the non-utilization of the IRDP asset-giving scheme. It reveals the need and importance of communication in bridging the gap between the planner and the beneficiary.

All the respondents said that their financial condition would have improved had they availed the scheme. They feel that it is a useful scheme.

Conclusion

The study reveals that awareness about the schemes is a crucial factor in availing and proper utilization of the schemes—DWCRA and IRDP. While all the beneficiaries of DWCRA and IRDP have awareness about these schemes, 36 per cent of the DWCRA target beneficiaries and 25 per cent of IRDP target beneficiaries, who have not availed these schemes, do not have awareness about the schemes. Those, who have awareness about these schemes, acquired this awareness through interpersonal and group communication channels—government officials, sarpanch, friends and family members. Interestingly, no single respondent mentioned mass media as source of information. 54 per cent of DWCRA non-beneficiaries could not avail the scheme, lack of awareness being one of the reasons. Where there is more awareness and initiative on part of the beneficiaries, there effectiveness of the scheme is found to be more. For example, DWCRA beneficiaries in Uttarpalli and IRDP beneficiaries of Pathuru, awareness and initiative have been found to be more. In their case, the respective schemes also have been utilized properly. In case of the majority of the DWCRA beneficiaries, there is some improvement in their financial condition, as every month they are saving some little amount of money. However, some beneficiaries are not in a position to pay the money every month, as their husbands continue to take liquor. Therefore, there is an indispensable need to create awareness and educate the people—both men and women—about the importance of regular savings and about the disadvantages of drinking habit, in case of IRDP asset-giving scheme.

The study reveals that the government officials have given adequate choice to the target beneficiaries to choose the asset they need. But since the selection of the beneficiaries is done by them, they have sanctioned the loan to those who are better-off and thus showed the bias in favour of rich applicants instead of providing opportunity to the poor for whom this scheme is meant. Thus, on the one hand in Uttarpalli beneficiaries failed to utilize the scheme, and on the other, in Pathuru, beneficiaries could well utilize the scheme, but already they had certain level of affluence. Over all the assets have been given to very limited number of people, which is a limitation of the scheme and which limited the impact of the scheme.

Though for 80 per cent of the respondents, there is no improvement in their quality of life, they feel now that there is change in their outlook, which is a commendable achievement of the scheme. Interpersonal and group communication among the members of the DWCRA groups have contributed significantly for this change.

7 Environmental Awareness Among the People of Medak District

Introduction

In the previous chapter, the role of communication in relation to the poverty alleviation programmes in Medak district was discussed. The present chapter deals with the awareness of environmental problems in the district. Unless the people have awareness about the environmental deterioration and its consequences, they cannot act upon it at their level. Therefore, it is pertinent to know the extent of environmental awareness among different sections and age groups of the people in the society. To make them well informed, conscious and responsible minded individuals about the environment, it is also important to know about their life style, their sources of information about the environment and their media habits. This chapter is divided into three Parts – Part I, Part II and Part III. While the environmental awareness, their life style, sources of information about various environmental issues have been dealt with in Part I, media habits of the people have been dealt with in Part II. Patancheru pollution being a major environmental problem in Medak district, the present study would be incomplete if the role of communication in Patancheru pollution is not analyzed. Therefore, this aspect has been dealt with in Part III.

Before going into the details of findings, it would be useful to present the profile of the villages and towns where the primary data was collected and the profile of the respondents from whom information was taken.

PART I

Section A

A Profile of the Study Area and the Respondents

The data was collected through a stratified purposive sampling technique from 200 respondents both men and women, in rural and urban areas belonging to different age groups, education, income, caste and religious backgrounds as shown in Tables 7.1 and 7.2.

Table 7.1 : Profile of the Respondents by Age and Education

Education	*Urban*								*Rural*								
	Below 15		*16-30*		*31-40*		*41 and above*		*Below 15*		*16-30*		*31-40*		*41 and above*		
	M	*W*	*M*	*W*	*M*	*W*	*M*	*W*	*M*	*W*	*M*	*W*	*M*	*W*	*M*	*W*	*Total*
Illiterates	4	0	1	1	2	2	2	3	0	1	2	2	3	3	4	2	32
V Class & below	4	3	0	1	0	0	2	3	5	10	2	4	3	0	2	3	42
VI – X	2	5	2	2	0	2	0	1	11	12	10	14	2	2	1	0	66
XI to Graduation	0	0	4	5	3	2	1	1	0	1	12	5	1	0	3	2	40
PG & above	1	0	5	1	1	2	4	2	0	0	1	0	0	2	0	1	20
Total	11	8	12	10	6	8	9	10	16	24	27	25	9	7	10	8	200

M = Men, W = Women.

Table 7.2 : Respondents by Religion and Income

Monthly Income	*Hindu*	*Muslim*	*Christian*	*Total*
Rs. < 1000	48	2	0	50
Rs. 1000-3000	75	2	5	82
Rs. 3000-6000	33	4	1	38
Rs. 6000-12000	13	4	3	20
Rs. >12000	8	1	1	10
Total	177	13	10	200

Areas of the Study

The data was collected from four urban areas Patancheru, Sangareddy, Medak and Siddipet and three villages Chitkul, Pathuru and Ponnala of Medak district. These towns and villages represent the urban and rural population in three revenue divisions of Medak district. Sangareddy and Patancheru being the headquarters of the district and nearby urban area overlapping with Hyderabad city, a total of 35 respondents were taken from these two towns. Medak and Siddipet being the major towns in these two revenue divisions, 20 respondents in each town have been taken. Thus a total of 75 respondents were covered in urban areas.

The village Chitkul is situated in Patancheru mandal. It is nearly six kilometers away from Patancheru and 20 kilometers away from Sangareddy, the district headquarters town. It is one of the villages worst affected by the Patancheru industrial pollution. The total population of the village is 2,925. Out of this, there are 1,471 men and 1,454 women. Literacy rate in the village is 50 per cent. The village is prone to air pollution, water pollution and soil degradation.

Pathuru is located in Medak mandal. It is 8 kilometres away from Medak and 60 kilometres away from Sangareddy, the district headquarters. As described in the previous chapter, the total population of the village is 2,332 out of which 1,113 are men and 1,219 are women. Literacy rate in the village is 20 per cent. Out of the total area of the village, 2,991 acres, the forests occupy 1,500 acres area. Two watersheds have been constructed in the village and there are Vana Samrakshana Samithis (VSS) to protect the forest area.

Ponnala is situated in Siddipet mandal. It is 5 kilometers away from Siddipet and nearly 170 kilometers away from Sangareddy. Total population of the village is 3,900, out of which 1,935 are males and 1,965 are females. Literacy rate in the village is 40 per cent. In this village, 5 tanks have been constructed under the Watershed Management Scheme. There is a watershed group to lookafter, the watersheds. As part of 'clean and green' programme, nearly 500 trees were planted in school compounds and main streets of this village. On every Saturday 'clean and green' programme is observed in this village.

Communication

Nearly 40 newspapers which include *Vaartha, Eenadu, Andhra Prabha* and *Andhra Bhoomi* are circulated in the village. There are more than 100 TV sets with cable connection and there are over 200 radio sets. Yearly 3-4 times traditional folk performances are given and developmental messages are disseminated through these performances.

Section B

Environmental Awareness about the Global Environmental Issues

Some environmental problems—Ozone layer depletion, green house effect and acid rains have thc impact on thc entire globe. There are the results of the activities of man across the globe and they call for the attention of all the global people for timcly action on their part. Therefore, people were asked about their awareness on these problems, reasons for these problems and effects of these problems.

Awareness about the Ozone Layer Depletion

Respondents were asked whether they have heard or read about the ozone hole. Very few people responded positively. Out of 200 respondents, 76 respondents (38%) said that they are aware of the ozone hole. This awareness is found to be more among the urban respondents (48%) than the rural respondents (32%). Similarly, more men (42%) are aware of the Ozone hold than women (34%). Education is one factor determining the awareness as shown in Table 7.3.

Table 7.3 : Awareness about the Ozone Layer Depletion (Percentage in Parenthesis)

Educational Background	*Urban*			*Rural*			*Total*
	Men	*Women*	*N*	*Men*	*Women*	*N*	*N Percentage*
Illiterate	0	1	1	2	0	2	[32] 3 (9.3)
V and below	2	1	3	3	4	7	[42] 10(23.8)
VI – X	3	3	6	4	10	14	[66] 20(30.3)
XI – graduation	7	7	14	12	2	14	[40] 28(7)
PG & above	7	5	12	2	1	3	[20] 15(7)
Total	19	17	36	23	17	40	[200] 76(38)

N—Total Number

Table 7.3 shows that more people (75%) among those who have done post-graduation are aware of the ozone layer depletion, followed by those who received college level education (70%), high school level education (30.3%), primary school level education (23.8%) and illiterates (9.3%). (This is because the more educated people have more access to and capability of using various sources of information).

Knowledge about the Ozone Hole

When it comes to the knowledge about the effects of the ozone layer depletion, though most of those who are aware of the ozone hole have the knowledge about one effect or other, very few people have thorough knowledge about the effects. Out of 76 respondents, only 26 respondents (34.2%) know thoroughly about the effects of ozone hole. According to them all the effects, sun rays directly falling on the earth, the process of photosynthesis in the plants getting affected, and occurrence of cancer are the consequences of the effect of ozone hole. Among other respondents, sun rays directly reaching the earth was mentioned by 33 (43.4%) respondents, 8 respondents gave multiple answers which were also included here. While occurrence of cancer was mentioned by 13 (17.1%) respondents, the process of photosynthesis in the plants getting affected was mentioned by 6 (7.8%) respondents as shown in Table 7.4.

Table 7.4 : Awareness about the effects of Ozone Hole

Sl.No.	*Effects*	*Urban*			*Rural*			*Grand Total*	
		Men	*Women*	*T*	*Men*	*Women*	*T*		*% age*
1.	Sun rays/UV rays will reach the earth directly	6	6	12	13	8	21	33	43.4
2.	It affects the process of photosynthesis	1	3	4	0	2	2	6	7.8
3.	It causes cancer	2	3	5	5	3	8	13	17.1
4.	All the above	8	3	11	8	7	15	26	43.2
5.	None of the above	1	0	1	1	1	2	3	3.9
6.	I don't know	1	0	1	2	0	2	3	3.9

In Table 7.4 options 1, 2 and 3 are also correct. But the 4th one, i.e., *all the above is appropriate one.* Out of those who have given the appropriate answer, 8 respondents (30.7%) are post-graduates, 9 respondents (34.6%) are those who received college education, 7 persons (26.9%) are those who received high school education and 4 respondents (15.3%) are those who received primary school education. Thus education is found to influence the awareness of the individuals.

Awareness about the Reasons for the Depletion of Ozone Layer

Among the responses given, emission from the industries was mentioned by 44 respondents (57.8%). While emission from air-conditioners and refrigerators was mentioned by 19 (25%) respondents remaining 13 respondents (17.1%) admitted that they did not know the reasons for the ozone layer depletion.

Table 7.5 : Awareness about the reasons for Ozone Hole Grand

	Urban			*Rural*			*Grand Total*	
Reasons	*Men*	*Women*	*Total*	*Men*	*Women*	*Total*		*%age*
Emission from air-conditioners and refrigerators	5	5	10	5	4	9	19	25.0
Emission from industries	10	12	22	12	10	22	44	57.8
I don't know	2	2	04	7	2	9	13	17.1
Total	17	19	36	24	16	40	76	100

As shown in Table 7.5, CFCS or emissions from air-conditioners and refrigerators being the reason for the depletion of ozone layer, has been mentioned by only 19 (25%) respondents. More men than women and more urban people than rural people have awareness about the reasons for ozone hole. This could be due to the explosure and access to the information. Generally men and urban people have more exposure and access to the source of information than their counter parts—women and rural people.

Global Warming

Compared to ozone hole, more people are aware of global warming. Out of 200 respondents 116 persons (58%) said that they are aware of global warming. About this problem also more men (62) than women (54) and more urban respondents (60%) than rural respondents (56.8%) have awareness. As shown in Table 7.6, educational background of the respondents contributes to a great extent to their awareness.

Table 7.6 : Awareness about the Global Warning

Educational Background	*Urban*			*Rural*			*Grand Total*	
	Men	*Women*	*Total*	*Men*	*Women*	*Total*	N	*%age*
Illiterate	4	0	4	2	2	4	32	8(25)
V and below	3	3	6	7	8	15	42	21(50)
VI – X	3	7	10	16	19	35	66	45(68)
XI- Graduate	6	5	11	10	3	13	40	24(60)
PG & above	9	5	14	2	2	4	20	18(90)
Total	25	20	45	37	34	71	200	116
	Urban – 60%			Rural – 56.8%			Total —58%	

Table 7.6 shows that 18 respondents (90%), who have done post-Graduation know about the global warming, followed by those who received or receiving high school and college education respectively. This is because for high school students, it is taught in the school. Comparatively, less number of respondents who received primary school education and no education (illiterates) know about the global warming.

Knowledge about the Effects of Global Warming

Out of 116 respondents, who are aware of the global warming, majority of the respondents (68%) know about the effects of global warming. But only 31 respondents (26.7%) have thorough knowledge about these effects as shown in Table 7.7.

Table 7.7 : Awareness about the effects of Global Warming

Sl. No.	*Urban*			*Rural*			*Total*	
	Men	*Women*	*T*	*Men*	*Women*	*T*		*%age*
1. It will heat up the earth's temperature	5	6	11	9	5	14	25	21.5
2. Ice (Caps and sheets will melt)	1	0	1	2	2	4	5	4.3
3. Both 1 & 2	9	4	13	5	11	16	29	25.0
4. Sea level will increase	0	1	1	18	4	22	23	19.8
5. All the above	6	7	13	10	8	18	31	26.7
6. None of the above	1	1	2	0	0	0	2	1.7
7. I don't know	3	1	4	3	4	7	11	9.4

In Table 7.7 though options from 1-5 are correct, the 5th one is the appropriate one, which was mentioned by only 31 respondents (30%) among those who have knowledge about the effects of global warming. The pattern shows that awareness is comparatively low about certain aspects of the problem.

Reasons for Global Warming

Though majority of the respondents (62%) know about one factor or other for the global warming a considerable number of respondents (38%) do not know the reasons for the global warming. Interestingly, as shown in Table 7.8 only 10 respondents (8.62%) have thorough knowledge about the reasons for the global warming.

Table 7.8 : Awareness about the reasons for Global Warming

Sl. No.	Urban			Rural			Grand Total	
	Men	Women	Total	Men	Women	Total		%age
1, Carbon dioxide	6	5	11	11	11	22	33	28.4
2, Chlorofloro carbons	2	2	4	1	1	2	6	5.1
3, Both one and two	5	5	10	2	8	10	20	17.2
4, Sulpher dioxide	1	0	1	2	0	2	3	2.5
5, All the above gases	2	1	3	6	1	7	10	8.6
6, None of the above gases	1	0	1	2	0	2	3	2.5
7, I don't know	8	7	15	13	13	26	41	35.3
Total	25	20	45	37	34	71	116	100

The above table shows that more respondents know about one main reason. But more reasons are known only to a few respondents. Among those who have given the appropriate answer, there are more men (8) than women (2) and there are more rural respondents (7) than urban respondents (3).

Awareness about the Acid Rains

Awareness about acid rains is comparatively very low. Out of 200 respondents only 72 (36%) said that they have heard or read about acid rains. More men (39) than women (33) and more urban respondents 34 (45.33%) than rural respondents 38 (30.4%) are aware of the acid rains.

Table 7.9 : Awareness about Acid Rains

Educational Background	Urban			Rural				Grand Total
	Men	Women	Total	Men	Women	Total		%age
Illiterate	1	1	2	4	1	5		7(21.8)
V & below	3	0	3	4	2	6		9(21.4)
VI – X	2	4	6	3	10	13		19(28.7)
XI-Graduate	4	6	10	8	2	10		20(4)
PG & above	8	5	13	2	2	4		17(8)
Total	18	16	34	21	17	38	200	72(36%)

Table 7.9 shows that awareness about acid rains also is determined by the educational background of the respondents. More respondents 17 (85%) among those who have done PG and above are aware of the

acid rains, followed by those who have received college level education 20 (50%) high school level education 19 (28.78%), primary illiterates 7 (21.87%).

Reasons for Acid Rain

Out of 72 respondents who are aware of acid rains, 50 respondents (69.5%) know one reason or other for the acid rain. While 30 respondents (41.6%) felt that industrialization is causing acid rains 6 persons (8.3%) said that power generation is responsible for acid rains. As shown in Table 7.10 only 14 respondents (19.4%) said that both industrialization and power generation are reasons for the acid rains, which is the appropriate answer.

Table 7.10 : Awareness about the reasons for Acid Rain

	Urban			*Rural*			*Grand Total*	
	Men	*Women*	*Total*	*Men*	*Women*	*Total*		*%age*
1. Industrialisation	11	8	19	6	5	11	30	41.6
2. Power Generation	0	0	0	4	2	6	6	8.3
3. Both 1 and 2	3	5	8	3	3	6	14	19.4
4. Other (Specify)	0	0	0	0	1	1	1	1.3
5. I don't know	4	3	7	8	6	14	21	29.1
Total	18	16	34	21	17	38	72	100

Table 7.10 shows that a considerable number of respondents (29.1%) do not know the reasons for the acid rain. Here more women (8) than men (6) and more urban respondents than rural respondents have given the appropriate answer.

Awareness about the Consequences of Acid Rains

Out of 72 respondents those who are aware of the acid rains 56 respondents (77.7%) have knowledge about the consequences of acid rain. Of these 56 respondents, 31 persons (55.3%) have thorough knowledge about the consequences, while among the remaining respondents 14 (25%) felt that acid rains will affect the crop productivity, 6 respondents (10.71%) said that it acidifies lakes and streams and 5 respondents (8.92%) said that it increases the soil acidity.

Out of 72 respondents who have heard or read about the acid rains 16 respondents (22.22%) do not know about the consequences of acid rains as shown in Table 7.11. It implies that more respondents have the awareness about the problem in general, but when it came to the specific aspects of the problem, comparatively few respondents have such awareness.

Table 7.11 : Awareness about the effects of Acid Rain

	Urban			*Rural*			*Grand Total*	
	Men	*Women*	*Total*	*Men*	*Women*	*Total*		*%age*
It increases soil acidity	2	1	3	2	0	2	5	6.9
It acidifies lakes and streams	0	2	2	2	2	4	6	8.3
It affects crop productivity	5	2	7	3	4	7	14	19.4
All the above	5	9	14	9	8	17	31	43.0
None of the above	2	0	2	0	0	0	2	2.7
I don't know	4	2	6	5	3	8	14	19.4
Total	18	16	34	21	17	38	72	

A Comparison of Awareness on Ozone Hole, Global Warming and Acid Rain

Among the global environmental issues, more respondents (116) are aware of global warming (58%) followed by ozone hole (38%) and acid rains (36%) as shown in Fig. 7.1.

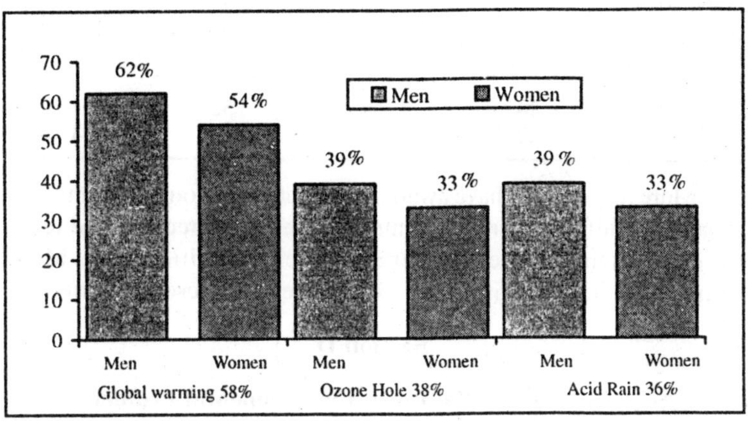

Fig. 7.1 : A Comparision of awareness on Ozone hole, global warming and acid rain

Figure 7.1 shows that more men than women have awareness on global warming. Awareness is found to be more on global warming.

Awareness is found to be more on global warming because, people are directly experiencing the increase of the temperature every year.

Section C

Awareness about Various Environmental Issues of Significance in India

As shown in Table 7.12 majority of the respondents are aware of all these issues. Among the environmental problems, known to the respondents, water pollution occupies the first position. It is known to 170 (85%) respondents, followed by air pollution (84%), deforestation (82%), sound pollution (79%), extinction of species (78.5%), renewable sources of energy (78.5%) and bio diversity (62%).

Table 7.12 : Awareness about the Various Environmental Issues of Significance in India

	Urban			*Rural*			*Grand Total*
	Men	*Women*	*Total*	*Men*	*Women*	*Total*	*% age*
Deforestation	29	31	60	55	49	104	164 (82)
Soil degradation	28	28	56	47	47	94	150 (75)
Air pollution	28	34	62	51	55	106	168 (84)
Water pollution	29	36	65	52	53	105	170 (85)
Sound pollution	25	30	55	51	52	103	158 (79.4)
Extinction of species	25	28	53	50	54	104	157 (78.5)
Renewable sources of energy	24	28	52	53	52	105	157 (78.5)
Bio-diversity	20	23	43	38	43	81	124 (62)

More respondents have awareness about the various environmental issues of significance, in the country. It is because directly or indirectly they are facing these problems in their localities also. Many respondents have the first hand experience with these problems.

Section D

Awareness about the Local Environmental Problems

In order to know the awareness about the local environmental problems both open ended and close ended questions were asked. Among the problems mentioned by the respondents water pollution occupies the first position told by 80 (40%) respondents, followed by air pollution (36%), sound pollution (16%), deforestation (6%), garbage accumulation (5%) and water scarcity (4.5%).

When close ended question was asked, garbage accumulation and stinking was mentioned by more number of people 123 (61.5%) followed by water scarcity (58.5%), water pollution (56%), air pollution (55.5%), deforestation (52%) and sound pollution (41.5%). Awareness about the local environmental problems in urban and rural areas is as shown in Figure 7.2.

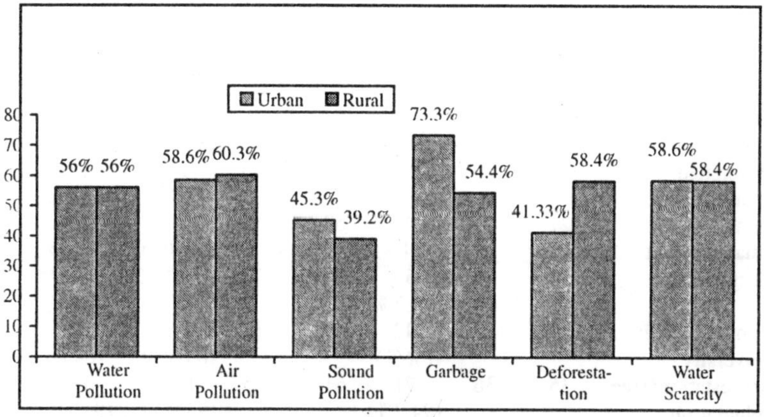

Fig. 7.2 : Awareness about the local environmental problems

Figure 7.2 shows that water pollution and water scarcity is found at same range in both urban and rural areas. Garbage accumulation and stink being the problem told by more number of respondents, was being more in the urban areas than rural areas. Similarly, air pollution and sound pollution are found to be more in urban areas than in rural areas. The problem of deforestation was mentioned by more rural respondents than urban respondents. This is because trees or forests grow more in rural areas than in urban areas.

Section E

Awareness about the Environmental Promotion Programmes/ Activities

In order to control the environmental deterioration and to take up the steps to promote the environment, people should be aware of various environmental promotion activities or programmes. Therefore, people were asked whether they were aware of various environmental promotion activities 'Clean and Green', Watershed Management, Joint Forest Management, Recycling, Conserving Bio-diversity,

Aforestation and Reducing the Wastage of Water, Electricity etc. or not? Interestingly, majority of the respondents, both men and women in urban as well as in rural areas know about these programmes as shown in Table 7.13.

Table 7.13 : Awareness about the Environmental Promotion Programmes (Percentage in brackets)

	Urban			*Rural*			*Grand Total*
	Men	*Women*	*Total*	*Men*	*Women*	*Total*	
Clean and Green Programme	26	34	60 (80%)	54	48	102 (81.6%)	162 (81%)
Watershed management	27	26	53 (70.7%)	52	46	98 (78.4%)	151 (75.5%)
Joint-forest management	21	27	48 (64%)	54	49	103 (82.4%)	151 (75.5%)
Recycling	26	30	56 (74.7%)	55	51	106 (84.8%)	162 (81%)
Conserving bio-diversity	19	23	42 (56%)	49	37	86 (68.8%)	128 (64%)
Aforestation/Tree plantation	35	36	71 (94.7%)	61	55	116 (92.8%)	187 (93.5%)
Reducing/Minimizing the wastage of water, electricity	32	37	69 (92%)	62	60	122 (97.6%)	191 (95.5%)

Table 7.13 shows that most of the respondents (95.5%) know about reducing or minimizing the wastage of water, electricity etc., followed by aforestation/tree plantation (93.5%), recycling (81%), clean and green programme (81%), watershed management (75%), joint forest management (75%) and the conservation of biological diversity (64%).

Most of the respondents have awareness about the need for minimizing the wastage of water, electricity etc. For this, in addition to environmental concerns, one reason could be the water scarcity. It is obvious that 58 per cent of respondents in both urban and rural areas have already mentioned that they have water scarcity. Remarkable increase in the electricity charges by the state government in the recent times too could be a reason for reducing the wastage of electricity. Tree plantation has occupied the second position. It is desirable that people are taught right from the childhood about the importance of tree plantation. Even the political leadership has taken such an initiative to inculcate environmental values to the people. On the eve of his birthday (20th April) the then Chief Minister of Andhra

Pradesh said that he would be pleased if each person can plant a sapling. (*Vaartha,* 21.4.2001) 'Clean and Green' as well as recycling take the next position. There was widespread dissemination of information and participation of people with regard to clean and green. While people come to know about the recycling by seeing those who purchase or collect the old papers, plastic, glass etc. respondents have come to know about the watershed management and joint forest management through their first hand experience and media publicity. Though majority of the people know about the biological diversity, comparatively, it occupies the last position. The possible reason could be that it has not been given wide publicity like other programmes that have been discussed.

Section F

Awareness about Family Planning

Most of the respondents 190 (95%) are aware of the need of family planning i.e., basically following the small family pattern. In Telugu the slogan, *Chinnakutumbam, Chintaleni Kutumbam* (a small family has no worries) was popularized. Many respondents, including the children are aware of this slogan.

Awareness about the Various Methods of Family Planning

Respondents were asked whether they know about the family planning methods—vasectomy, tubectomy, oral pills, condoms, copper-T and

Table 7.14 : Awareness of Family Planning Methods

	Urban			*Rural*			*Grand Total*
	Men	*Women*	*Total*	*Men*	*Women*	*Total*	
Vasectomy	29	32	61 (81.33%)	59	52	111 (88.8%)	172 (86%)
Tubectomy	33	35	68 (90.66%)	62	56	118 (94.4%)	186 (93%)
Oral pills (Mala-D)	28	28	56 (74.66%)	51	43	94 (75.2%)	150 (75%)
Condoms (Nirodh)	29	28	57 (76%)	50	38	88 (70.4%)	145 (72.5%)
Copper-T	17	25	42 (56%)	29	32	61 (48.8%)	103 (51.5%)
Loop	17	24	41 (54.6%)	33	30	63 (50.4%)	104 (52%)

loop. Among these methods, most of the respondents 186 (93%) know about tubectomy operation, followed by vasectomy operation 172 (86%), oral pills 150 (75%), condoms 145 (72.5%), loop 104 (52%) and copper-T 103 (51.5%).

As shown in Table 7.14, comparatively less number of respondents know about copper-T and loop. Because these methods are adopted by very few respondents and the publicity given about these methods also seems to be low.

Number of Children

In order to know the pattern of having children in general and in different religious groups in particular, information has been collected from the respondents about the number of children they have. As shown in Table 7.15 there are 100 respondents who have children. Out of these 100 respondents 22 respondents have only one child, 29 respondents each have 2 and 3 children respectively, 14 respondents have 4 children and 7 respondents have 5 children and more.

Table 7.15 : Number of Children of the Respondents Belonging to Different Religious Groups

Religion	*No.of Child-1*		*No.of Child-2*		*No.of Child-3*		*No.of Child-4*		*No.of Child-5*		*Total*
	Urban	*Rural*	*Urban*	*Rural*	*Urban*	*Rural*	*Urban*	*Rural*	*Urban*	*Rural*	
Hindu	6	14	10	15	8	18	4	5	1	4	85
Christian	2	0	1	1	2	0	0	0	0	0	6
Muslim	0	0	2	0	1	0	3	1	1	1	9
Total	8	14	13	16	11	18	7	6	2	5	100

Total = 100.

Table 7.15 shows that among those who have more than two children, there are 40 (47%) Hindus, 2 (33%) Christians and 7 (78%) Muslims.

Here though more percentage of the Muslim respondents have more than 2 children family planning is also adopted by more Muslim respondents as shown in Table 7.16. It reveals that more Muslim respondents have consciousness about the family planning, but they are adopting it late.

Adoption of Family Planning

Out of 100 respondents, those who have children, 73 persons have adopted permanent family planning. They had undergone either tubectomy or vasectomy operation. Among those who adopted the permanent family planning methods 62 (72.94%) respondents are Hindus, 4 (66.6%) respondents are Christians and 7 (77.7%) respondents are Muslims. As shown in Table 7.16 more urban respondents than the rural respondents have adopted family planning.

Table 7.16 : Adoption of Family Planning

	Urban			*Rural*			*Total*
	Men	*Women*	*Total*	*Men*	*Women*	*Total*	*%age*
Hindu	9	14	23	21	18	39	62(72.9)
Christian	0	3	3	0	1	1	4(66.6)
Muslim	2	3	5	2	0	2	7(77.7)
Total	11	20	31	23	19	42	73

Among those 27 respondents who have not adopted family planning, 20 respondents said that they are expecting or waiting for another child and 7 respondents said that naturally without any effort their reproduction system was stopped.

Gender Preference

Gender bias is leading to a number of social and environmental problems which effect the sustainable development. Unless people change their attitudes, gender equality cannot be achieved. Therefore, respondents were asked about their preference in terms of the gender of their children. Those who are unmarried were also asked as to whom they prefer, boy or girl, even kids were asked whether they like younger brother or sisters.

87 respondents (43.5%) said that they treat both a boy and a girl equally 59 respondents (29.5%) said that they prefer boy while 54 (27%) respondents said that they prefer a girl. Table 7.17 shows that a boy is preferred more in rural areas and low income groups than the urban areas and higher income groups.

It reveals that the overall gender preference bends towards the boy. The situation calls for the change in the attitude of people in

Table 7.17 : Gender Preference

Income	*Boy*		*Girl*		*Equal*		*Total*	
	Urban	*Rural*	*Urban*	*Rural*	*Urban*	*Rural*		*Percentage*
Below Rs.1000	5	9	4	5	5	17	45	22.5
Rs.1000-3000	9	20	5	13	7	28	82	41.0
Rs.3000-6000	2	6	6	9	9	5	37	18.5
Rs.6000-12000	2	4	6	4	5	5	26	13.0
Rs.12000 and above	2	0	2	0	6	0	10	5.0
Total	20	39	23	31	32	55	200	100

favour of the girl to achieve the gender equality which constitutes an important element in sustainable development.

Section G

Lifestyle of the Respondents in Relation to Environment

Participation in 'Clean and Green' Programme

Clean and Green programme is a major environmental promotion programme initiated by the government of Andhra Pradesh. It aims at promoting the environment through a massive public participation. As described in Section-E a total of 162 respondents (81%) are aware of this programme. When it came to the participation level 146 respondents (73%) have participated in it. As shown in Table 7.18 more men (77%) than women (69%) and more respondents (75.2%) in rural areas than urban areas 69.3 participated in this programme. Generally people are more acquainted with the need for growing of trees; availability of more space and manageable atmosphere and size of the population could be reasons for the participation of more respondents in rural areas than the respondents in urban areas.

Participation of People in Clean and Green Programme by Age

Table 7.18 shows that more respondents (86.6%) in the age group of 31-40 have participated in the programme, followed by the respondents in 41 and above age group (77.7%) below 15 years age group (76.2%) and 16-30 years age group (63.5%). Similarly, more exposure and freedom that male have in the society could be reason

Table 7.18 : Participation of People in Clean and Green Programme by age

Age	*Urban*			*Rural*			*G. Total*		
	Men	*Women*	*Total*	*Men*	*Women*	*Total*		*N*	*Percentage*
Below 15	6	7	13	13	19	32	45	59	(76.2)
16-30 years	8	7	15	21	11	32	47	74	(63.5)
31-40 years	3	7	10	11	5	16	26	30	(86.6)
41 and above	7	7	14	8	6	14	28	37	(77.7)
Total	24	28	52	53	41	94	146	200	

Men—77%, Women—69%, Total—73% Rural—75.2%, Urban—69.3%

for the participation of more male respondents than female respondents.

Works done as Part of Clean and Green Programme

The activities taken up by the respondents as part of the clean and green programme were planting the saplings, watering the saplings and cleaning the surroundings. As shown in Figure 7.3, among those who have participated in clean and green programme, 36 respondents (24.65%) planted the saplings, 24 respondents (16.43%) cleaned the

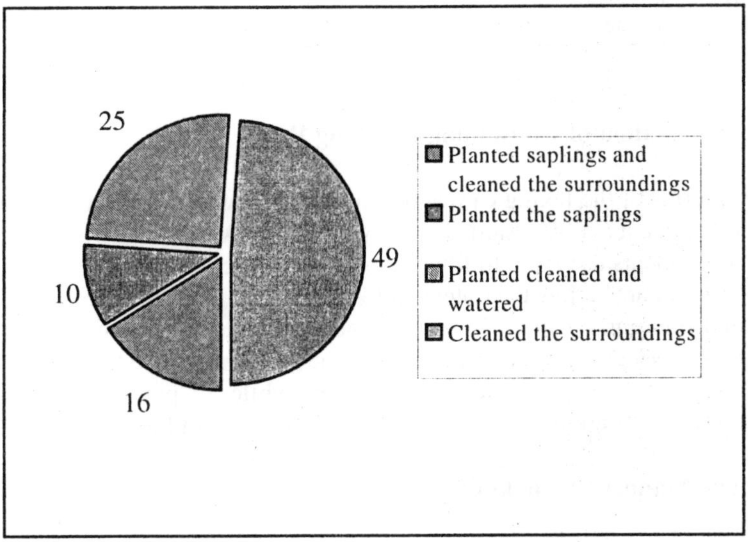

Fig. 7.3 : Works done as part of Clean and Green Programme

surroundings, 72 respondents (49.31%) did both planting the saplings and cleaning the surroundings and 14 respondents (9.58%) did all these three works.

Source of Drinking Water

In spite of many efforts by the governments, still a large number of people do not have access to safe drinking water world wide. In Medak district, people were asked about their sources of drinking water. As shown in Table 7.19 majority of the people (70.5%) are consuming drinking water which is supplied by the municipality or panchayats, 26 respondents (13%) bore water and 9 respondents (4.5%) followed by well water. Remaining 24 respondents (12%) said that they are using both boring pump water and municipal water. From this it seems that all the respondents have access to safe drinking water.

Table 7.19 : Source of Drinking Water

Source	*Urban*	*Rural*	*Total*	*Percentage*
Well	3	6	9	4.5
Boring water	10	16	26	13.0
Supply water	56	85	141	70.5
Boring water and supply water	6	18	24	12.0
Total	75	125	200	100

The Method of Consuming Drinking Water

In terms of the taking care about the drinking water, majority of the respondents (60%) said that they filter the water. Most of these respondents use cloth to filter the water. Four respondents (2%) said that they are boiling the water and 14 respondents (7%) are both boiling and filtering. As many as 54 respondents (27%) are neither boiling nor filtering. Over all 73 per cent of the respondents are taking care about the water in one way or other, while 27 per cent of the respondents are not taking care about it as shown in Figure 7.4.

The Manner of Cooking

The Source of our cooking (stove) also affects the environment. As shown in Table 7.20, gas stove is being used by more urban respondents

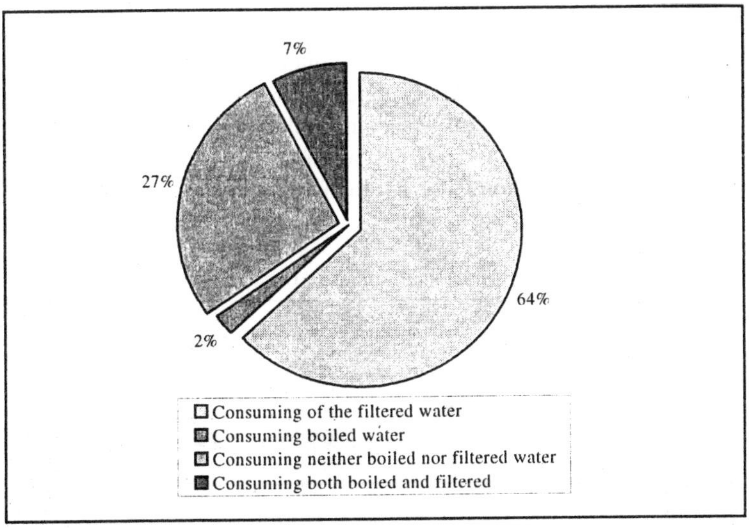

Fig. 7.4 : The method of purifying the drinking water before consumption

Table 7.20 : The Source of Cooking (Types of stoves used by family's monthly income)

Types of Stove	*Below 1000*		*1001-3000*		*3001-6000*		*6001-12000*		*12000 and above*		*Total*
	Urban	*Rural*	*Urban*	*Rural*	*Urban*	*Rural*	*Urban*	*Rural*	*Urban*	*Rural*	
Gas Stove	5	8	10	10	10	9	11	6	6	0	75
Kerosene Stove	2	2	2	1	1	0	1	0	1	0	10
Both Kerosene & Gas	2	1	3	2	1	1	2	1	1	1	15
Fire wood stove	6	26	9	35	2	9	0	2	1	0	90
Smokeless fire wood stove	0	4	0	6	0	0	0	0	0	0	10
Total	15	41	24	54	14	19	14	9	9	1	200

than rural respondents and fire wood stove is used by more rural respondents than urban respondents.

Table 7.20 also shows that in high income group more respondents are using gas stove and in low income groups, more respondents are using the firewood stove.

Possession and Use of Toilets

Out of the 200 respondents, 100 respondents (50%) have toilets. As shown in Table 7.21 more respondents (80%) in urban areas have toilets than the respondents (32%) in rural areas. More respondents in high income groups have toilets than the respondents in low income groups. Except 3 respondents in rural areas, all other respondents who have toilets are using these toilets.

Table 7.21 : Possession of Toilets in Urban and Rural Areas

Income in Rs. Monthly	*Urban*	*Rural*	*n*	*Total*
Below Rs.1000	9	9	50	18 (18%)
1000-3000	15	15	82	30 (36.5%)
3000-6000	16	10	38	26 (70.2%)
6000-12000	12	6	20	18 (69.2%)
12000 and above	8	0	10	8 (80%)
Total	60	40	200	100 50%

Disposing of Household Wastage

The method of disposing the household wastage impinges on the environment. While certain methods are environment-friendly, others lead to environmental deterioration too. For example, while re-using and composting are environment-friendly methods, throwing the garbage in streets and on the roadside leads to the environmental deterioration. Therefore, people (respondents) were asked as to how they dispose their household wastage. The respondents are disposing the household wastage as shown in Table 7.22.

Vegetable and Fruit Peelings

Majority of the respondents (64%) said that they are composting the vegetable and fruit peelings. Among those who are composting, there are more respondents (89.6%) in rural areas than (21.33%) in urban areas. A total 67 respondents (33.5%) are dumping this wastage in the municipality bin. More urban respondents (76%) than the rural respondents (8%) are dumping in the municipal bin. Five respondents – 2 (2.66%) in urban areas and 3 (2.4%) in rural areas are throwing the fruit and vegetable peelings on the road side or away from their homes.

Table 7.22 : The Method of disposing the household wastage

Mode of Disposing	*Vegetable and fruit peeling*		*Carry bags*		*Glass*		*Plastic*		*Paper*	
	Urban	*Rural*	*Urban*	*Rural*	*Urban*	*Rural*	*Urban*	*Rural*	*Urban*	*Rural*
Sell	0	0	0	0	23	39	27	55	40	40
Reuse in the house	0	0	10	19	14	47	15	40	13	53
Compost it	16	112	11	72		31	2	24	2	25
Dump in the Municipality bin	57	10	50	10	32	6	27	4	18	4
Any other	2	3	4	2	6	2	4	2	2	3
Total	75	125	75	103*	75	125	75	125	75	125

*22 respondents that they are not using carry bags (all belong to rural areas).

Plastic Carry Bags

A total of 29 respondents (14.5%) said that they reuse the carry bags. As many as 83 respondents (41.5%) are composting, of these 72 respondents (87.8%) belong to rural areas. Carry bags are dumped in municipality bin by 60 respondents, out of whom 50 respondents (83.33%) belong to urban areas and 10 respondents (16.66%) belong to rural areas. Among others, while 4 respondents (2%) said that they are throwing distantly or on the roadside. 2 respondents (1%) said that they burn the carry bags. And 22 respondents (11%) said that they are not using the carry bags. All these 22 respondents belong to rural areas.

Glass

Pertaining to the disposing of glass 62 respondents (31%) are selling 61 respondents (30.5%) are reusing it in house, 31 (15.5%) respondents are composting it and 38 respondents (14%) are dumping it in the municipality bin, while 8 respondents (4%) are throwing distantly in the bushes. Thus, while 122 respondents (61.5%) are disposing the glass in an environment-friendly manner, others are disposing in an environmentally unproductive manner.

Plastic

A total of 82 respondents (41%) said that they sell the waste plastic. While 55 (27.5%) respondents said that they are reusing the waste plastic for one purpose or other. 26 respondents (92.3% of who belong to rural areas) are throwing the plastic also in the compost items. Among others, 31 respondents (of whom 87.9% are urban respondents) are dumping it in the municipality bin and 8 respondents (4%) said that they throw it on the road side or at a far off place. Thus still a good number of respondents in rural areas are composting the plastic items and in urban areas they are being dumped in the municipality bin.

Paper

A total of 80 respondents (40%) said that they sell the waste paper. 66 respondents, out of whom 53 are rural respondents, said that they reuse the paper in the house. 27 respondents (13.5%) told that they compost the paper. Out of these 22 respondents (11%) said that they dump the waste paper in the municipality bin, and 5 respondents (2.5%) said that they dump the waste/old papers on the roadside or at a distant place.

The above findings show that respondents are disposing the household wastage in both environment-friendly as well as in a counter productive manner. It may not be always deliberate, but respondents are contributing for the promotion of environment through selling the waste items—glass, plastic and paper, which are generally recycled. By re-using the waste items also they are acting in an environment-friendly manner. Composting is also environment-friendly method of disposing the waste materials. But all materials are not desirable to be composted. For example, carry bags, glass and plastic materials are not to be composted. Though, by dumping the waste materials in municipality bin environmental cleanliness can be maintained, people should look beyond that to contribute to sustainable development. Re-using and recycling of materials are the better methods to be more environment friendly. Therefore, a good number of people are yet to get the awareness about the importance of re-using and recycling the wastes.

Section H

Sources of Information on Various Environmental Issues

For the better understanding of the role of communication in environmental protection, for formulating the effective communication strategies for promoting environment, it is important to know the environmental awareness of people and their sources of information

Table 7.23 : Sources of Information on Environmental Issues

	Issues	*NP*	*TV*	*Radio*	*Magazines*	*Cinema*	*Books*	*TFM*	*First Hand Experience*	*NGO*	*Friends*	*Family Members*	*Being a member of any argn.*	*Others*
1.	Global warming	29	43	11	12	1	36	–	10	–	1	2	2	5
2.	Ozone hole	28	29	9	11	1	40	–	1	–	2	1	–	8
3.	Acid rains	21	23	11	6	–	31	–	17	–	4	1	1	4
4.	Deforestation	36	63	17	3	1	38	–	64	--	14	6	–	12
5.	Water pollution	40	46	22	7	–	38	–	107	–	13	5	1	10
6.	Air plloution	44	59	17	7	1	44	1	99	–	3	3	–	8
7.	Soil degradation	37	45	8	6	–	34	–	68	–	7	5	–	12
8.	Sound pollution	37	55	12	8	–	23	–	107	–	5	4	–	11
9.	Recycling	40	44	12	6	–	14	–	91	1	8	12	–	5
10.	Clean and Green Programme	55	75	20	4	1	10	–	78	1	9	6	16	14
11.	Watershed management	53	58	17	8	–	11	–	89	1	6	7	1	6
12.	Joint forest management	58	87	27	8	1	16	–	61	1	2	4	3	11
13.	Aforestation	52	86	19	5	1	11	–	93	1	4	3	3	18
14.	Family planning	52	74	25	9	3	29	–	57	2	28	21	2	18

Note: NP – Newspapers, TFM – Traditional Folk Media, NGO – Non-Governmental Organisation.

on various issues. Therefore, respondents were asked about their sources of information on different specific environmental issues. Most of the respondents told that they have come to know about various issues that were specified through multiple sources as shown in Table 7.23.

Table 7.23 shows that on global warming, joint forest management and family planning, television was mentioned as source of information by more respondents followed by newspapers, books, first hand experience and others. On ozone hole and acid rains, books were named as source of information by more respondents, followed by television, newspapers, radio and others. On deforestation, water pollution, air pollution, soil degradation, sound pollution, recycling clean and green programme, watershed management and aforestation, more respondents said that they came to know about these issues through first hand experience, followed by television, newspapers, books, radio and others. Since the respondents are involved in respect to these issues in one way or other, they have awareness about them through first hand experience. Among the sources of information on various issues, first hand experience, television, newspapers and books have occupied significant positions. Magazines, friends, family members and teachers were also mentioned as source of information by a few respondents. Though there are over 25 non-governmental organizations, their presence was hardly felt during the survey and their role as a source of information is negligible.

PART-II

MEDIA HABITS

Introduction

Today directly or indirectly our world view is moulded by media. They provide information, entertainment, education, guidance etc., and thus they influence our actions, reactions and over all lifestyle to a great extent. There are different media. All people do not use the same media for the same purpose. Different people use different media for different purposes. Since media have the potentialities of moulding a sustainable lifestyle, it is important to know the media habits of people in general and different sections of people in particular. Therefore, information has been collected from the respondents, on their media habits and the findings have been presented in this part.

Section A

Newspaper Reading Habit Among the Respondents

Newspaper reading habit is high among the respondents. Out of 200 respondents, 144 persons (72%) read the newspapers. More male respondents (81%) than female respondents read newspapers (63%). Interestingly, as shown in Table 7.24, more respondents (75.2%) in rural areas are read newspapers than urban respondents (66.6%).

Table 7.24 : Newspaper Reading Habit Among the Respondents

	Men	*Women*	*Total*
Urban	26 (70.27%)	24 (63.15%)	50 (66.66%)
Rural	55 (87.30%)	39 (62.90%)	94 (75.2%)
Total	81 (81%)	63 (63%)	144 (72%)

Names of the Newspapers Read by the Respondents

Among the newspapers read by the respondents, *Eenadu* (a Telugu daily) occupies the first position. It is read by 96 respondents (66.66%) among those who read newspapers (144). It is followed by *Vaartha* (a Telugu daily), ready by 83 respondents (57.63%), *Deccan Chronicle* (an English daily) read by 19 respondents (13.19%), *Andhra Bhoomi* (a Telugu daily) read by 12 (8.33%) respondents, *Andhra Jyothi,* read by 9 (6.25%) respondents, *Siasath* (an Urdu daily) read by 8 (5.55%) respondents and *The Hindu,* read by 6 (4.16%)

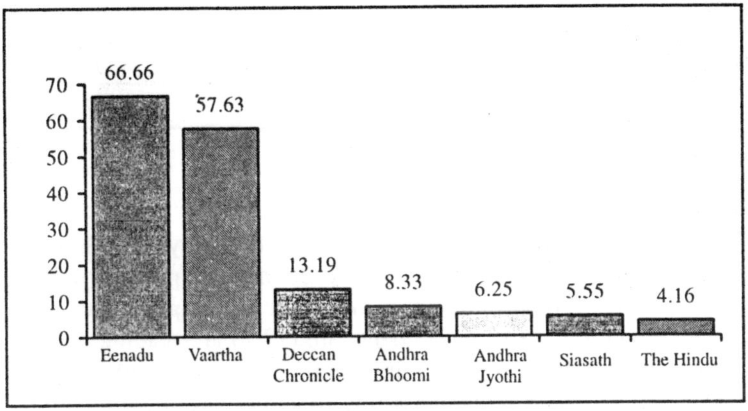

Fig. 7.5 : Newspapers Read by the Respondants

respondents as shown in Figure 7.5. From this, it is evident that majority of the respondents read Telugu language newspapers.

Subscription to the Newspapers

Out of those who read newspapers (144 respondents), only 52 respondents (36.11%) subscribe to the newspapers. Among those who subscribe to newspapers, more respondents belong to urban areas and high income groups as shown in Table 7.25.

Table 7.25 : Subscription to Newspapers in Rural and Urban Areas by Income

Income (Rs.)	*Urban*	*Rural*	*n*	*Total*	*Percentage*
Below 1000	1	4	50	5	(10.0)
1000-3000	4	9	82	13	(15.8)
3000-6000	9	7	38	16	(42.1)
6000-12000	8	5	20	13	(65.0)
12000 and above	5	0	10	5	(50.0)
Total	27 (54%)	25 (26.59%)	200	52	(36.11)

Among the newspapers that are subscribed, Eenadu gets the top position, followed by *Vaartha, Deccan Chronicle* and *Andhra Bhoomi* as shown in Table 7.26

Table 7.26 : Subscription to Various Newspapers in Urban and Rural Areas

Newspaper	*Urban*	*Rural*	*Total*	*Percentage*
Eenadu	13	20	33	52.3
Vaartha	12	10	22	34.9
Andhra Bhoomi	1	1	2	3.1
Deccan Chronicle	4	2	6	9.5
Total	30	33	63	100

Frequency of Reading Newspapers

Majority of the respondents read the newspapers everyday. While 81 respondents (56%) said that they read newspapers daily, 24 respondents (16.66%) told that they read newspapers twice in a weak. Among others, 19 respondents are (13%) are reading once a week: 9 respondents (6.25%) are reading once a month and 11 respondents (7.6%) are reading rarely (reading with more than one month gap). The frequency of reading newspapers is shown in figure 7.6.

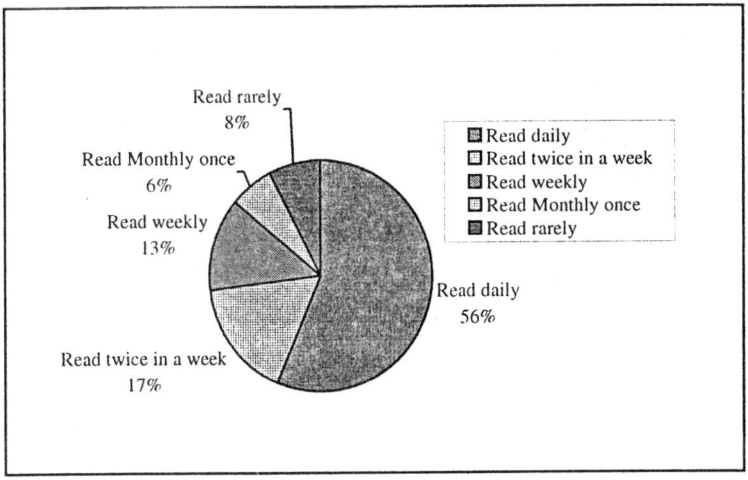

Fig. 7.6 : Frequency of Reading Newspapers

Magazine Reading Habit

Compared to newspapers, magazines are read by less number of respondents. A total of 81 respondents (40.5%) read the magazines. As shown in Table 7.27 more urban respondents (46.66%) than the rural respondents (36.8%) read the magazines. The magazine readership is also more among men (45%) than women (36%).

Table 7.27 : Magazine Reading Habit

Area	*Men*	*Women*	*Total*
Urban	18	17	35 (46.66%)
Rural	27	19	46 (36.8%)
Total	45	36	81 (40.5%)

Among the magazines read by the respondents, *Swathi* occupies the top position. It is read by 48 respondents (59.25%) out of those who read magazines. *Swathi* is followed by *India Today, Andhra Jyothi, Andhra Bhoomi* and others as shown in Figure 7.7

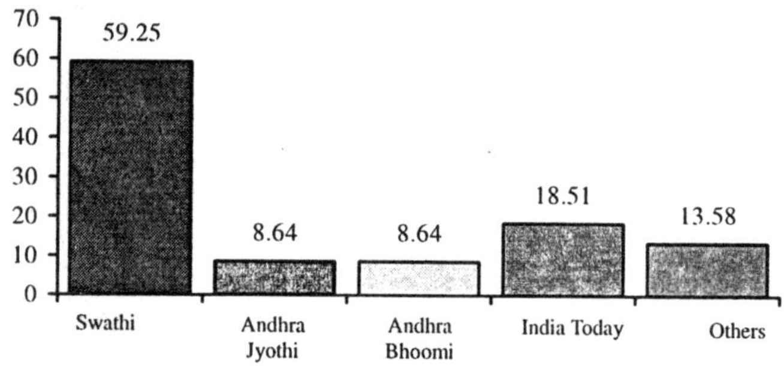

Fig. 7.7 : Readership of Various Magazines

Section B

Film Viewing

Most of the respondents see the films. Out of 200 respondents 184 (92%) said that they see films. Among them as shown in Table 7.28 more rural respondents (92.8%) than urban respondents (90.6%) and more male respondents (94%) than the female respondents said that they see films.

Table 7.28 : Film Viewing

	Urban	*Rural*	*Total*
Men	34	60	94
Women	34	56	90
Total	68 (90.6%)	116 (92.8%)	184 (92%)

Mode and Frequency of Seeing Films

Majority of the respondents said that they see the films both in the cinema hall and on television. Out of 182 respondents, who see films 152 (83.51%) go to cinema halls. Out of these respondents 5 persons (3.28%) see weekly twice, 20 respondents (13.15%) see weekly, 16 respondents (10.52%) see fortnightly, 78 respondents (51.31%) see monthly and 33 respondents (21.71%) see quarterly. As shown in Table 7.29, 157 respondents (85.32%) see films on television. Out of them 92 respondents (58.59%) see daily, 20 respondents (12.73%)

see weekly twice, 37 respondents (23.56%) see weekly, 4 respondents (2.5%) see fortnightly and another 4 (2.5%) respondents see films monthly once on television. It is to be noted, some respondents see films both in Cinema Halls and television.

Table 7.29 : Mode and Frequency of Viewing Films

Mode of seeing	*Daily*	*Weekly twice*	*Weekly*	*Fortnightly*	*Monthly*	*Quarterly or yearly*	*Total*
In Cinema ball	0	5	20	16	78	33	152
On TV	92	20	37	4	4	0	157
Cassettes/CDs	3	0	2	3	4	0	12

Table 7.29 also shows that 12 (6.52%) respondents see films through CDs or cassettes. Out of them, 3 respondents (25%) see daily, 2 respondents (16.66%) see weekly, 3 respondent (25%) see fortnightly and 4 respondents (33.33%) see film CDs or cassettes monthly once. Majority of the respondents said that they see the films with a family story followed by comedy films, devotional films and patriotic films.

Viewership of Newsreels

Among those who see films in cinema halls, 122 respondents (80.26%) said that they see newsreels with interest. The remaining 30 (19.73%) respondents said that they do not see newsreels with any interest, because of the boring nature of these films, and due to the feeling that it is a disturbance before the main film.

Section C

Radio Listening

Comparatively, radio is used by less number of respondents. A total 106 respondents (53%) said that they listen to the radio. As shown in Table 7.30 more men (56%) than women (50%) and more rural

Table 7.30 : Radio Listening Habit

	Urban	*Rural*	*Total*
Men	14	42	56
Women	19	31	50
Total	33 (44%)	73 (58.4%)	106 (53%)

respondent (58.4%) than the respondents (44%) in urban areas listen to radio. Quite a few respondents said that since television is providing all the information and entertainment, they are not using radio.

Television Viewership

Comparatively, more number of respondents are watching television. A total of 177 respondents (88.5%) said that they watch television. Television viewership is almost equal in both urban and rural areas. As shown in Table 7.31 more men (90%) than women (87%) are watching television.

Table 7.31 : T.V. Viewing

Gender	*Urban*	*Rural*	*Total*	*Percentage*
Men	34	56	90	90.0
Women	32	55	87	87.0
Total	66 (88%)	111 (88.8%)	177	(88.5%)

Possession of TV Sets

Majority of the respondents who watch television have got their own TV sets. Out of 177 respondents, who watch television, 139 respondents (69.5%) have their own television sets. As shown in Table 7.32 more urban respondents (77.3%) than rural respondents (64.8%) own television sets.

Table 7.32 : Possession of TV Sets by the Respondents

Income (Rs.)	*Urban*	*Rural*	*n*	*Total*	*Percentage*
Below 1000	7	18	50	25	(50.0)
1000-3000	15	42	82	57	(69.5)
3000-6000	16	13	38	29	(76.3)
6000-12000	12	8	20	20	(100.0)
12000 and above	8	0	10	8	(80.0)
Total	58	81	200	139	(69.5%)

Table 7.32 shows that the possession of TV sets is more in high income groups than in the low income groups. Most of these television sets have cable connection.

Viewership of Different Programmes

Among the television programmes watched by the respondents, serials occupy the top position. Out of the 177 respondents, who watch television, 146 respondents (84.48%) said that they watch serials, followed by the news and current affairs (81.92%), films (76.83%), film songs (55.93%), educational programmes (37.28%) and documentaries (5.08%). Viewership of different programmes is shown in Figure 7.8.

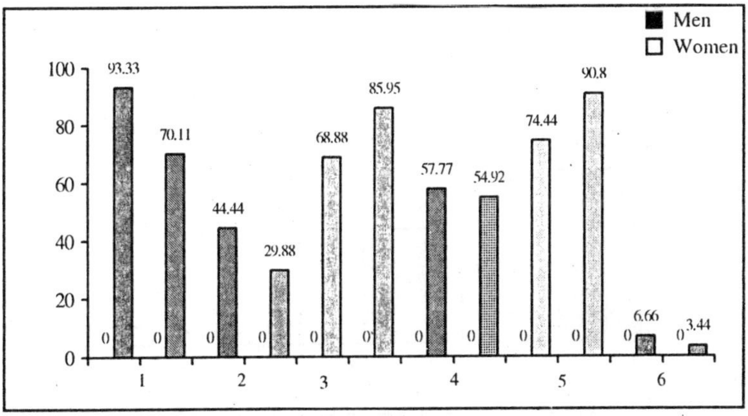

Male = N (90) Female = N (81) Total = N (177)

Fig. 7.8 : Viewership of different programmes by gender

1. News and current affairs
2. Educational programmes
3. Films
4. Film songs
5. Serials
6. Documentaries

News and current affairs: 81.72

Educational Programmes 37.16%, Films 76.16%, Film Songs 55.89%, Serials 82.89%, Documentaries 5.05%.

The above figure shows that news and current affairs, educational programmes, film songs and documentaries are viewed by more male respondents than female respondents. In case of films and serials this pattern is reverse. These are viewed by more female respondents than male respondents. This programme viewership pattern reveals that while more male respondents tend to watch information and educational programmes, female respondents watch entertainment programmes.

Different Television Channels Viewed by the Various Respondents

Among the television channels viewed by the respondents, Gemeni and Teja (Combination) Channels occupy the top position followed by ETV, Doordarshan, Sony, Star and other channels as shown in Figure 7.9.

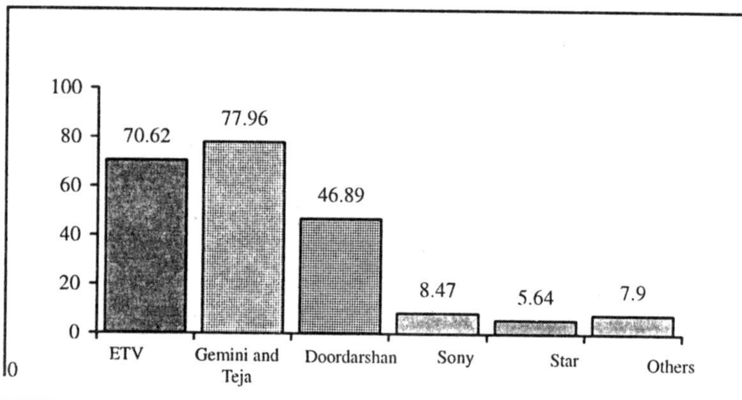

Fig. 7.9 : Different television channels viewed by the various respondents

The figures show that more respondents watch Telugu channels, than others. While over 70 per cent of the respondents watch ETV and Gemini TV, only less than 10 per cent of the respondents watch Sony, Star and other channels.

Section D

Traditional Folk Performances

Traditional folk media are part and parcel of rural life. But their viewership is getting gradually reduced. With regard to attending and seeing the folk performances, 90 respondents (45%) said that they see traditional folk performances. As shown in Table 7.33 more male respondents (49%) than female respondents (41%) and more rural respondents (50.4%) than urban respondents (36%) see the traditional folk performances.

Those who do not see these performances told that due to lack of interest, time and want of performances, they do not attend the traditional folk performances. Those who go to see these performances do so occasionally. For example, on the occasion of Dasara, Sankranti, Ugadi, etc. Folk performances and their viewership is more prevalent in Siddipet area than Sangareddy and Medak. Some respondents told that the developmental messages were also incorporated in the performances that they had seen.

Table 7.33 : Seeing of Traditional folk Performances

Gender	*Urban*	*Rural*	*Total*
Men	13	36	49
Women	14	27	41
Total	27 (36%)	63 (50.4%)	90 (45%)

Using Different Media by the Respondents: A Comparison

Different media are used by different people according to suitability of the media to their needs. While one medium is used by more number of people, another one is used by comparatively less number of people. The media are used by the respondents in the Medak District as shown in Figure 7.10.

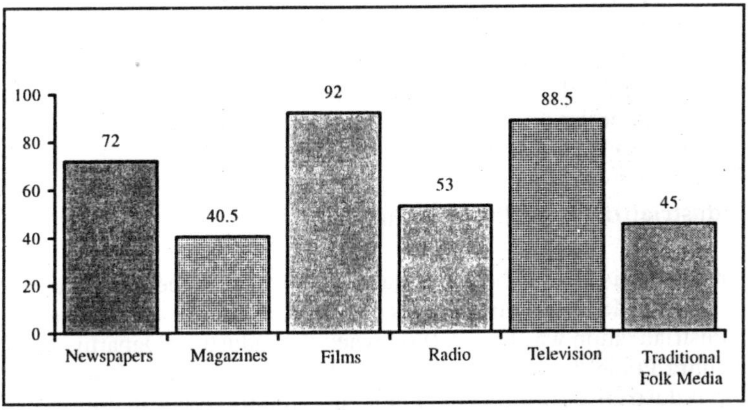

Fig. 7.10 : Using of different media by the respondents : A comparison

The above figure shows that films are seen by more respondents (92%) followed by television (88.5%), newspapers (72%), radio (53%), traditional folk media and magazines (40.5%).

PART-III

ROLE OF COMMUNICATION IN COMBATING THE PATANCHERU INDUSTRIAL POLLUTION IN MEDAK DISTRICT

As discussed in Chapter-3, communication is of crucial importance in promoting the cause of environment. Communication media played their due role in relation to Chipko Movement, dangers to Tajmahal, Silent Valley project etc. Patancheru area of Medak district has witnessed the worst form of pollution. The industrial pollution in this area led to a myriad of dangerous consequences—air pollution, water pollution, soil degradation, loss of live stock, disorder in the reproductive system of women, loss of lives etc. It was wondered whether the industralization of Patancheru was development or anti-development? Two environmental organizations, Citizen Against Pollution (CAP) which is a state level organization and Patancheru Anti-Pollution Committee (PAPC) which was formed specifically with regard to the problems of pollution in Patancheru, organized a strong environmental movement against Patancheru industrial pollution (Reddy, D.P., 1992). It resulted in the setting up of common effluent treatment plant at Patancheru (Akhileshwari, R., 1989) closure of 18 chemical industries (*Mathuku Seema* : 1-3-2001) and in the construction of 18 kms. pipeline to carry the industrial wastes from Patancheru common effluent treatment plant to sewerages treatment plant at Fathenagar (*Vaartha* dated 24.4.2001). With regard to organizing the environmental movement, communication played very important role. Therefore, the role of communication in relation to combating pollution in Patancheru has been analyzed in this part of the present chapter.

Industrialization of Patancheru

Patancheru is one of the industrial areas located in the surroundings of Hyderabad. It is situated in Medak district. The foundation for the industrialization was laid in 1962 when the Industries Department of Andhra Pradesh earmarked an area of 56.26 acres near Patancheru for industrial development. Later on, Andhra Pradesh Industrial Infrastructure Corporation which was formed in 1973 further developed the area in five phases. Production in this industrial area includes chemical, pharmaceutical, paper, paints, cellulose, steel, etc. products.

Pollution of Patancheru

The effluents emitted from the industries gradually polluted Nakkavagu, a stream which was a source of water for drinking and cultivation to the people of 15 villages near by Patancheru. Hundreds of livestock died after consuming the polluted water. Even micro-organisms in the soil died due to the pollution of water. Birds and fish died due to the pollution. A number of fishermen and washermen lost their livelihood as they were out of their traditional occupations due to the water pollution (Reddy, 1992). Farmers lost their crops owing to the deterioration of quality because of the soil pollution. With the contamination of ground water, availability of pure drinking water for villages became a distant dream. Due to the air pollution, water pollution and solid wastes, health condition of nearly 50,000 people has been affected by diseases like epilepsy, skin and throat problems, respiratory diseases, conjunctivitis, glaucoma, cancer, leukemia and paraplegia. Besides, due to the disorders in the women's reproduction system some women even could not give birth to children. The condition of people became miserable. Therefore, a strong environmental movement was organized against the Patancheru industrial pollution.

Movement against Pollution and Role of Communication

A movement itself is a manifestation and communication of feelings in different ways. Communication is a crucial element in any movement and it plays a vital and determining role. During India's freedom movement, Indian press, public meetings etc., played a vital role. Like Indian freedom movement, Patancheru Anti-Pollution Movement was also peaceful. At no time, industries were targeted. In Patancheru Anti-Pollution Movement also various communication channels played informing, educating, supporting, campaigning, mediating and mobilizing role and contributed to the success of the movement.

The way Patancheru Anti-Pollution Movement took place is close to the model of self-reliance. The concern of this model was its focus on basic needs of people, catalyzing individual and group participation. This becomes a challenging arena for making participatory communication a part of the dynamics as an important activity to develop self-reliant individuals who are confident enough to speak up with their own points of view, unite together to define community needs and have a strong voice in setting priorities and action agendas. (Shirly A. White, 1994, p.26). When individuals become self-reliant, their behaviour will change from apathy to action, from dependence to independence, from alienation to involvement, from intolerance to tolerance, from powerlessness to assertiveness, from defensiveness to supportiveness, from manipulation ableness to self-determination, from outer directed to inner directed, from the ignorant to the knowledgeable. A community of self-reliant people will be capable of disposing its own problems, of developing innovative solutions, and of fostering development diverse which is relevant, culturally sensitive and ecologically sound and sustaining.

In a democratic system, political parties, people's representatives and other interest groups are the chief vehicles to carry over the people's problem. In Patancheru, these conventional articulating structures failed to prevent environmental pollution. Initially all main political parties like Congress and Telugu Desam got associated themselves with the activities of the Patancheru Anti-Pollution Committee. Later on they became apathetic to the problem (reasons for which most probably could be interdependent relationship between political parties, politicians and industrialists).

Dr. Krishna Rao, who runs a private hospital in Patancheru area found that pollution was causing skin diseases, respiratory problems, asthma etc., in his patients. As a reaction to this, an agitation was started under the leadership of Dr. Krishna Rao, which gained momentum with the formation of Patencheru Anti-Pollution Committee.

The impact of industrial pollution in Patancheru was (first) noticed by the Citizens Against Pollution (CAP), the first environmental group in Andhra Pradesh, which was formed on 14th April, 1985; following a newspaper report of a gas leak at M/s. Volhro Ltd., a pesticide factory on 9th July, 1986. Thus a newspaper report attracted the attention of the environmentalists and triggered action in them. This is how a newspaper report became a source of information and motivation for starting the movement.

Dr. Krishna Rao, who was already aware of pollution problems became a focal point for CAP in Patancheru. Initially the leadership, (which is non-local) took up an awareness campaign in the villages to explain the link between their recently noticed health problems and the coloured water passing through their village. Even though most of the villagers are illiterates, this educational campaign spurred them into action.

Under the leadership of Dr. Krishna Rao along with farmers and industrial workers a *dharna* was organized before Volhra factory. This action was the first step of organized protests by pollution victims. Then the Patancheru Anti-Pollution Committee was formed in 1986 and in the same year it organized *dharnas* for immediate steps to control pollution. Though initially all main political parties got associated with the movement, they could not continue to support it. The failure of conventional interest articulating structures, provided the scope for the people affected by the industrial pollution to get organized themselves into some action groups. Thus it led to self-reliance.

To keep the issue in the limelight, action groups invited several journalists to visit the areas for a first-hand account of the hardships faced by the villagers (Reddy, 1992). Misery caused by the high rate of pollution to the human population was highly reported in the news media (*Ibid.*) According to Dr. Purushottam Reddy, Convener of the Citizens Against Pollution, their biggest ally in the struggle was the press, especially the Telugu language press. He said "The Press was 100 per cent supportive. It gave a big boost to our struggle and has been in fact nourishing it (Akhileshwari, 1989, p.12).

Seminar is another method of communication that PAPC sought to highlight the environmental problems. The PAPC attempted to strike at a common ground through a seminar held on 24th March, 1989, on "Industrial Development and Environment" which was attended by officials, scientists, some people's representatives in the local bodies and the anti-pollution activists. It wanted this forum to serve as an interface between the activists and the administration. Another channel of communication that was felt necessary by the action groups was to have their representative in the legislature, as the established channels and structures failed to air the grievances of the farmers. In a move previously unknown, they decided to contest the Lok Sabha elections held in mid-1991. Though its candidate lost the election, the voting pattern suggested the wide spread support to the leadership.

Another communication medium that was used in the movement is Burrakatha was a traditional folk form of Andhra Pradesh. A three member Burrakatha team was prepared to propagate about the Patancheru Industrial Pollution. The team gave the performances, narrating the sad story of environmental pollution (Uma Rao, 1992).

The important methods that were used to express the feelings and demands of people are, strikes, hunger strikes, the '*pada yatras*', challo Assembly programmes etc. Since the district administration did not respond in any concrete manner, on 16th August 1986, nearly 500 farmers collectively went to the legislative assembly and demanded that the Patancheru Pollution should be immediately controlled. Again on 26th August 1986, PAPC organized a bandh in Patancheru. Continuous pressure yielded results as district administration served notices to 22 industries. Though initially industries obtained stay orders, finally they got six months time to install individual Effluent Treatment Plants (ETP's) in March 1987 by approaching the High Court.

The deadline fixed by the court ended on 3rd September, 1987 and industries did not seem to have moved an inch towards setting up ETPs. The Collector's assurance failed. The farmers under the leadership of CAP and PAPC announced their second phase of public protest— 'Race Against Pollution' on September 12th, 1987 to focus the attention of authorities on the hazards posed by the industries. About 500 bullock carts blocked the Hyderabad-Bombay National Highway for over 6 hours.

This continuous pressure yielded some results. Compensation was given to the farmers and villagers were provided with the supply water and common effluent treatment plants were setup. Closure of 18 polluting chemical industries was ordered. Dr. Krishn Rao described it as people's victory (*Methuku Seeema*, 2001). The government's decision (APPCB's) to construct 18 kms. pipeline from Patancheru to Fathenagar (*Vaartha*, 2001) is another landmark achievement of the Anti-Pollution Movement towards solving the problem. For further details on the Patancheru Anti-Pollution Movement and the role of communication in it Dr. A. Krishna Rao who has been spearheading the movement from the beginning as interviewed.

Q. You were the first person to identify and establish the relationship between the ill-health in your patients and the Patancheru industrial pollution. Under your leadership *dharnas* were organized and a movement was started against the industrial pollution. How did you create the awareness to mobilize the people?

Ans. In June 1986, there was a leakage of toxic gas from a pesticide unit. Around 20 of us went to the unit and gave a questionnaire to the management, asking various details about the unit. Again in the month of August, there was a flood in which the industrial effluents over flowed along with the water causing a number of health problems. Then we started a relay hunger strike for the redressal of the problem. The hunger strike continued for 10 days. We educated and mobilized the people through street corner meetings, pamphlets and public meetings.

Q. Citizens Against the Pollution (CAP) and Patancheru Anti-Pollution Committee (PAPC) organizations played a dynamic role against the industrial pollution. Is there any difference in the strategies of these organizations?

Ans. There is no difference in the strategies of these organizations. It became a common issue for both the organizations. Therefore, both of us fought together. Gradually a number of others started supporting us. Especially, India Council for Enro Legal Action (ICELA), whose President and General Secretary are the former Chief Justice of India, Justice Bhagawati and the renowned lawyer-*cum*-environmentalist, Justice M.C. Mehta, respectively, save enormously helped our environmental movement. They took up the case in the Supreme Court and fought there on our behalf.

Q. What was the role of different media in Patancheru anti-pollution agitation?

Ans. The movement received good support from the media. In the beginning, press, especially '*Udayam*' gave us a good support. The pollution issue was also covered in *Illustrated Weekly, Frontline, New York Times* etc. The movement also attracted the attention of the press in Germany and New Zeland. Television channels —Doordarshan, ETV, STAR TV, Zee TV, City Cable etc., have telecasted the programmes on Patancheru Pollution. ETV's programme called 'Prathidhwani' started with Patancheru Pollution issue. Radio also extended its support by broadcasting programmes on Patancheru Pollution.

Q. Could you please provide some information about the progress of the movement in 1990s ?

Ans. In 1990s also we continued to organize the agitation through public protests. In 1994 there was a rigorous movement. Therefore, to deter the movement false cases were filed against us. At that time I was also in jail for a short period. We collected 5000 signatures and sent a representation to the Primc Minister.

Q. To what extent do you think the movement has succeeded in getting solved the pollution problems?

Ans. Though our environmental movement could not solve the problems completely, achievements of the movement are remarkable. This movement has sustained itself for a long period of 15 years and even now it is alive. We have been successful in creating awareness among the people. Recently for a public hearing, people belonging to different walks of life, came on their own and said in one voice "No Industries, No Pollution". Besides, government is also giving importance to us. Now we are in the Committees, such as, advisory committees, monitoring committees etc., appointed by the government. Citizens' participation in the implementation of the court orders is a new concept.

Q. What is the present position of pollution in Patancheru?

Ans. It is not totally clean, but now, the situation is better. There is some improvement. Air pollution and water pollution has decreased. Effluent treatment plants, which would not work earlier, are working now. But permanent damage has been done to the genetics in this area. Children are born with deformities.

Various communication channels played a significant role in Patancheru anti-pollution movement, which led to a number of steps that were taken by the government to control the pollution.

Conclusion

On global environmental issues, environmental awareness is confined to, relatively, less number of respondents. Only less than half of the respondents know about ozone hole and acid rains. While over 50 per cent of the respondents know about global warming. Awareness varies depending upon the educational background, gender and the area of living. This awareness is found to be more in educated, urban and male respondents than uneducated, rural and female respondents. It is so because, these sections of the people do have more exposure and access to the sources of information than their counterparts. But with regard to the environmental issues in the country, majority of the respondents have awareness about those issues, many respondents having first hand experience with these problems being a reason for this. At local level also majority of the respondents are facing the environmental problems—water pollution, air pollution, sound pollution, garbage accumulation and stink, deforestation and water scarcity. Majority of the respondents know about the environmental promotion programmes, acts and behaviour—aforestation, clean and green programme, watershed management, reducing the wastage of water and electricity, recycling, joint forest management and conservation of biological diversity.

Majority of the respondents participated in clean and green programme. Tree plantation, watering the trees already planted, and cleaning the surroundings; were the activities taken up by the respondents. It is a positive sign that people are not sitting idle. Instead they are participating in programmes of this kind.

Majority of the respondents are now consuming water supplied by the government. Very few respondents are also consuming water drawn from wells and boring pump. It implies that people have access to safe drinking water. No respondent said that he or she is consuming the water drawn from a tank, canal, pond etc. 74 per cent of the respondents are taking care about the water in one way or other—boiling, filtering, and both boiling and filtering. Here, the inclination towards cleanliness is clearly reflected.

In terms of the stove that is used by the respondents firewood stove is used by more number of respondents (45%) followed by gas stove (37.5%), kerosene stove (5%) and smokeless firewood stove (5%). Certainly gas stove is more comfortable and environment-friendly. In fact, the government of Andhra Pradesh is planning to run even buses with gas as it does not emit smoke. But the financial condition of people is a crucial factor in determining the use of gas stove. Gas stove is used by more respondents in high income groups and firewood stove is used by more respondents in low income groups. In order to encourage the use of gas stove, people are to be financially supported. One positive situation is, the government of Andhra Pradesh is distributing the gas stoves through DWCRA groups.

Though half of the respondents have toilets, remaining half of the respondents do not have toilets. In general more than half of the respondents are not using the toilets. Here, there is a need on the part of the government, NGOs and all those are the agents of development in society to encourage the construction and use of toilets. The present endeavour of the government with regard to construction of toilets as part of the 'clean and green' programme should be fully materialized.

In terms of disposing the house hold wastage; vegetable and fruit peelings as well as paper are disposed in reasonably proper manner. But with regard to the disposing of waste plastic, carry bags and glass, people are still disposing them in an environmentally unfriendly manner. A good number of respondents are composting these materials and dumping them in the municipality bins though these are not compostable.

With regard to the awareness on various environmental issues in the country first hand experience contributed for the environmental awareness in case of more respondents, followed by television, newspapers, books, radio, magazines, friends, family members and others. On global issues, television and books have been mentioned as main sources by majority of the respondents followed by newspapers, radio, magazines, teachers, friends and family members. Thus first hand experience, television, newspapers, books, radio and magazines, friends, teachers and family members are the sources of information in the order of priority. Generally NGOs are considered as the agents of development. Unfortunately, even the existence of any NGO was hardly felt in the present study.

Among the mass media used by the respondents, films are seen by more respondents (92%) followed by television (88.5%), newspapers (72%), radio (53%), traditional folk media (45%), and magazines (40.5%). Most of the literates are reading the newspapers. The using of radio got reduced, mainly due to the influence of television. TV has emerged as a dominant medium. Traditional folk media are confined to certain occasions, such as, festivals or visits of the government officials. Comparatively, magazines are read by less number of the respondents. Films being the source of entertainment are seen by most of the respondents. Thus each medium has got its own potentialities as well as the limitations. Taking this aspect into consideration, each of these media can be used in a suitable manner, for the promotion of sustainable development.

Patancheru industrial pollution being the worst form of pollution, a strong environmental movement was organized against the pollution. In strengthening the movement and in making the movement successful, various communication channels—Press, T.V., Radio, street corner meetings, public meetings and seminars have played a significant role. Thus, communication is of crucial importance in achieving the various goals of sustainable development. Various communication channels were highly supportive in Patancheru Anti-Pollution Movement. The agitation, which emanated from the people was strengthened and encouraged by communication, which yielded results.

The findings reveal that it is communication that created awareness about the global environmental issues. Respondents came to know about the global environmental issues through books, television, newspapers, radio and magazines in that order of priority. The findings also reveal that though these communication media created awareness, the role played by the media in creating awareness is inadequate as majority of the respondents, still do not have awareness about these issues. Again with regard to the specific dimensions of the problems, such as, affects of the ozone hole or reasons for the ozone hole, awareness is found to be low. It indicates that there is a need to take up a rigorous campaign by the media about these issues, their effects and the solutions to overcome these problems. Though media have contributed for the awareness on various environmental issues of significance in India, more respondents came to know about the issues through first hand experience. It is an indication of the gravity of these issues. Therefore, various communication media have a responsible role to play in educating and sensitizing the people about various dimensions of these problems on one hand and in focusing the attention of the government towards solving these problems on other hand.

Though communication is of crucial importance in promoting the environment-friendly lifestyle, it will be effective only when it is supported by other factors, such as, financial condition of the people, some basic amenities like municipality bin in the surroundings, etc. For instance, unless the people have the conducive financial condition, they cannot go in for the construction and use of toilets. On the other hand communication is a crucial and potential component in changing the attitudes of the people. For instance, even if government prohibits the using of carry bags, such prohibition will not be effective unless people realize the adverse effects of carry bags. In the present study also it has been found that many respondents are disposing of the carry bags in an environmentally unfriendly manner. Therefore, communication media have a catalistic role to play in influencing the decisions of the government on one hand and in sensitizing the people and contributing for the social acceptance of the environment-friendly behaviour on other hand. So also with regard to the disposing of other wastages. Thus, communication itself has its own limitations. It should be accompanied by the other supportive elements to promote the environment-friendly and sustainable lifestyle.

Most of the respondents have the required awareness about need for family planning. Media have contributed significantly in creating this awareness. But out of hundred respondents who have children, 49 respondents have more than two children. That means, nearly half of them have adopted the family planning methods late. Therefore, the role of media should not be confined merely to creating awareness. Various channels of communication should further contribute in sensitizing the people and promoting one or two children family pattern through constant campaigning.

All media should accept the sustainable development as a common goal. Since television has penetrated even into the villages and emerged as a dominant medium, its potentialities should be utilized for propagating and educating about various issues of sustainable development. Similarly, films, newspapers, radio, magazines, traditional folk media etc., have specific advantages in disseminating specific kind of messages or ideas. All such advantages should be utilized and used in a suitable manner.

REFERENCES

Akhileshwari, R.(1989), "Environment and the Media", *Vidura,* May-June, p.12.

Methukuseema (2001), "Kalushyam Vedajalluthunna 18 Rasayana Parisramala Musivethaku Utharvulu" (Closure of 18 polluting chemical industries ordered) News Item – dated 1.3.2001, p. 4.

Reddy, D.N., (1992) Public Policy for Environmental Protection: A Study of its Implementation in an Industrial Area, M.Phil. Dissertation, Department of Political Science, University of Hyderabad, pp.133.

Rao, B.V.S. *et al* (1990). *Andhra Pradesh Paryavarana Paristhithi : Praja Nivedika* (Status of Andhra Pradesh Environment : A Citizens' Report), p.139.

White, Shirly A. (1994), "The Concept of Participation: Transforming Rhetoric to Reality" in Shirly A. White *et al* (eds.) *Participatory Communication: Working for Change and Development,* Sage, New Delhi, pp. 25-26.

Uma Rao, Sunil (1992), Documentary film on Patancheru Industrial Pollution, Submitted to University of Hyderabad.

Vaartha (2001) "Kalushya Korala Nundi Patancheru Thwaraloo Vimukthi" (very soon Patancheru will be free from pollution) (a news item), Hyderabad edition, April 24, p.12.

Vaartha (2001), Mukhyamantri Janmadina Vedukalu (Chief Minister's Birthday Celebrations) News Item, 21 April, Hyderabad.

8 Summary, Conclusion and Recommendations

Last five decades have witnessed a shift in the meaning and focus of development, as also a remarkable progress in communication. Satellite communication technologies have brought about a revolution in the communication systems. Thus, the concern for development has broadened into sustainable development and, the channels of communication and their potentialities have increased significantly. Therefore, in sustainable development, not only big media, even small media, interpersonal communication channels and group communication channels, traditional folk media and NGOs have specific roles to play in specific conditions.

There is no medicine to AIDS, prevention is a solution to keep AIDS at bay. Informed and conscious citizens can take precautions to prevent the disease. Similarly, informed and conscious citizens can take steps to avert the danger to the environment and can take steps to promote safety to environment. Therefore, communication can play an important role in sustainable development by creating awareness, educating the people, translating the technical knowledge into people's language, conscientizing the people, facilitating people's expressions and interaction at grassroots level.

In 1950s and 60s, development was considered to be basically transformation of the Third World countries so as to resemble the already developed countries like US, UK, etc. through industrialization, urbanization and modernization. Communication was considered to be a missing link in the development chain, while mass media were thought to be magic multipliers that blow the winds of modernity into the Third World countries to replace the traditional elements in these societies. Increase in the agricultural production being a prerequisite for industrialization, to modernize agriculture and industry, the modernization of human resources was thought to be more important. Therefore, in order to modernize the human resources in the third world countries, education and mass media were given utmost importance.

During this period, the communication model that was followed was the bullet media or hypodermic needle model with an optimism that mass media would at a time reach a large number of people and they would change the attitudes and behaviour of people in the third world countries. Thus, the communication flow was expert-oriented, top down, authoritative and hortatory in nature.

In 1970s, realization dawned that the development as well as communication models that were followed in 1950s and 60s could not work in developing the underdeveloped world. Though many third world countries followed the model of dominant paradigm, the gap between the developed and underdeveloped countries as well as between rich and poor within the underdeveloped countries did not decrease. Rather, it widened. Mass media could not blow the winds of modernity into the third world traditional societies and they could not bring about uniform and powerful effects on the peoples of these countries as assumed. Besides, by giving more importance to industrialization, urbanization and modernization, more pressure was put on the natural resources. The over-exploitation of natural resources resulted in the environmental degradation in various ways—pollution of atmosphere, deforestation, soil degradation, loss of bio-diversity, etc. Therefore, the global community reacted and responded to the environmental degradation. The result is the emergence of the concept of sustainable development.

Colonization, which, according to some scholars, made some countries developed and some countries underdeveloped, was overlooked in this approach. Besides, though bullet media theory was discarded even in the West, where mass societies existed, this communication model was applied for the development of the third world countries, which were predominantly traditional societies and remained at far distance from the mass societies. The concept of sustainable development assumed significance in different stages. It was first introduced by the IUCN and subsequently, firmly established by the Brundtland Commission (WCED) (1987). It was further strengthened by the Earth Summit, 1992.

Sustainable development is a broader concept compared to the earlier concepts and trends of development. It is intended not merely for the third world countries, but it is for the entire globe into a distant future. It is a holistic approach. It encompasses all activities of human beings and it calls for the participation of people at individual, local, national and global levels. It is broader and different from the earlier trends of development as the earlier concepts and theories of development were concerned with only the development of the third world countries. The aim was to make these countries grow on par with already developed countries such as UK, USA, etc. Development was quantified and measured through the GNP and per capita income. But the aim of the sustainable development is not confined to merely the Third World countries. It emerged out of the concern shown in international conferences and commissions in which both developed and underdeveloped countries have been the partners and all have the common responsibility to fulfill the various objectives. Besides, it is aimed at helping not only for the present generations, but also the future generations.

As the concept of sustainable development is broader and different from the earlier trends of development, so also is the role of communication in sustainable development. The role of communication in sustainable development is much wider compared to the role of communication in earlier development (or dominant paradigm's approach of development).

Sustainable development has multiple implications for communication. As it is the development that aims at meeting the needs and aspirations of the present generations without compromising the ability of future generations to meet their own needs; eradication of poverty from the face of the earth is an indispensable requirement to enable the present generations to meet their needs and aspirations. Millions of people are starving and dying due to the diseases caused by hunger, not because of food grains not being available. Though food grains are available in more than the required quantity, the people are not in a position to afford to have the food grains owing to their poverty.

Communication in general and various media of communication in particular have a responsible role to play in eradicating poverty. It is through creating awareness among the target groups about the various poverty alleviation programmes meant for them, helping and encouraging their self-development efforts and by drawing the attention of the government towards the problems of poverty. For example, the news item about the hunger deaths of handloom weavers at Sircilla of Karimnagar district, Andhra Pradesh, was brought out by the major newspapers in the state. It not only led to the debate in various circles, it also attracted the attention of the Prime Minister* and resulted in the Prime Minister showing concern for hunger deaths in Sircilla (*Hindu,* 11-4-2001). In addition, the possession of large areas of land by a few deprived the rights of the millions of people from meeting their basic needs. Therefore, various media of communication have to accept and campaign for the land reforms to facilitate the equitable distribution of the land and its efficient management.

Sustainable development calls for a change in the quality of growth, to make it less material and energy-intensive and more equitable in its impact. Communication media, especially various intellectual fora of communication have a potential role in achieving this objective.

Environmental protection is another broad area where communication has a vital role to play. The quality and quantity of production depends upon the quality of the environment. Environmental protection is inevitable for the survival and welfare of the present as well as the future generations. Conservation of biological diversity, sustainable use of natural resources, using the renewable sources of energy, prevention and control of pollution, deforestation, desertification and soil erosion, waste management, and using appropriate technologies are some dimensions of the environmental protection. With regard to all these aspects, awareness among the people and their participation is inevitable. It is the communication, which has got potentiality to create awareness and consciousness and make people to work towards the fulfilment of these goals.

Population control and stabilization is another important concern of sustainable development, where communication is of crucial importance in creating awareness about the importance of family planning, and the different temporary as well as permanent family planning methods. Human rights, gender equality, social welfare and women's upliftment and promoting the peaceful and harmonious relationship among individuals, communities and nations being other important concerns of sustainable development, communication has a crusading role to play with regard to these aspects by informing, educating and creating a common understanding among people.

---

* *The Hindu* (2001), "Vajpayee to call for report on plight of Sircilla Weavers" (news item), 11-4-2001, Hyderabad, p. 4.

Achieving the intra-generational equity and inter-generational equity being the broad goals of sustainable development, in fact, there is a need to mould a 'lifestyle' that is productive, equitable and harmonious with Nature, all over the world. Communication has a crucial role in moulding such a lifestyle, which takes care of the environment from purchasing, consuming to campaigning and crusading for conservation of environment.

Sustainable development being a holistic approach calling for the participation of people—individuals, communities and organizations at individual, local, regional, national and global levels, in facilitating the participation of people, communication is of crucial importance. Communication in general and various communication channels in particular have a vital role to play in achieving the goals of sustainable development—poverty eradication, environmental protection, population control, etc. by creating awareness among people, educating the people and by conscientizing the people so as to enable them to think globally and act locally with regard to various aspects of these goals. Translating the technical knowledge into people's language, facilitating people's expressions and interaction at grassroots level, changing the attitudes and behaviour of the people in favour of promoting sustainable development, supporting the organizations and movements for the environmental protection, focusing the attention of the government on various issues, supporting the developmental projects and activities and creating the consensus among the global countries are some of the ways in which communication has a role to play in sustainable development.

Lifestyle is a crucial element in sustainable development. One's lifestyle can contribute for the promotion or deterioration of the environment. Similarly, it can be equitable or of exploitative nature and it can be productive or counter-productive. Sustainable development calls for a lifestyle that is productive, equitable and environment-friendly. Various communication channels have a potential role to play in moulding such lifestyle throughout the globe.

Newspapers, magazines and journals being the conventional channels of communication to the large number of people and scholars respectively and the press being the fourth estate, a channel of communication between people and government, it has a vital role to play in sustainable development by popularizing various issues, creating awareness on these issues among people, and through constructive criticism and suggestions. The Press played a crusading role with regard to the hazards of pollution to Taj Mahal, Bhopal gas tragedy, Silent Valley Project, etc.

Television as a medium of mass communication has got immense potentialities to work for sustainable development. It has emerged as a dominant medium presenting the programmes from local level to global levels. Television being an informative, educational and entertainment medium, through all these means, it can contribute in moulding a sustainable lifestyle. VCRs and VCD players are highly useful tools to educate people about various environment and developmental programmes. Video conferencing is another means to accentuate the sustainable development. It facilitates avoiding delay and helps the speedy implementation of various developmental programmes.

Radio being the cheap and simple medium, it is an important means of reaching the people in rural areas. Though its listenership is getting reduced with the rapid expansion of television, still the radio is a source of informatio , education and entertainment to a large number of people. Therefore, these potentialities of radio are utilized for sensitizing the people through information, education and entertainment on various aspects of sustainable development.

A cinema hall is the place where different sections of people sit together and view the film. It is a place to educate even illiterates and unorganized people about various facets of environmental protection, poverty alleviation programmes, family planning, etc. through newsreels and short films. By incorporating the stories and characters, which function as role models to promote the sustainable lifestyle, feature films can influence a large number of people and thus they can contribute for the promotion of sustainable development.

Along with these mass media, traditional folk media, telematics, posters, calendars, religious organizations, literature, educational organizations and NGOs as means of communication are of crucial importance in educating and sensitizing the people so as to adopt a sustainable lifestyle in their day-to-day activities.

Though the concept of sustainable development is relatively a new one, various policies and programmes towards the fulfilment of its various goals were initiated by the Indian Government even before the emergence of this concept. As far back as in 1938, Jawaharlal Nehru's National Planning Committee stated that getting rid of appalling poverty and providing people with food, clothing, housing and every other essential requirement of human existence was India's primary goal. In the post-Independent India, programmes like Community Development Programme (1952), the Intensive Agricultural District Programme (1960-61), the Intensive Agriculture Area Programme (1964) and High-Yielding Varieties Programme (1966-67) were introduced in 1950s and 60s in this direction.

Realization in the late sixties that any indirect policy measure would not be of much help to the rural poor, led to the introduction of the direct beneficiary-oriented programmes. Small Farmers Development Agency (1969), Food for Work Programme (1977), National Rural Employment Programme (1980), Rural Landless Employment Guarantee Programme (1983), Integrated Rural Development Programme (1978-79), Swarna Jayanti Gram Swarojgar Yojana (1999-2000) are the directly beneficiary-oriented poverty alleviation programmes, introduced by the Government of India in this direction. Besides, land being the source of income and wealth for poverty eradication, land reforms were also introduced at different stages. Though all these programmes were introduced for the eradication of poverty, owing to a number of loopholes in the implementation, the benefits from these schemes trickled down to the beneficiaries to a very limited extent. Lack of awareness among the target beneficiaries about the programmes, meant for them, is found to be one of the important reasons for the failure of these schemes. For instance, with regard to the impact studies of Small Farmers' Development Agency (SFDA), Ram Reddy and Haragopal (1985) noted thus: "Most of these studies maintain that the benefits did not percolate to the target groups. Ineffectiveness of the agency is traced to lack of awareness about the agency on the part of the target groups to take government loans, misutilization of the loan amount and cornering of the benefits by richer sections".

India became the first country to adopt an official policy to reduce population growth by promoting family planning. In all the five year plans, concern has been shown for the population growth and family planning. A centre for testing and developing contraceptives was established in Bombay during the First Five Year Plan, and 1649 family planning centres were opened during the Second Five Year Plan. In addition to that, research in the fields of demography, reproduction physiology, motivation and communication was undertaken. The Third Plan aimed at the stabilization of the population growth. The Fourth Five Year Plan targeted the reduction of crude birth rate from 32 per thousand. During the Fifth Plan, an integrated approach, i.e. integrating family planning with health, maternity, child healthcare and nutrition services at all levels was adopted. During the emergency period, coercive methods were adopted for family planning. But during 1977-80, the Janata Government gave up coercive methods and adopted persuasive methods. In the subsequent five year plans also, concern has been clearly shown towards family planning. In the new population policy declared in February 2000, the need for population control to meet the goals of sustainable development was clearly stated. In all the plans, communication was recognized as an important element that can contribute for the success of the family planning programme by changing the attitudes of the people in favour of family planning.

Environmental protection being another broad goal of sustainable development, the Government of India initiated certain policies and programmes for the protection of environment. Though government took steps to protect the environment even before Independence, as in many other countries, environmental planning took formal shape in India as a consequence of the Stockholm Conference held in 1972.

Legislation is one of the methods through which government sought to protect the environment. In the pre-Independent India, Acts such as the Orient Gas Company Act, 1857, the Northern India Canal and Drainage Act, 1873, the Indian Forest Act, 1927, etc. were introduced to protect the environment. In the post-independent India, Acts like Wildlife Protection Act, 1972, the Water Prevention and Control of Pollution Act, 1974, the Forest (Conservation) Act, 1980, the Air (Prevention and Control of Pollution) Act, 1981, Environment (Protection) Act, 1986, etc. have been enacted to protect the environment. But unfortunately, these Acts were confined to the statute books only. Even after these Acts were enacted, pollution increased unabatedly in areas like Patancheru and Bollaram in Andhra Pradesh.

Another way the government sought to protect the environment was by setting up the Pollution Control Boards. Though initially the Central and State Pollution Control Boards were established to advise the central and state governments respectively, after the amendment to the Water (Prevention and Control of Pollution) Act, 1974 in 1988, the boards have been given powers to close or stop the supply of water and electricity to the offending establishments. Besides, powers were also given to give clearance to the coming up a new establishments and to receive the criminal complaints. But as Narasimha Reddy (1992) observed, in case of the deterioration of the environment in Medak District, the pollution control boards could not react and take action promptly. It took a long time for them to find solutions to the problem. People could be mobilized because wide circulation of news through media and public meetings.

The setting up of the Department of Environment for planning, promotion and coordination of environment in 1980 is a landmark event. Through an integrated department of environment, forests and wildlife, which was created in 1985, the government is now seeking to promote the protection of environment. The government also set up the Department of Non-Conventional Energy Sources, National Wastelands Development Board, National Parks and Sanctuaries, Special Projects for Endangered Species, etc., for ensuring the protection and promotion of the environment.

As people's participation is important for the protection of environment to provide environmental education, the Centre for Environmental Education (CEE) was established in Ahmedabad. It has countrywide network. In addition, by incorporating the environmental education in school syllabus, also an attempt is being made to educate the children about various aspects of the sustainable development. Indeed, it is a systematic approach to create environmental awareness. It has been observed during the survey that the high school students have more environmental awareness, because they are taught in the school about this aspect. Thus, in various ways, government is endeavouring to protect and promote the environment. The awareness can be brought about only through communication. It is communication that can conscientize the people and make them to act, within their purview.

Medak District being one of the backward districts in the state, various poverty alleviation programmes such as IRDP, DWCRA, TRYSEM, SGSY have been implemented in the district for poverty eradication. Though communication alone cannot make a programme succed, it is found to be of crucial importance in availing and proper utilization of the poverty alleviation programmes. In Uttarapalli and Pathuru of Medak District, while all the respondents who are the beneficiaries of the scheme are aware of the scheme, 36 per cent of the non-beneficiaries do not have the awareness about the scheme. More than half of the non-beneficiaries said that they could not avail of the scheme due to the lack of information and motivation. While for those who have availed themselves of the scheme government officials are the source of information, for the majority friends have been the sources of information about the scheme. It reveals that while the beneficiaries received information directly from the government personnel, non-beneficiaries received the information about DWCRA through friends. The close communication between the beneficiaries and government personnel, and the communication gap between the non-beneficiaries and government personnel has understandably determined the availing or not availing of the scheme.

Where there is more awareness and initiative, there the scheme is going on well. In Uttarapalli where women themselves discussed, decided and formed the DWCRA groups, the scheme is going on well. In Pathuru, where majority of them were 'motivated'. In this village some other groups are not functioning well.

Since every month women are saving some little amount of the money, 54 per cent of the respondents feel that there is a little improvement in their financial condition. But 80 per cent of the respondents admitted that there is no improvement in their quality of life even after joining DWCRA. It is evident that the amount saved by the women is too little to improve the quality of life. Nevertheless, under the DWCRA scheme, women in the villages have been well-organized in the form of groups. According to some women of Uttarapalli, though there is no remarkable improvement in their financial condition or the quality of life, their outlook has changed. Now, they are coming out from their houses, discussing various issues and thus, they are sharing their views with others. They are now receiving education and many of them have become literate women.

With regard to the IRDP asset-giving scheme, while all the beneficiaries in Uttarapalli and Pathuru are obviously aware of the scheme, 25 per cent of the non-beneficiary respondents do not have awareness about the scheme. Unlike in case of DWCRA, to a majority of the beneficiaries as well as non-beneficiaries of IRDP in these villages, government personnel have been the source of information. Interestingly, 73 per cent of non-beneficiaries also tried for the asset-giving scheme. But they could not get through. Here, in case of these respondents, awareness is not a problem. But opportunities are very limited.

As in case of DWCRA, among IRDP beneficiaries also, where there is more awareness, there the scheme has been utilized successfully. In Pathuru, more initiative was shown on the part of the beneficiaries. Whereas, in Uttarapalli, they were 'motivated'. In terms of the improvement in financial condition and quality of life, such improvement has taken place in case of the respondents in Pathuru, there is no improvement at all in the financial condition or quality of life of the IRDP beneficiaries in Uttarapalli. But there is some contrast between the beneficiaries of Pathuru and Uttarapalli. While the beneficiaries in Pathuru are already rich, the beneficiaries in Uttarapalli are by and large poor. The nature of the assets also could be a factor in the utilization or non-utilization. While sheep units, which were given in Uttarapalli, are easily disposable, the submersible bores and pump sets, given in Pathuru, are not easily disposable. Thus, though communication alone cannot make a scheme successful, but it is of crucial importance in proper utilization of various poverty alleviation schemes.

Environmental awareness among people varies depending upon whether the problem is a local, national or global one. On issues like global environmental issues—Ozone hole, acid rain, global warming —less number of people have awareness. While over 50 per cent of the respondents are aware of the global warming, only over 35 per cent of the respondents are aware of the ozone hole and acid rain. The respondents who have awareness about these issues are relatively more educated, urbanite and male respondents compared to the less-educated, rural and female respondents. Interestingly, this awareness is found to be more among the respondents those who have received or receiving the high school education than those who have received the college level education. It is because these aspects are taught now at the high school level. Thus, those who have more exposure and access to the sources of information have more awareness than their counterparts.

Majority of the respondents have awareness about various environmental issues of significance in India like air pollution, water pollution, soil degradation, sound pollution, etc. Many respondents had first hand experience with these problems. These problems were observed by the respondents even in their localities. In addition to the awareness created by the mass media and books about various environmental issues of significance in the country, the first hand experience of the people with these problems in their localities has contributed to a great extent for the awareness among respondents. Patancheru area of Medak District is a glaring example for water pollution, air pollution, soil degradation, etc. Therefore, whoever visits Patancheru is likely to become aware of air pollution, water pollution, soil degradation, etc.

Among the local environmental problems mentioned by the

respondents, garbage accumulation and stinking has occupied the top position followed by water scarcity, water pollution, air pollution, deforestation and sound pollution. These problems affect human life everyday. Therefore, these problems cannot be neglected any longer and authorities concerned should immediately take steps to combat these problems.

Majority of the respondents have awareness about the various environmental promotion programmes and acts—clean and green, aforestation, minimizing the wastage of water and electricity, watershed management, joint forest management and the conservation of biological diversity. This awareness, they acquired, not necessarily for environmental consideration, but directly to get benefited from such acts, as minimizing the waste of electricity, growing trees in their compounds, checkdams (watersheds), etc.

Family planning is known to most of the respondents. Majority of the respondents have awareness about vasectomy, tubectomy, oral pills, condoms, copper-T and loop. But comparatively, less number of respondents are aware of copper-T and loop. Among those who are married and have children, majority of the respondents have adopted the family planning method. They have undergone either tubectomy or vasectomy operations. Among those who have children, while 50 per cent of the respondents have one or two children, remaining 50 per cent of the respondents have more than two children. This pattern reveals that though half of the respondents are aware about the family planning, they are late in adopting it. With regard to the gender preference, there is a bent towards the male. Therefore, the situation calls for a change in the attitudes of people with regard to family planning and the gender preference.

Pertaining to the lifestyle of the people, majority of the people have participated in clean and green, an environmental promotion programme. This gives an optimistic picture. Though respondents mentioned the problem of water scarcity in their locality, all the respondents have access to safe drinking water and majority of the respondents are purifying the water by filtering, while a few respondents are boiling it also. It reveals that the respondents have consciousness about consuming the clean and safe drinking water.

Among the sources of cooking, more respondents are using the firewood stove, followed by gas stove, kerosene stove and the smokeless firewood stove (improved *chullah*). While the gas stove is used by more respondents in urban areas, the firewood stove is used by more respondents in rural areas. Besides, while the using of gas stove is prevalent in high income groups, firewood stove is prevalent among the respondents of low income groups. Here, financial condition of the respondents is a determining factor with regard to the type of the stove the respondents use.

Half of the respondents have toilets. Similar to the use of gas stove, more respondents in high-income groups and living in urban areas have toilets compared their counterparts. With regard to the possession and use of the toilet also, the place of living and the financial status of the respondents are the determining factors. It shows that with regard to the using of gas stove and toilets, unless the people are financially empowered, using of these items become highly difficult.

The household waste is disposed of in both environment-friendly manner as well environmentally unfriendly manner. Though it may not be always done deliberately, respondents are contributing for the promotion of environment by composting the vegetable and fruit peelings and by selling the glass, plastic and paper materials. But composting of carry bags, glass and plastic is not a desirable method of disposing the household waste from the point of view of the environmental protection. Though by dumping these materials in the municipality bin, cleanliness can be maintained, people should look beyond that to contribute for sustainable development through reusing and recycling these materials.

Respondents have come to know about various environmental issues through different sources. While on global environmental issues, television, books and newspapers have been the main sources of information, on various environmental issues in India and in local areas, first hand experience, television, newspapers and radio have been the main sources of information. Television being a medium that is used by most of the respondents, it has served as a source of information to more number of respondents, followed by newspapers, books, radio, magazines, teachers, friends and family members. Here, there is a slight variation compared to the findings of Graham Chapman, *et al.* According to the environmental awareness is more among those who read English newspapers. Here also, though newspapers are the sources of information to a good number of people, it is the television that has occupied the first position. Newspapers are next only to the television in giving environmental information to the respondents. Radio and magazines also have been mentioned as sources of information on environment by a limited number of respondents. Compared to television and newspapers, radio and magazines have served as sources of information to less number of respondents. Teachers, friends and family members have served as sources of information to nearly 13 per cent of the respondents. Thus, it is clear that mass media and books are serving as main sources of information to respondents on environment. Though there are over 25 NGOs in Medak District, their existence was hardly felt in the study areas of Medak District.

Among the media used by the respondents, films occupy the first position followed by television, newspapers, radio, traditional folk media and magazines. Films being the primary source of entertainment to the people, most of the people go to the films whether in cinema halls or on television, people are used to watching movies. Therefore, films have got immense potentialities to play a vital role in moulding the lifestyle that is imperative for sustainable development through stories and characters, which can be the role models to the people. Television has emerged as a dominant medium. It is viewed by all sections of the people. Even those who do not have television are also watching television. However, 69 per cent of the respondents have their own television sets. Besides, most of the respondents who own television sets also have the cable connection. TV was mentioned as one of the main sources of information on environment by the respondents. So, TV, which has a number of channels and a variety of programmes is of vital importance in promoting the sustainable development.

Most of the literate people, including the children, read newspapers. Out of 72 per cent of the respondents, who read newspapers, 56 per cent of the respondents read newspapers daily. While majority of the respondents read Telugu newspapers—*Eenadu, Vaartha* and *Andhra Bhoomi*—few respondents read English and Urdu newspapers—*The Hindu*, *Deccan Chronicle* (English) and *Siasat* (Urdu). Newspapers being the source of information to 72 per cent of the respondents, they have a crucial role to play in achieving the goals of sustainable development. Already it has been mentioned as one of the main sources of information on various environmental issues. Newspapers can play a crusading role in promoting the sustainable development by adopting the news values from the viewpoint of sustainable development.

Compared to films, television and newspapers, radio listening is found to be low. Listening to radio has decreased in recent times. Quite a few respondents said that they are not listening to radio, because television is fulfilling their needs. It implies that the expansion of the television has affected radio listening significantly. Nevertheless, 58 per cent of the people in rural areas are listening to the radio. Among the mass media sources on environment, radio also has been mentioned as a source of information by a good number of the respondents. Therefore, radio should be used more effectively to promote the sustainable development by giving priority to various dimensions of sustainable development in different radio programmes—news, commentaries, plays, songs, discussions, etc.

Traditional folk media are attended by 45 per cent of the respondents. But the respondents are attending to these media only occasionally. With regard to the environmental awareness or awareness about the poverty alleviation programmes, the role of traditional folk media as sources of information is insignificant. Yet, since a considerable number of respondents 45 per cent said that they are interested in traditional folk media, the potentialities of the traditional folk media cannot be underestimated/undermined. Their advantages can be harnessed to the fullest extent to disseminate messages about sustainable development and in moulding the sustainable lifestyle.

Compared to newspaper readership, magazine readership is very low. While 72 per cent of the respondents read the newspapers, only 40 per cent of the respondents read the magazines. Majority of the respondents read Telugu language magazines—*Swathi, Andhra Bhoomi, Andhra Jyoti, India Today, Suprabhátam, Eenadu, Sunday Magazine*, etc. Though magazines too have been mentioned as a source of information on the environmental issues by the respondents, their number is less. Yet, they are serving as one of the sources of information on environment. Magazines serve as the source of information and entertainment. Especially, magazines like *Swathi, Andhra Bhoomi* are more of entertainment-oriented than giving information. Therefore, alongwith the informative as well as entertainment items of these magazines, the element of imparting knowledge about the environment and development can be incorporated to prepare the people to follow the sustainable lifestyle in their personal lives.

In the wake of the analytical and empirical research that has been carried out, a communication strategy for the sustainable development has been intended to be formulated as follows:

Communication Strategy for Sustainable Development

While formulating a communication strategy for sustainable development, we need to take into consideration both the scope of sustainable development and the potentialities of communication in general and various communication channels in particular. As discussed in the earlier chapters, the scope of sustainable development is very broad. It is not merely meant for the third world countries, but for the entire globe and into the distant future. It calls for the participation of people at different levels—individual, community, local, regional, national and international. Its goals range from poverty alleviation to evolution of sustainable lifestyle, which is productive, equitable and environment-friendly. Its concern is establishing commonness among the global people.

On the other hand, the tremendous progress that has taken place in the field of communication offers us opportunities to communicate at any range—individual, local to global level. Communication is an essential and potential element in fulfilling the task of sustainable development, as it requires the people to 'think globally and act locally'. In promoting such global thinking and local actions, various communication channels are of crucial importance. Besides, for moulding the 'sustainable lifestyle' throughout the globe, media are the potential agents.

While planning for communication strategy for sustainable development, we need to take into consideration the aspects of diversity. As people, problems, programmes and purposes of communication are different, we need to use different types and various channels of communication so as to suit to communicate with different types of people in different situations, different types of messages and for different purposes; sustainable development being the overall goal. Thus, in relation to sustainable development, multimedia communication approach is the suitable approach. Different mass media, traditional folk media, Internet, group communication channels, educational institutions, literature, etc. have to be used systematically to disseminate information and to conscientize the people on specific aspects of sustainable development, taking into consideration the relevance and suitability of messages and media, respectively, to the audience as follows:

Mass Media

Mass media have the potentiality of reaching a large number of people at a time. They have become inseparable part of our lives. Directly or indirectly, our world view is shaped by them. We use one media or the other or all for one purpose or other. Even among mass media, one medium is not completely alternative to another medium. Every medium has got its own advantages and limitations. We need to use these media taking into consideration their suitability to the message to be disseminated and audience to be reached.

As newspapers and magazines are very important sources of information to the public, they have a significant role to play in fulfilling the goals of sustainable development by informing, educating, conscientizing and sensitizing the public relating to various aspects of sustainable development. While applying the news values, selecting the angle and focus, journalists should see the events from the perspective of environment and development. Cartoons and photos being attractive centres, issues such as environment and poverty should be highlighted in photos and cartoons. Like sports news and business news sections, environment and development should form a regular feature in newspapers and magazines. Apart from conscientizing and sensitizing the public and supporting the popular movements, newspapers and magazines should bring to the notice of government various issues and wherever necessary, they should offer constructive criticism and offer productive suggestions.

Journals being the channels of communication, carrying the research results and advancements in various disciplines, journals of various disciplines are of crucial importance in strengthening and promoting the cause of sustainable development. They enlighten and enrich the intellectuals, who, in turn, play an important role in society. The issues relating to sustainable development should not be confined to the specialized journals and magazines like *Down to Earth* or *Paryavarana Bharati*, but other general magazines and journals need to present various items, which are within their purview from the angle of sustainable development. For example, campaigning against dowry, contributing for the gender equality, human rights, etc. also lead to the fulfillment of some goals of sustainable development. Therefore, magazines like *Swathi* and *Andhra Bhoomi* need to give priority to stories, poems, serials, jokes, etc., which promote equitable and environment-friendly lifestyle.

Television

Television has emerged as a dominant medium. It has penetrated into the rural areas with a number of channels. As sustainable development calls for the involvement of people at individual, regional, national and global levels, so is the television as a medium of communication capable of disseminating messages at all these levels. The informative, entertainment and educative potentialities of television need to be systematically utilized in conscientizing the people and for promoting sustainable lifestyle. For this, care should be taken to disseminate the messages of relevance to audiences.

In television news also, while applying news values, in selecting the angle and focus, newsmen should give priority to environment and development. Like sports news and business news, environment and developmental news should become an integral part of each news bulletin. Various messages, aiming at creating awareness and moulding attitudes and lifestyles can be given to people through public service advertisements or quickies and spots in television. For example, the advertisement showing smoke with the slogan Pollution... If we don't kill it, it will kill us in Doordarshan and the advertisement Clean Air is Your Right to live in Sony TV have such appeal.

Majority of the respondents in the present study said they watch entertainment programmes like serials, films, etc. The entertainment potentiality of the television need to be utilized to change the attitudes and outlook of the people through the programmes such as serials, which have pro-development themes, stories and characters. Like *Hum Log*, which is a pro-development serial, there is a need to give priority to edu-tainment in the serial. Especially, in campaigning for the equal status for women and girl children, human rights, etc., the entertainment programmes like serials are the suitable means. Television can be used to educate people through the programmes of educative nature, such as *Living on the Edge, Turning Point, Heads and Tails*, etc. Besides, the subjects relating to sustainable development should be given priority in educational television programmes—Countrywide Classroom, *Tarang*, etc. of various disciplines.

VCRs or VCD Players

The VCRs and VCD players can be used to screen the programmes of educational or edu-tainment nature to the small groups. Through this means of communication, visitors are educated about various aspects of environment at Manjira Sanctuary in Medak District. Video cassettes and CDs can be used to educate even illiterate people about various practices, which would promote sustainable development.

Radio

Radio being the source of information and entertainment for a large number of people, its various programmes need to be used to convey the messages related to different aspects of sustainable development to its listeners. In different genres—news, radio plays, discussions, serials, etc., messages and values that would conscientize people about the need for sustainable development need to be incorporated. Since radio offers us the opportunity to reach the people from local to global level, it can be used in such a way that while it imparts knowledge about the national and global issues, it should also concentrate on activating people at local level.

Film

Films are inseparable part of our lives whether in cinema halls or in television. Films, film songs and scenes are primary entertainment to many people from illiterate villagers to elite urbanites. Perhaps, a cinema hall is the only place where mass and class people sit together and enjoy. Film being the audio, visual, intimate and ubiquitous medium, it can communicate effectively to the people. Often, we find the common people imitating the film heroes and heroines. Therefore, the potentialities of the film should be utilized for the promotion of sustainable lifestyle. This can be done in the following two ways :

1. Information and educational short films can be screened before the commencement of the main film. Taking into consideration the target audience of the main film, the short film, which would be relevant to such audiences, can be screened. For example, before screening a women-oriented film, a short film on DWCRA; before screening an adult film, a short film on AIDs can be screened.
2. Sustainable lifestyle can be promoted through feature films, which depict the sustainable development oriented themes such as stories and characters reflecting the real life. Since the film heroes and heroines are role models to the people, by creating such roles, which are environment-friendly or which stand for poverty eradication, awareness can be created among people about those issues. Films like *Tamanna* (Hindi) expose the gender discrimination, while *Vimukti Kosam*

(Telugu) (For Salvation) shows the exploitation of the poor. *Banani* (Assamese) deals with the subject of conservation of forests. These kinds of films should be produced and encouraged to contribute for the sustainable development.

Computers

Computers being the source of information reception, storage and transmission through various networks and Internet, information about various dimensions of the sustainable development can be disseminated and received through Internet. Therefore, more and more information on sustainable development should be made available on Internet.

Extension Communication

Extension workers like demonstrators and health workers should be used effectively to communicate various messages to different sections of people, conscientize and activate them so as to enable them to practice in their localities. Demonstrators can be used to impart knowledge about sustainable agricultural methods to the farmers. Similarly, health workers can be used to motivate the people to adopt family planning. In Pathuru of Medak District, health workers have played an important role in promoting the adoption of family planning. These extension workers can also function as a link between policy-makers and the people at grassroots level.

Traditional Folk Media

Traditional folk media have many advantages in creating awareness among the people in rural areas. Like the *Burrakatha* team that was prepared to narrate the story of Patancheru industrial pollution, teams of various folk forms are needed to be prepared to disseminate information on various aspects of sustainable development.

Voluntary Organizations

Voluntary organizations can be effective in conscientizing the people within their jurisdiction. They have to be encouraged as channels of communication to people. By directly dealing with the people, voluntary organizations can contribute for the promotion and success of various poverty alleviation, family planning and environmental protection programmes.

Educational Institutions

Educational institutions are the formal and systematic means of imparting knowledge. These institutions are an important means to educate people about the sustainable development. Environmental awareness is found to be more among the high school going children than their counterparts in colleges in the present study, because they are specifically taught about various environmental issues in the schools. Therefore, the educational organizations have to be utilized to optimum level for promoting environmental consciousness and the sustainable lifestyle. At all levels, various dimensions of sustainable development, have to be included in the syllabus. The Chief Minister of Andhra Pradesh announced the formation of 'Green Brigades' in the schools. Like NCC or NSS, such 'green brigades' should become an integral part of educational institutions. Books being the chief sources of knowledge, educational institutions should encourage the environment and development-related book reading within and outside the syllabus. Seminars and symposia at different levels can be organized from time to time-to-impart knowledge on the latest developments in relation to various aspects of sustainable development.

Non-formal means of education, for instance, adult literacy centres or night schools have to be used to create awareness among the uneducated sections of people about different aspects of sustainable development.

Literature

Poets, short story writers, etc. have to respond to the need of the world today. Already, many writers have started writing poetry, short stories, songs and novels on environmental issues. Such a trend has to be intensified and it should become a part of movement for protecting the environment, eradication of poverty, etc. Green themes have to be encouraged by the publishers of periodicals and books.

Religious Organizations

Since religious organizations play an influential role in our lives, these organizations also have to be used as means of communication to mould the sustainable lifestyle among different religious groups. The religious organizations and leaders have to be conscious of their responsibility in fulfilling the various goals of sustainable development and orient their members about sustainable lifestyle.

Gram Sabha (Village Assembly)

Gram Sabhas function as two-way communication between the people in the villages and the government officials. From time-to-time, by organizing such *Gram Sabhas*, there can be a regular interaction between the people and government officials on various aspects of sustainable development. For implementing various poverty alleviation or environmental promotion programmes, these *Gram Sabhas* can be utilized to the maximum extent.

In addition to the above means of communication, posters, calendars, hoardings, etc., also need to be used to promote sustainable lifestyle. Not only government, but media organizations, NGOs, educational institutions, writers, different sections of leaders, etc. should accept their responsibility in helping to materialize the goals of sustainable development. They all, rather, we all have to create a 'way of life' with common attitudes, values and behaviour to promote sustainable development to protect the globe and to protect us.

Often, questions are asked as to who is responsible for the environmental degradation; is it innocent and common people or the few industrialists? Who should be educated about sustainable development? The importance of communication cannot be undermined in dealing with the industries or industrialists. The role played by various communication media in fighting against the Patancheru industrial pollution is a glaring example. Press, television, radio, pamphlets and seminars have played a significant role in building a strong environmental movement against the industrial pollution, which yielded good results. Similarly, in the areas where there is similar industrial pollution—along with media advocacy, street corner meetings, pamphlets, public meetings, seminars of different levels—can be used to organize the people and to build a strong environmental movement against industrial pollution.

Sustainable development being goal that calls for the people to think globally and act locally, and communication being an important element in meeting this goal, the following interactive model has been developed to describe how the commonness is established among global people with regard to promoting the cause of sustainable development.

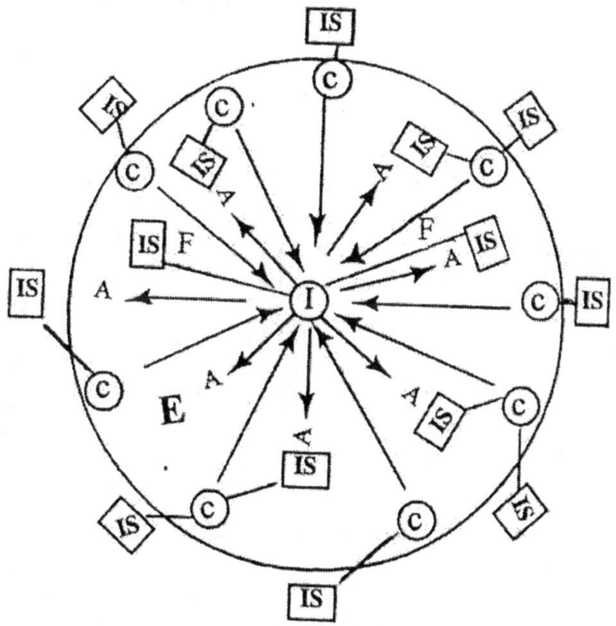

E—Environment
I—Individual
IS—Issues related to sustainable development
C—Channels of communication
A—Activities of an Individual
F—First hand experience

Fig. 8.1 : An informed individual acting in his/her environment

In the above model I is an individual, E is environment, C means various channels of communication, IS means various issues related to sustainable development, F means first hand experience. An individual living in an environment is communicated through different communication channels about various issues relating to sustainable

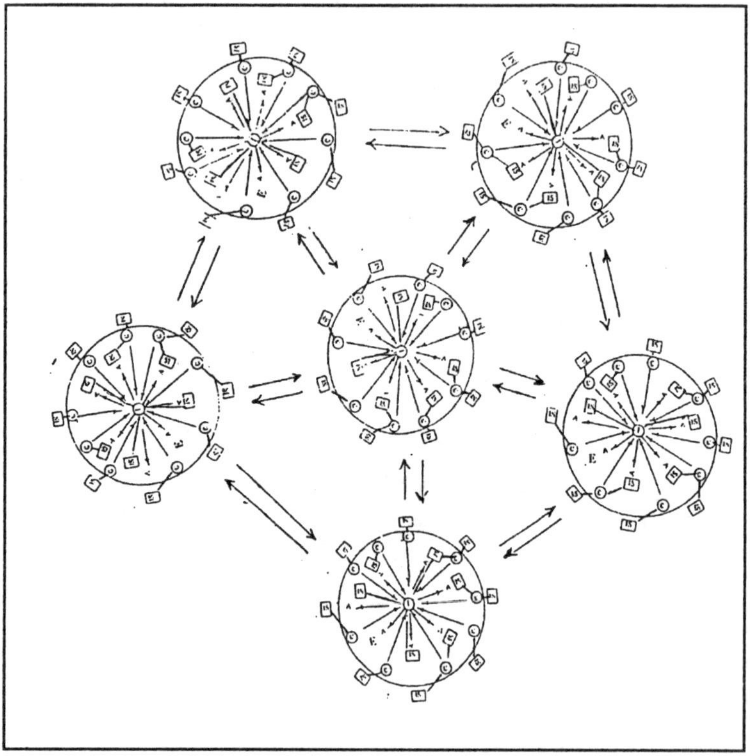

Fig. 8.2 : Individuals in a social system interacting with each other

development. These communication channels can be of different types—mass media, traditional folk media, *Gram Sabha* meetings, educational institutions, literature, NGOs, etc. In addition to getting information through these channels of communication, individuals also perceive certain issues related to sustainable development through first hand experience. The channels of communication play a significant role in creating awareness and in influencing the activities of the individual. While the mass communication channels are more important in creating awareness about the issues related outside the individual's environment, interpersonal and group communication channels are more important in creating awareness and motivating the individual to act locally. In the model, 'a' indicates the various activities of the individual. An individual, after perceiving about various issues, acts in his or her life through different activities. There

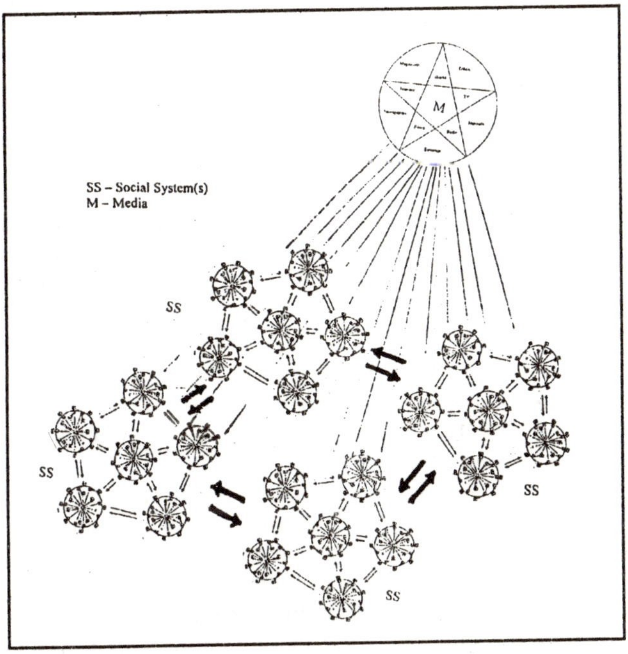

Fig. 8.3 : Social systems interacting with each other

need not be an immediate effect in this communication process, as the Lasswell's model of communication describes. Thus, this model does not resemble the *bullet media* or hypodermic needle model. There will be a gap between individual's perception and action. It takes some time for the individuals from the stage of perception to evaluate, to get convinced and to implement in the various activities of the individual. In this respect, this model resembles the model of the diffusion of innovation. Again, the rate of adopting the sustainable development-related behaviour may vary from person to person. The rate of adopting the sustainable lifestyle is influenced by a number of factors. For example, alternatives to the existing counterproductive practices, availability of proper waste disposing facilities, financial condition of the people etc. If these factors are working negatively, mere communication may have limited impact. Therefore, both communication as well as these factors should be conducive to influence the individual behaviour.

In the next stage such informed individuals in a social system interact with each other and share the common concerns.

Figure 8.2 shows the interaction of the individuals in a social system. This interaction may take place through the interpersonal communication or group communication. And thus, individuals in a social system share their common concerns. Individuals interact in a social system on two types of concerns. One, the issues and programmes in their localities, in regard to which, they also involve in facilitating this kind of interaction, interpersonal communication, group communication, pamphlets, public meetings, local media, etc. play an important role. Two, interaction on the issues and programmes, outside the environment of the individuals. Mass media play an important role in facilitating the interactions among the individuals about the issues and programmes outside their environment.

In the next stage different social systems within and across the boarders interact with each other and share their concerns. By informing and sensitizing the people in these social systems different media facilitate the interaction between the social systems as shown in Figure 8.3.

Figure 8.3 shows the interaction of social systems within and across the frontiers. They share their common concerns through mass media, Internet, seminars, summits, symposia, etc. Here, mass media have a significant role to play in establishing the commonness. This interaction of the social systems facilitates the representatives of these social systems or countries to set the common goals to implement them in their respective social systems so as to promote the global thinking and local actions. Thus, commonness, i.e. communication, is established among the global people about the sustainable development. The goals of sustainable development establish commonness or common concerns among the global people and indeed that is the goal of communication too. Thus, the mass media and other channels of communication can play a significant role in meeting the goals of sustainable development.

The following recommendations can be considered by the government and other parties concerned to make communication more effective in achieving the various goals of sustainable development :

(a) The film being a popular medium, the potentialities of the cinema hall as a means of communication should be utilized for educating the people. In every cinema hall, showing educational films, especially relating to the sustainable development for 10-15 minutes before the starting of the film, should be made compulsory. Seminars and symposia should be organized for the film personnel to orient them about their role and importance in creating awareness about the sustainable development. Besides, film personalities should be invited to the seminars and symposia on different dimensions of sustainable development. The festive occasions too can be utilized for motivating the film personalities. Film critics and journals should highlight the importance of films like '*Banani*' (Assamese).

(b) Seminars and workshops should be conducted to the media personnel on various aspects of sustainable development.

(c) Special attention should be paid to the environment and developmental journalism in communication and journalism departments.

(d) Environmental education should be an integral part of our education at all levels. Special attention should be paid to the areas of environment and development in teachers' training and orientation courses.

(e) Since the religious institutions are also important sources of communication, influencing the lifestyle of the individuals, religious leaders and priests also should be given orientation to encourage the sustainable lifestyle.

(f) Literature with environment and developmental content should be encouraged.

In this book, a modest attempt has been made to analyze the role of communication in sustainable development in general with reference to Medak District in particular. Sustainable development being a very broad area, all its dimensions and sub-dimensions could not be paid special attention in the present study. In order to explore further, the role of communication with regard to various specific issues of sustainable development, many more research studies can be taken up and carried out. This strengthens the area of development of communication in communication discipline and also helps the people of the world to protect the globe with life-sustaining system as well as to protect ourselves.

REFERENCES

The Hindu (2001), 'Vajpayee to call for report on plight of Sircilla Weavers', (news item), Hyderabad, April 11, p. 4.

The World Commission on Environment and Development (WCED) 1987, *Our Common Future,* Oxford University Press, New Delhi.

Bibliography

Agarwal, Anil (1999), "Getting Greener" *Down to Earth,* New Delhi, February, p. 22.

Agarwal, Anil (2000), "A Drought of the Mind, Not Water", *Times of India,* Calcutta, April 30, p. 11.

Ahana (1995), "How Forests were once conserved", *The Hindu,* Hyderabad, March 4.

Akhileshwari, R. (1989), "Environment and the Media", *Vidura,* May-June, pp. 11-12.

Ambekar Yadav, J.B. (1992), *Communication and Rural Development,* Mittal Publications, New Delhi, pp. 151-157.

Amulya K.N. Reddy (1997), "Energy Sustainable Strategies", *The Hindu Survey of the Environment,* Chennai, p. 27

Arundhati Roy (1999), "The Greater Common Good", *Outlook,* New Delhi, May 24, pp. 54-72.

Ascroft, Joseph and Sipho Masilela (1989), "From Top-Down to Co-equal Communication: Popular Participation in Development Decision-Making" paper presented at the seminar on Participation: A Key Concept in Communication and Change, University of Poona, Poona.

Ascroft, Joseph and Sipho Masilela (1994), "Participatory Decision Making in Third World Development" in Shirly A. White, Sadanandan Nair and Jeseph Ascroft (eds.) *Participatory Communication: Working for Change and Development,* Sage, New Delhi, pp. 259-292.

Ascroft, Joseph and Sipho Mesilela (1994), 'Participatory Decision Making in Third World Development' in Shirly A. White, *et al.* (eds.) *Participatory Communication Working for Change and Development,* Sage, New Delhi, pp. 259-311.

Asthana, D.K. and Asthana Meera, (1998), *Environment Problems and Solutions,* S. Chand and Company, New Delhi, p. 221.

Balakrishna, P. (1995), "Pedala Sthithi Maralante Samskaralanala Gathi Marali", *Yojana* (Telugu) Publications Division, Sumputi 22, Samchika:12, Hyderabad, p. 34.

Bhakshi, P.M. (1997), *The Constitution of India: With Selective Comments*, Universal Law Publishing Co., Delhi, pp. 35-45.

Bharara, L.P. and S.K. Verma (1998), 'Social Issues of Environment for Sustainable Development' in Joshi, Y.G. and D.K. Verma (eds.) *Social Environment for Sustainable Development,* Jaipur and New Delhi, Rawat Publications.

Bhardwaj, C. and Tara Satyavathi, C. (1998), "Bio-diversity Key to Food Security", *Employment News,* New Delhi, 17-23 October, p. 1.

Bhatt, S.C. (1998), *The Encyclopedic District Gazetteers of India*, Gyan Publishing House, New Delhi, Vol. 1, pp. 241-256.

Bos, E., M.T. Vu, A. Jevin, R. Bulatao, (1992) *World Population Projection* 1992-93, Edition, John Hopkins University Press, Baltimore, MD, Published for the World Bank.

Brookfield, H. (1975), *Interdependent Development*, Methuen, London. Cited by BSS Rao (1992), *op. cit.* p. 21.

Brown, L.R., Flavin, C. and Postel, S. (1991), "From Growth to Sustainable Development" in cited by Reid David (1998), *op. cit.,* p. 4.

Calender (1999), *Power Grid Corporation of India Ltd.*, North Eastern Region, Shillong.

Centre for Environment Education (CEE) 1993-94, *Annual Report*, Nehru Foundation for Development, Ahmedabad, pp. 1-20.

Chakrabarty, N.K. (1994), *Environmental Protection and the Law*, Ashish Publishing House, New Delhi, pp. 53-68.

Chakravarthy, T.K. (1980), *Development of Small and Marginal Farmers and Agricultural Labourers: An Overview of Policies and Programmes,* NIRD, Hyderabad, p. 24.

Chapman, Graham Keval. J. Kumar, Cordine Fraser and Ivor Yaber (1997), *Environmentalism and the Mass Media: The North-South Devide,* Routledge, London, pp. 221-274.

Chatterjee, P.C. (1991), *Broadcasting in India,* Sage, New Delhi, pp. 51-130.

Chitepo, Victorio (1986), quoted in WCED's, *Our Common Future, op. cit.*, p. 34.

Clean and Green Folder (N. D.), "Pudamithaliki Pachathoranam Prajalandariki Arogya Aabharanam" Department of Public Relations, Government of Andhra Pradesh, Hyderabad.

Compendium of instruction on SFDA/MFAL (1975) Government of India, Ministry of Agriculture and Irrigation, Department of Rural Development, September, p. 1.

Dahlan Alwi, M. (1989), "The Environmental Approach to Mass Media Coverage", *Media Asia,* Vol. 16, No. 4, pp. 219-222.

Daly (1992), Steay-State Economics, Earth Scan, London. cited by David Reid (1995) *op. cit.* xvii.

Dandekar, V. M. and Nilakantha Rath (1971), *Poverty in India,* Sangam Press, Pune, p. 15.

Daniels, Walter, M. (1951) *The Point Four Programme,* H. W. Wilson, New York, p.11, cited by Melkote, S. R. (1991), p. 28.

Defleur, Melvin L. and Dennis, Everett E. (1991), *Understanding Mass Communication,* Goyl Saab, New Delhi, p. 8.

Devito, Joseph A. (1994), *Human Communication: The Basic Course,* Harper Collins College Publishers, New York, pp. 32-389.

Dilli, K. T. (1996) "Poverty the Worst From of Pollution" *Third Concept,* New Delhi, January, pp. 25-29.

Dissanayake, W. (1984), "A Buddhist Approach to Development: A Srilankan Endeavour" in Wang. G and Dissanayake, W. (eds.), *Continuity and Change in Communication Systems,* cited by Melkote (1991), pp. 204-205.

Down to Earth (1999), January 15, New Delhi, pp. 16-17.

Down to Earth (2000), "The Hole Truth" Centre for Science and Environment, New Delhi, p. 13.

Down to Earth, (1999), February 15, 1999, "Chandrababu of Hyderabad" Analysis, pp. 40-43.

Down to Earth (1999), "Cyberbabu of Hyderabad", February 15, Centre for Science and Environment, New Delhi, pp. 40-41.

Eddie Girdner (1992), "In the Valley of Shadow of Death" Third Concept, *An International Journal of Ideas,* Vol. 6, No. 67, (September 1992) cited by Madhavi, C. (1993), *op. cit.,* p. 14.

Eighth Five Year Plan 1992-97 (1992), Planning Commission, Government of India, New Delhi.

First Five Year Plan (1951), Planning Commission, Government of India, New Delhi.

Fjes, Fred (1976), 'Communication and Development' An unpublished paper, College of Communications, University of Illinois, Urbana-Campaign, cited by Melkote, S. R., (1991) *op. cit.,* p. 38.

Fourth Five Year Plan (1969-74), Planning Commission, Government of India, New Delhi.

Gaddar (1992), Bhopal, *Gaddar Kavithalu,* Jana Natyamandali Publications, Hyderabad, p. 49.

Ganesh, E. V. and Mohan, V. V. K. (1998), "Paripurnath Saadhinchina Praja Udyamam" (People movement that achieved perfection) *Andhra Pradesh,* January, p. 7.

Ganguly, J. B. (1996), *Sustainable Development in North-Eastern Region of India,* ICSSR, Shillong, pp. 11-15.

Garga, B. D. (1996) *So Many Cinemas: The Motion Picture in India,* Eminence Designs Pvt. Ltd., Mumbai, p. 307.

Gerbner, G. (1967), 'Mass media and human communication theory' in Dance, E. F. X. (ed). *Human Communication Theory* cited by Denis Macquil and Sven Windahl (1982) *op. cit.* p. 3.

Gerard C. Rowe, (1991) 'International Environmental Sustainability: Policy and Law', the Science of the Total Environment, 108, p. 31, cited in Pradipto Ghosh and Akshay Jaitly (eds.) *The Road from Rio* (1993), *op. cit.,* p. 29.

Ghosh and Malhotra (1993), "Implications of Agenda 21 – An Overview in Pradipto Ghosh and Akshay Jaitly (eds.) *The Road from Rio*, TERI, New Delhi, p. 80.

Giriappa, S. (1992). "IRDP and Poverty Alleviation", *Journal of Rural Development,* NIRD, Hyderabad, p. 486.

Goodland Robert and Ledec, George (1987), Neo-classical Economics and Principles of Sustainable Development", Ecological Modelling, Vol. 38, p. 36, cited by Akshay Jaitly (1993), *op. cit.*, p. 29.

Government of A. P. (N. D.), Programmes of Poverty Alleviation in Andhra Pradesh, Panchayati Raj Rural Development and Relief Department, Hyderabad.

Green, C. (1992), "The Environment and Population Growth Decade for Action", *Population Reports*, Series, M. No. 10, p. 11.

Gupta, S. P. (1995), "Economic Reform and Its Impact on Poor" *Economics and Political Weekly,* June 3, New Delhi.

Gupta, V. S. (1989), "Environmental Reporting", *Vidura*, May-June, pp. 3-7.

Hazari, M. A. M. (1996), Working Plan for the Forests of Medak District, Forest Department, Government of Andhra Pradesh, Hyderabad, pp. 46-47.

Holmberg, J. and R. Sandbrook (1993), 'Sustainable Development: What is to be Done? in J. Holmberg (ed.) *Policies for a Small Planet,* Earth Scan London, pp. 19-38.

Human Development Report (1991), United Nations Development Programme, Oxford University Press, New Delhi.

Human Development Report (1994), United Nations Development Programme, Oxford University Press, New York, pp. 1-27.

Indian Penal Code, 1860.

IUCN – The World Conservation Union, United Nations Environment Programme and World Wide Fund for Nature, *Caring for the Earth*, IUCN, UNEP and WWF, Switzerland, 1991, cited by Akshay Jaitly, (1991), *op. cit.*, p. 29.

Jacobson Thomas, L. (1994), "Modernization and Post-Modernization Approaches to Participatory Communication for Development in Shirly, A. White *et al.*, (eds.) 1994, *op. cit.*, pp. 60-73.

James Gustove Speth (1989), "The Environment: The Greening of Technology, *Development*, Vol. 2, No. 3, cited by Akshay Jaitly (1993), *op. cit.*, p. 29.

James, Sybil L. (1994), "Facilitating Communication Within Rural and Marginal Communities: A Model For Development Support in Shirly. A. White *et al.* (eds)., *Participatory Communication: Working for Change and Development*, Sage, New Delhi, p. 332.

Jaitly, Akshay (1993) 'An Overview of Post-Rio Political Economy Issues' in Pradipto Ghosh and Akshay Jaitly (eds.), *The Road from Rio*, TERI, New Delhi.

Jeffery Leonard and Katrina Edie Brandon (1990), "Biological Wealth and Human Poverty: A Tragic Embrace?", *Media Asia,* Vol. 17, No. 1, p. 44.

John Bongaarts (1994), "Population Policy Options in the Developing World", *Science,* Vol. 236, 11th February.

Johnson, Ch. (1998), "Samachara Saakha Nuthana Prachara Prakriya – Keelaka Rangalapai Dhristi" (New Information Dissemination Process of Information Department – Focus on Key areas) *Andhra Pradesh* (Telugu), August, Hyderabd, pp. 39-40.

Joni, C. Joseph (1997), *Mass Media and Rural Development,* Rawat Publications, New Delhi, pp. 217-218.

Jos Chathukulam and Kuriour V. K. (1995), "Jawahar Rozgar Yojana : An Assessment ?" *Economic and Political Weekly*, February 4, pp. 343-344.

Joshi, P. C. *et al.* (1985), *An Indian Personality for Television*, Vol. 1, Publications Division, New Delhi, pp. 42-43.

Juan Diaz Bordenave (1994), "Participatory Communication as a Part of Building the Participative Society" in Shirly, A. White, *et al.* (eds.) 1994, *op. cit.*, pp. 35-47.

Kantowski, D. (1980) *Sarvodaya: The Other Development,* Vikas Publishing House, New Delhi, cited by Melkote (1991) *op. cit.*, p. 204.

Kirkby John, *et al.* (1995), *The Earth Scan Reader in Sustainable Developmen*, Earth Scan, London, p. 1.

Kothari, Ashish (1997), "Biodiversity in India, Deep Slumber," *The Hindu Survey of the Environment,* Chennai, pp. 41-44.

Krishnathray Pradeep (1989), "Environmental Journalism" *Vidura*, May-June, New Delhi, pp. 13-14.

Kumar, Keval, J. (1994), "Communication Approaches to Participation and Development: Challenging the Assumption and Perspectives" in Shirly. A. White, *et al.* (eds), *Participatory Communication: Working for Change and Development*, *op. cit.*, pp. 76-80.

Labour Enquiry, Summary Report (1974-75), Labour Bureau, Chandigarh, Ministry of Labour, p. 15.

Laskar, S. I. (1998), *Directive Principles of State Policy in Indian Constitution*, Deep and Deep Publishers, New Delhi, pp. 26-29.

Lavanya, Banda (1999), Medak Zilla (Mana Zillaalu series) Andhra Pradesh, March 99, Department of Information and Public Relations, Hyderabad, pp. 63-65.

Lerner, Daniel (1958), *The Passing of Traditional Society,* Glencoe, Free Press, cited in Rao, BSS, *Television for Rural Development (1992), op. cit.*, p. 45.

Lutz, M. (1992), "Humanistic Economics: History and Basic Principles" in P.E. Kins and M. Max Neef (eds.) *Real Life Economics: Understanding Wealth Creation*, Routledge, New York, p. 102.

Mac Bride, Sean, *et al.*, (1980) *Many Voices One World*, UNESCO, London, 1980, p. 3.

Mac Neill, J. (1989), "Strategies for Sustainable Economic Development" *Scientific American*, pp. 105-113, cited by Reid David (1995), *op. cit.*, p. 4.

Madhavan, P.K.S. and Rao G.S. (1988), "Voluntary Action in A. P. : An Appraisal" AWARE, Hyderabad, p. 70, cited by Prasad, S.D.J.M. in Role of Voluntary Organizations in Rural Development, M.Phil. Dissertation, Department of Economics, University of Hyderabad, Hyderabad, 1992.

Madhavi, C. (1993), Impact of Industrial Pollution on Social Relatons: A Case Study of Sultanpur, M.Phil. Dissertation, Department of Sociology, University of Hyderabad, pp. 28-49.

Madhavi, C. (1993), Impact of Industrial Pollution on Social Relations: A Case Study of Sultanpur, M.Phil Dissertation, Department. of Sociology, University of Hyderabad, Hyderabad, pp. 31-49.

Maithani, B.P. and Haloi, K. (1988), "Implementation of IRDP: Nagaland Experience", *Journal of Rural Development,* NIRD, Hyderabad.

Malhan, P.N. (1985), *Communication Media: Yesterday, Today and Tomorrow*, Publications Division, New Delhi, p. 156.

Manasa, N. (1995), 'Global Fight Against the Hunger is Confined Only to the Lip Service' *Eenadu* (a Telugu daily) 13, March, Ushodaya Publications, Hyderabad.

Martin, P. (1998), River Pollution in India: An Overview", *Employment News,* New Delhi, 28 March-3 April, p. 1.

Mcquail, Denis and Sven Windahl (1981), *Communication Models,* Longman, New York, pp. 3-10.

Mcqual, Denis (1987), *Mass Communication Theory*, Sage Publication, New Delhi.

Meenakshi Subramaniam (1989), "Crusading Role of the Media", *Vidura,* May-June, pp. 9-10.

Mehta, M. C. *vs.* Union of India (1987) Supp. SCC 131 : AIR 1987 SC 1080 cited by Bhakshi, P. M. (1997) *op. cit.*, pp. 35-45.

Melkote Srinivas, R., Chandrasekhar Vallath, Syed Amjed Ahmed, D. S. Poornanda, (1992), *Communication Gap in India*, Rawat Publications, New Delhi, pp. 59-60.

Melkote, Srinivas, R. (1991), *Communication for the Development in Third World Countries*, Sage, New Delhi, pp. 21-263.

Methukuseema (2001), "Kalushyam Vedajalluthunna 18 Rasayana Parisramala Musivethaku Utharvulu" (Order for Closure of 18 Polluting Chemical Industries) News Item, dated 1.3.2001, p. 4.

Morley Mohan Lal, G. (1988), *Poverty Alleviation: The Indian Experience*, Himalaya Publishing House, Bombay, pp. 53-60, 288-324.

Mukharjee, A.K. (1999), "Environment and Sustainable Develop-ment", *Technorama*, January, Vol. 48, Institution of Engineers' India, Calcutta, pp. 4-6.

Mukharjee, Amitava and Agnihothri, V.K. (1993), *Environment and Development: Views from the East and West*, Concept Publishing Company, New Delhi, pp. 574-577.

Muley, Vijaya (1979) "Films for Development and Education" *Symposium on Cinema in Developing Coundties*, Publications Division, pp. 142-149.

Murphy, G., L.B. Murphy and T.M. Newcomb (1937), *Experimental Social Psychology: An Interpretation of Research upon the Socialization of Individual*, Harper and Row, New York, p. 889 as quoted by Severin, *et al.* (1988) *op. cit.*

Nancharaiah, G. (1998), 'Social Environment and Economic Development' in Joshi, Y.G. and D.K. Verma (eds.), *Social Environment for Sustainable Development*, *op. cit.*, p. 87.

Narasimha Reddy, D. (1992), Public Policy for Environmental Protection: A Study of Its Implementation in an Industrial Area, M.*P*hil. Dissertatoin, Dept. of Political Science, University of Hyderabd, Hyderabad, pp. 70-78.

Narendra Kumar *vs.* State of Haryana LJT (1994) 2 SC 94 quoted by Bhakshi, P.M. (1977) *op. cit.* p. 40.

Narula, Uma (1994), *Development Communication: Theory and Practice*, Har-Anand Publications, New Delhi, pp. 18-139.

Neazil, Mark and Willam Kovarik (1996), *Mass Media and Environ-mental Conflict: America's Green Crusade*, Sage, New Delhi, pp. 9-10.

Ninawe, A.S. (1995), "Environment and Ozone Depletion", *Employment News*, New Delhi 16-22 December, p. 1.

Osgood, C.E., Suci, G.T. and Tannenbaum, P.H. (1957) *The Measurement of Meanings*, Urbana : University of Illinois Press cited by Dends Mcquail and Sven Widahl (1982) *op. cit.* p. 3.

Pandey, G.P. (1999), "Traditional Folk Media and Development: The Only Effective Way to Diffuse Messages", *Communicator*, New Delhi, July-September, pp. 35-36.

Pandey, K. N. Dubey, V.K. and Choubey, P.N. (1990), "Media and Environment: A Case Study of Doordarshan Kendra, Lucknow and All India Radio, Varanasi", *Media Asia*, Vol. 7, No. 1, pp. 40-42.

Parikh, Kirit, S. (1999-2000), *India Development Report,* Oxford University Press, New Delhi, p. 5.

Praveen Kumar, Oddi Raju (1998), "Pachaga Molakethudam", *Andhra Pradesh* (Telugu), Department of Information and Public Relations, Hyderabad, November, p. 13.

Pearce, David, Anil Markandya and Edward B. Barbier (1989), *Blue Print for a Green Economy,* Earth Scan, London, pp. 1-40

Pradeep Thomas (1994), "Participatory Development Communication: Philosophical Premises" in Shirly, A. White, *et al.*, (eds.) *Participatory Communication: Working for Change and Development, op. cit.,* pp. 49-59.

Prasad, Kamta (1985), *Planning for Poverty Alleviation*, Agricole Publishing Academy New Delhi, pp. 31-153.

Prasad, Mani Shanker (1996), "Need for Environmental Awareness" *Third Concept,* January, 1996.

Prasad Rajendra, R.J. (1994), "Computers to Assess Forest Wealth", *The Hindu,* Hyderabad, December 17, 1994.

Prasad, Gargi (1995), "Cutting the Ground Under Land Reforms", *The Hindu,* November-12, p. 17.

Prince Stephen (1997), *Movies and Meaning : An Introduction to Film,* Allyn and Bacon, London, pp. 362-3.

Quebral, Nora (1975), "Development Communication; Where Does it Stand Today? *Media Asia,* Vol. 2 (4) 197-202, cited by Narula, Uma (1994), *op. cit.,* pp. 18-19.

Rahim, Syed (1994), "Participatory Development Communication as a Dialogical Process" in Shirly, A. White, *et al.* (eds.), 1994, pp. 117-136.

Rajamani, R. (1999), Quoted in *Down to Earth,* February 15, *op. cit.,* p. 42.

Rajasekhar, N. (1995), Role of Voluntary Organisations in Rural Development: A Case Study of Deccan Development Society, M.Phil. Dissertation, University of Hyderabad, 1995, p. 54.

Rajasekhar, N. (1995), Role of Voluntary Organisations in Rural Development: A Case Study of Deccan Development Society, M.Phil. Dissertation, University of Hyderabad, Hyderabad, p. 134.

Ram Reddy, G. and Haragopal, G. (1985), *Public Policy and the Rural Poor in India,* Centre for Economic and Social Studies, Hyderabad, pp. 11-92.

Rama Krishna, T. (2000) "Jeevana Parirakshanaki Vanyaprani Samrakshane Dhweyam" (The purpose of conserving wildlife is to conserve the life sustaining system), *Yojana* (Telugu), October, Hyderabad, pp. 2, 42-43.

Ramanamma, M.V. (1997), "Green Journalism: A Social Imperative", *Comunicator*, Indian Institute of Mass Communication, October-December, pp. 17-18.

Ramireg Recardo (1999), "Communication"— a Meeting Ground for Sustainable Development", A paper presented in University of Guelph, Ontario, Canada, pp. 1-2.

Ramudu, Sripathi (1996), Anti-Arrack Movement in Andhra Pradesh (1992), M.Phil. Dissertation, Department of Political Science, University of Hyderabad, p. 44.

Rao, M.S.R.K. (2000), "Grameena Bharata Punarnirmanam: Parivarthana Kosum Pathakalu" (Reconstruction of Rural India: Schemes for the Changes) *Yojana,* (Telugu), October, Hyderabad, pp. 10-14.

Rao, B.S.S. (1992), *Television for Rural Development,* Concept, New Delhi, pp. 21-175.

Rao, B.V.S. *et al.*,(1990) Andhra Pradesh Paryavarana Paristhithi (The States of Andhra Pradesh Environment) *Praja Nivedika*, Academy of Gandhian Studies, p. 138.

Rao, Laxmana, Y.V. (1963), Communication and Development: A Case Study of Two Indian Villages, Ph.D. dissertation, University of Minnesota, cited by Melkote (1991), *op. cit.*, pp. 84-85.

Rao, Pran S.M. (1995), *Neelipapa*, Visalandhra Publishing House, Hyderabad.

Rao, B. V. S., *et al.* (1990), *Andhra Pradesh Paryavarana Paristhithi: Praja Nivedika* (Status of Andhra Pradesh Environment: A Peoples Report) Academy of Gandhian Studies, Hyderabad, pp.133-270.

Rao, P.L.V. (1997), 'Drought in Telangana' in S. Simhadri and P.L. Vishweshwara Rao (eds.) Telangana : Dimensions of Under Development, Centre for Telangana Studies, Hyderabad, p. 105.

Rao, P.L.V., (1993), 'Public Relations as a Two Way Communication Process', in Abdur Rahim, *et al.* (eds.) *Public Relations and Development*, Dr. B.R. Ambedkar Open University, p. 9.

Ray, C.N. (1992), Journal of Rural Development, NIRD, Hyderabad, pp. 97-98.

Reddy, D.N. (1992), Public Policy for Environmental Protection : A Study of Its Implementation in an Industrial Area. M.Phil. Dissertation, Department. of Political Science, University of Hyderabad, Hyderabad, pp. 70-80.

Reddy, D. N. (1994), "Patancheru Industrial Pollution", *Paryavarana*

Bharathi (Telugu), Society for Information and Dissemination on Environment 605, Hyderabad, March-June, pp. 8-9.

Reddy, D. N. (1994), Patancheru - Parisramika Kalushyam (Patancheru Industrial Pollution) *Paryavarana Bharathi*, Hyderabad, March-June, pp. 8-9.

Reddy, Rammanohar, C. (1995), "Towards a Better Life" *The Hindu*, Hyderabad, 5th March.

Reddy, Sphurthi (2001), "Janam Janam Prabhanjanam" (People, People, Over Number of People) *Vaartha* (Telugu) Sunday Magazine, 8th April, pp. 12-15.

Reid David (1995), *Sustainable Development: An Introductory Guide*, Earth Scan, London, pp. XV-175.

Research Journal of Chemistry and Environment, Vol. 2 (3) September, 1998, New Records in Ozone Depletion, Indore, p. 55

Riti, M.D. (1998), "Doing What Comes Naturally", *The Times of India*, Sunday Review, New Delhi, October 18.

Rogers, Everett, M. (1976), 'The Passing of Dominant Paradigm – Reflections on Diffusion Research' in Schramm oud D. Learner (eds.) *Cummunication and Change.* University Press of Hawaii, cited by Kelkote, S.R. (1991) *op. cit.*, pp. 56-57.

Rogers, Everett, M. (1983), *Diffusion of Innovations*, The Free Press, New York, pp. 1-392.

Rowe, Gerard, C. (1991), "International Environmental Sustainability Policy and Law" Cited in Pradipto Ghosh and Akshay Jaitly (eds) *Road from Rio* (1993) *op. cit.*, p. 31.

Sadanandan Nair, K. and Shirly, A. White (1994), "Participatory Development Communication : A Cultural Renewal", in Shirly A. White, *et al.* (eds.) (1994), pp. 138-189.

Sarangi Satish and Gary Cohen (1995), "A Tale of Two Industrial Estates" *Economic and Political Weekly,* June 17, pp. 1419-1421.

Sasireha, S. (1995), "Contribution of Traditional Media in Creating Awareness", *Communicator*, Indian Institute of Mass Communication, July-September, 1995, p. 29.

Satyanarayana, S.V. (1998), *Telugu Saahityamlo Abhyudayam Velugulu*, (Telugu) [The Light of Progress in Telugu Literature], Andhra Pradesh (Telugu Weekly), Department of Information and Public Relations, Hyderabad, May 1998, p. 31.

Savita Varmani (1989), "Land Reforms in India: Evaluative Study of Surplus Land Distribution Allotters in Haryana, in M.L. Sharma and R.K. Punia (eds.) *Land Reforms in India,* Ajantha Publication, New Delhi.

Schramm, Wilbur (1964), *Mass Media and National Development*, Stanford University Press, Stanford, California, cited by Ascroft and Masilela (1994) *op. cit.* pp. 271-272 and Melkote, S.R. (1991), p. 92.

Schumachar, E.F. (1973), *Small is Beautiful: A Study of Economic as if People Mattered*, Abacus edition, Sphore Books, London, p. 138.

Second Five Year Plan (1956), Planning Commission, Government of India, New Delhi.

Sethi, Indrajit, Sethi, M.S. and Iqbal, S.A. (1991), Environmental Pollution: Causes, Effects and Control, Common Wealth Publishers, New Delhi, 1991.

Seventh Five Year Plan, 1985-90 (1985), Planning Commission, Government of India, New Delhi.

Severin, Warner J. and James W. Tankard Jr, (1988), *Communication Theories: Origin, Methods and Uses*, Lognman, New York, p. 458.

Shanti Kumari (2001), " Itu Jala Samrakshana – Atu Ceiling Bhoomula Abhivruddi" ("on one hand the water haravesting and on the other hand the development of ceiling lands.) District Collector of Medak, Shanti Sumari's interview with News Today, *Eenadu* (Telugu) March 15, Medak District edition, Sangareddy.

Sharma, P. D. (1994), *Ecology and Environment,* Rastogi, New Delhi, pp. 340-467.

Sharma, S.L. (1995), "Towards Sustainable Development in India: Issues and Perspectives" a paper presented at ICSSR, North Eastern Regional Centre, Shillong.

Sharma, S.L. (1998), "Sustainable Development: Socio-Cultural Imperatives" in Joshi. Y.G. and Verma, D.K. (eds.) *Social Environment for Sustainable Development*, Rawat Publications, Jayapur, p. 36.

Shirly, A. White (1994), Introduction – "The Concept of Participation: Translating Rhetoric to Reality in Shirly, A. White, *et al.* (eds.) *Participatory Communication: Working for Change and Development,* Sage, New Delhi, pp. 15-31.

Shiva Vandana (1991), *Ecology and the Politics of Survival,* Sage, New Delhi, p. 1.

Singh Yashpal and Anju Aggarwal (1998), "Environmental Crisis: A Challenge Ahead", *Employment News*, 30 May- 5 June, New Delhi, pp. 1-2.

Singh, D.V., Jagadish Chand and Tulsiram (1989), "Impact of Land Reforms on the Socio-Economic Structure of Farming Families – A Case Study in Himachal Pradesh" in M.L. Sharma and R.K. Punia (eds.) *Land Reforms in India*, Ajanta Publication, New Delhi, pp. 12-18.

Singhal Arvind and Everett M. Rogers (1989), *India's Information Revolution*, Sage, New Delhi, pp. 205-206.

Sixth Five Year Plan, 1980-85 (1980), Planning Commission, Government of India, pp. 374-375.

Sri Sri (1939), Keka and Pedalu, *Maha Prasthanam,* Visalandhra Publishing House, Hyderabad, 1950, pp. 82-84.

Srinivas, Satya, G. (1994), Paryavaranamu – *Sthree* ("Environment and Woman") *Paryavarana Bharathi,* March-June, p. 15.

Srinivasan, C. (1979), "Search for Identity", Symposium on *Cinema in Developing Countries*, Publications Division, New Delhi, p. 91.

Subhash, *vs.* State of Bihar, AIR 1991 SC 420 cited by Bhakshi, P.M. (1997) *op. cit.* pp. 35-45.

Sudha Prasad (2000) – "World Religions Summit: A Confluence of All Faiths", *Civil Services Chronicle*, New Delhi, November, p. 28.

Sujatha, Gottipati (1998), "Paryavarana Samatulyataku Vanyapranule Pranam" (Wildlife is lifeline to maintain environmental equilibrium) *Andhra Pradesh* (Telugu), Hyderabad, October issue pp. 31-33.

Suresh Kumar Garlapati (2000), "Methuku Seemalo Porapatudhorani", *Suprabhatam,* 4th Nov. p. 15.

Suryakumari Manukunda (1998), "Deenabandhu", *Andhra Pradesh*, Department of Information and Public Relations, Hyderabad, November 1999, p. 23.

Swarnajayanti: Gram Swarojgar Yojana (SGSY) Guidelines, Government of India, Ministry of Rural Development, New Delhi.

Tandon, P.K. (1995), "Impact of New Economic Policy on Peasantry", *Third Concept,* February, New Delhi.

Technorama, (1999) January, Vol. 48, Institution of Engineers India, Calcutta, p. 41.

Tewari, I.P. (1997), *Communication Technology and Development*, Publications Division, New Delhi, pp. 96-100.

The Hindu (1992), The New Environmental Policy Announced Article: *The Hindu*, 22 February, cited by Madhavi,C. (1993), *op. cit.,* p. 41.

The Hindu (2001), "Vajpayee to call for report on plight of Sircilla Weavers" (News Item), 11-4-2001, Hyderabad, p. 4.

Theodorson, S.A. and Theodorson, A.G. (1969) *A Modern Dictionary of Sociology,* New York, Cassell, cited by Denis Mcquail and Sven Windahl (1982) *op. cit.*, p. 3.

The World Commission on Environment and Development (WCED) (1987), *Our Common Future*, Oxford University Press, New Delhi, pp. 3-141.

Third Five Year Plan (1961), Planning Commission, Government of India, New Delhi, p. 7.

Times of India (1998), "Shooting Stars" (Editorial), New Delhi, October 14, p. 12.

Udayam (1991), Hyderabad, 29 April, pp. 1-2,

Uma Rao, Sunil (1992), Patancheru Pollution (Documentary Film) produced by University of Hyderabad.

UNDP (1994), Human Development Report, Oxford University Press, New Delhi, p. 27.

Upadhyaya, Ramesh (1995), "Poverty Alleviation Tops Agenda: Mishra" an Interview with Dr. Jagnnatha Mishra, *The Hindu,* Hyderabad, July 12, p. 15.

Vaartha (2001), Mukhyamanthri Janmadina Vedukalu (Chief Minister's Birthday Celebrations) News Item, April 21st, Hyderabad.

Vaartha (2001), "Kalushya Korala Nundi Patancheru Thwaraloo Vimukthi" (Very Soon Patancheru will be free from Pollution) [News item], Hyderabad edition, April, 24, p. 12.

Verma, Jag Mohan Singh (1998), 'Bio-Sociocentric Model for Sustainable Development' in Joshi, Y.G. and D.K. Verma (eds.) *Social Environment's for Sustainable Development*, Jaipur and New Delhi, Rawat Publications, p. 97.

Vijaya Mulay (1979), "Films for Development and Education", Symposium on Cinema in Developing Countries, Publications Division, New Delhi, 1979, p. 143.

Vision 2020 (1998), *Pragathi Vijayalatho Swarnandhranu Nirmiddam* (with the Victories of Progress, Let us build the Golden Andhra Pradesh), Department of Information and Public Relations, Hyderabad, pp. 57-58.

Waston James and Hill Anne (1989), *A Dictionary of Communication and Media Studies*, Universal Book Stall, New Delhi, 1989, pp. 32-40.

White Robert (1994), "Participatory Development Communication as a Social Cultural Process" in Shirly. A. White, *et al.* (eds.) *op. cit.*, pp. 95-114.

Wolfenson, James, D. (1998), Preface, World Development Report, Oxford University Press, New York, pp. iii-iv.

World Development Report, 1992, Oxford University Press, New York, p. 2.

Yadav, J. S. (2000) "An Indian Perspective: Communication and Development" *Communicator*, MC, New Delhi, October-December 1999 and January –March 2000, pp. 30-33.

Index